GLOBAL FEAST
Cookbook

Edited by Annice Estes
Illustrated by Lauren Jarrett

Published by: Mystic Seaport Museum Stores
                47 Greenmanville Avenue
                Mystic, Connecticut 06355

Library of Congress Number: 94-071298
ISBN: 0-939510-25-1

Designed and Manufactured in the United States of America by:
Favorite Recipes® Press
P.O. Box 305142
Nashville, Tennessee 37230
1-800-358-0560

Recipes tested in Favorite Recipes® Press test kitchen

Printed in the United States of America

Additional copies of this book may be obtained by using the order form in the back of the book, by writing to the Mystic address listed above, or by calling 1-800-331-BOOK. To order *Global Feast Cookbook* for re-sale purposes, call 1-800-248-1066.

Your purchases directly support the maritime preservation work of Mystic Seaport Museum.

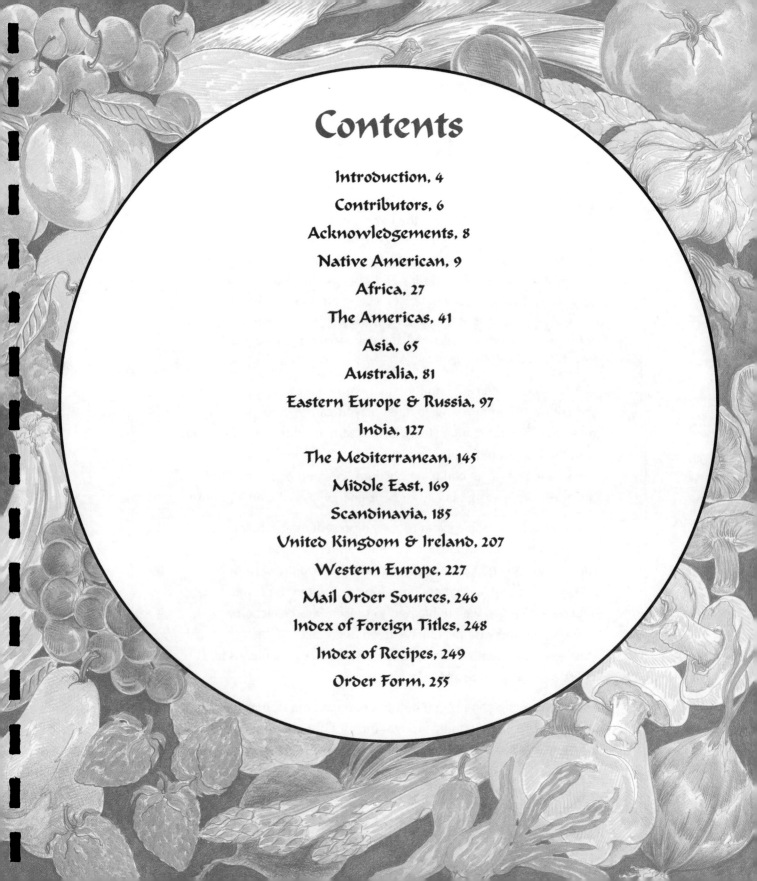

Contents

Introduction

Every Sunday, up to a dozen tiny bodies would settle themselves on the stairs overlooking the large eat-in kitchen at my grandmother's house. Aromas and conversations mingled and rose up the stairs as quickly as the children's plates had been filled. We would sit on those stairs, cousins and siblings alike, eating and giggling, watching aunts and uncles seated around the large table below. The food was as simple as our lives. Prepared with care, the dishes were savory and plentiful and echoed my grandparents' French-Canadian birthplace.

After dinner, Mémère and the other women lingered over dishes and coffee while the young children played games, using their imaginations more than anything else. Hearty laughter would ring out from the living room, where fun-loving uncles recounted tales of pranks and posturing, and older children dreamed of joining their circle. We were a large family and our energy filled the entire house.

This cookbook is filled with recipes representing the collective memories of countless families like mine. After all, the best contribution any ethnic group brought to this country was the tradition of strong family ties. Since food was often the cement that bound us together, we are pleased to present this collection of recipes that otherwise might have been been taken to the grave—secrets that now can be shared with other generations and lovers of good food of all kinds.

Indeed, immigration is one of the great maritime stories in our history. A harsh sea journey brought most of our ancestors here, and for some, the sea became a workplace. In 1841, the listing of the first crew of the whaling ship *Charles W. Morgan* (now preserved at Mystic Seaport) included a variety of international surnames. New England's fishing fleet, as represented by the schooner *L. A. Dunton*, also at Mystic Seaport, had a long tradition of using immigrant labor. The Portuguese influence we witness today in the commercial fishing fleet of Stonington, Connecticut, was present on the *Morgan* and many other ships. And in Mystic, the shipbuilding and whaling industries attracted immigrant workers even before textiles brought Germans and other Europeans to the area. The tide of immigration has ebbed a bit since the great flood of the nineteenth and early twentieth centuries, but an ever-changing mix of new people continues to keep this nation vital and our cuisine choices interesting.

While most of us are descendants of immigrants, Native Americans hold a special place in our history. New England was home to many Native American tribes who extended the hand of friendship and whose help enabled the Pilgrims to adapt and survive in their harsh, new surroundings. In this book we are pleased to offer recipes from tribes all over the United States, and it is only fitting that they are featured in the opening chapter. As the first inhabitants of this land, their harvesting and preparation of numerous indigenous foods dramatically altered cuisines around the world.

In closing, I would like to say a word about part of the design of this book's cover. The starburst pattern actually represents the compass rose long featured on navigational charts. We hope this traditional symbol will magically steer us all in the right direction—perhaps pointing the way to a warm family gathering centered around a large kitchen table.

Annice Estes

Contributors

Thomas H. Aageson
Binti Ackley
Mikki Aganstata
Jane Akins
Sonia Alling
The American-Scandinavian Foundation
Liz and Enrique Arellano
Australian Consulate General
Australian Meat & Livestock Corporation
Australian Wheat Board
Caryn Balamaci
Elaine L. Bauer
Kenneth Beatrice
Belgian Endive Marketing Board
Barbara Bergman
Ruth Bettendorf
Josephine Billeci
Jolene Blair
Acee Blue Eagle
Joan R. Booker
Mary Lou Bosco
Leslie A. Boswell
British Information Services
Maria Elena Brooks
Ann Burdick
Cabazon Band of Mission Indians
Mr. & Mrs. William Campbell
Ann F. Carroll
Frank J. Carter
Kay Chapin
Cherokee Publications
Chickasaw Nation of Oklahoma
Joan Christensen
Mrs. Frederick S. Claghorn
Gloria Coleman
Midge Condaxis
Consulate General of the
    Commonwealth of the Bahamas
Consulate General of Denmark
Consulate General of Morocco
Consulate General of Sweden
Gwen R. Coomber
Phyllis B. Crosby
Barbara Curphey
Leona Ayashume Dabney
Thomas DeBartolo

Diana Restaurant
Patricia Haughey DiGrigoli
Mrs. Sam Donato
Sheila Drometer
Doris Duggan
Helen Dunion
Binh Duong
Louise Durej
Helen F. Dykun
Nancy D'Estang
Josephine Eckman
Joanne J. Erickson
Margaret Jones Farris
Finnish Consulate
Evgeni and Alla Fokine
Carolyn Frances
Edith R. Frankel
Lehka Gai
Glenda Galvan
Gail Gaspar
Judy Georg
Athena George
Rae Anna Gray
Greek Food and Wine Institute
Nancy Horn Grubin
Kathleen Hanning
Beatrice M. Hartung
Amy Havens
Christine Hayes
Dot Hazlin
India Mahal Restaurant
Indo-China Mobile Education Project
Paul Ingenito
Cathy Jensen
Arthur V. Johnson
Susannah Jordan
Michael F. Jubinsky
Mary Kao
Janet Kazo
Hardu and Sloan Keck
Margaret Kilcoyne
Patricia Kilcoyne
Birgitta Kirk
Marilyn Kollmeyer
Sheryl Kuempel
Sunil Kumar

Mrs. Alex Lake
Margaret Fahnestock Lewis
Joan Lillquist
Myra Lucas
Berit Lunde
Rosanne Maggio
Robert Malicki
Jean M. Marra
Margaret Mason
Irene McDade
Bill McEvoy
Kathy McGuire
Sue McMillan
Jo Merrill
Marianne Meyer
Justine Millovitsch
Mississippi Band of Choctaw Indians
Bonita Mockler
Eric Moscahlaidis
Narragansett Indian Tribe
Raquel Nasser
Christine Nelson
Marie H. Neville
Northfield Mount Herman School
Lady Oakes
Mrs. William Ogilvie
Beatrice Ojakangas
Order of Ahepa-Daughters of Penelope
Carol Ortiz
Betty Panarites
Lilliam Pancorbo
Mary E. Pappas
Michael Patrone
Irene M. Patterson
Sherman Paul
Maria Pease
Elaine Pelliccio
Himilee Perez
Permanent Mission of the Azerbaijani
    Republic to the U.N.
Permanent Mission of the Republic
    of Cyprus to the U.N.
Watie Pettit
Susan Pire
Jo Plant
Pauline Poehlmann
Mrs. Joseph E. Pucci
Mrs. J. Rae
Clayton Reeves
Anne J. Richardson

Claudia Richartz
Nancy Richartz
Rosemarie Riechel
Irene Rioux
Pauline Rix
Beverly Welmas Roosevelt
Royal Norwegian Consulate General
The Russian Embassy
The Russian Tea Room
Silvia Salvari
Louis E. Scarmuzzo
Valerie Schacter
Jan Scottron
Victor Scottron
Francine Seiden
Victoria Bychok Seitz
Ella Sekatau
Senegal Tourist Office
Margaret S. Sentz
Jessica Shah
Eleanor Smith
Alice Solovy
Alzira Souza
Diana Stadtmiller
Paul and Patti Stannard
Connie Stein
Anna Stracuzzi
St. Regis Mohawk Indian Reservation
Thelma A. Swody
Nancy Tapley
Dwight Terrance
Lowie E. Treco
Tule River Indian Reservation
Tatu Tuohikorpi
Mikelene Vakulick
Kathy Van Arsdale
Mrs. F. C. Van Winkle
Carmen Verrier
Catherine P. Ware
Judith Sandstrom Wayland
Sophie Webber
Mike Welder
Scott Whitehouse
Florence B. Wilson
Dede Wirth
Judith Woodman
Audry Wooten
Mary Zastrow
Anthony Zeppieri

Acknowledgements

Special thanks are extended to the following persons, whose assistance greatly facilitated the tasks at hand:

Andy German
Glenn Gordinier
Sandy Jubinsky
Trish LaPointe
Alex Matthiessen
Sally McBee
Dede Wirth

We gratefully acknowledge the following authors and publishers who gave permission to reprint certain recipes or provided historical background.

Cateora, Nancy and Sheryl Kuempel. ***The Colorado Cookbook***. Self-published, ©1981.

Daughters of Penelope. ***International Hellenic Cuisine***. Self-published, ©1992.

Gwaltney, Frances, comp. ***Corn Recipes from the Indians***. Cherokee Publications, ©1988.

Mississippi Band of Choctaw Indians. ***Food for Choctaw Families***. Self-published.

Ojakangas, Beatrice. ***Scandinavian Feasts***. Stewart, Tabori and Chang, ©1992.

Randelman, Mary Urrutia and Joan Schwartz. ***Memories of a Cuban Kitchen***. Macmillan, ©1992.

Sekatau, Ella Thomas. ***Narragansett Indian Recipes, Traditional and Contemporary***. Self-published, ©1975.

A Selection of British Menus and Recipes. Food from Britain, ©1989.

Wright, Jeni. ***The Encyclopedia of Asian Cooking***. Octopus Books Limited, ©1980.

Native American

*T*he excellent inhabitants of North America made good use of the natural ingredients found in abundance all around them. Fishing and hunting supplied the bulk of their diet, and crops such as squash, corn, and beans supplemented it. They gathered nuts, roots, and berries; seasoned dishes with wood ashes, herbs, and flowers; and preserved by drying and smoking that which they couldn't immediately use. We will be forever grateful for the Indians' contribution of the clambake and barbecue methods of cooking.

For many tribes the main meal was served in the late morning, though there was always something cooking over a fire or dried foods for snacking throughout the day—necessary also because a strong sense of hospitality dictated that visitors should be fed upon arrival.

It was the spiritual nature of the Indians that gave rise to celebrations before and after a successful buffalo hunt or harvest. Even everyday occurrences warranted acknowledgement of nature as a bountiful provider. After eating a salmon, for example, Indians of the Northwest would arrange the bones in a careful manner so that the fish could return to life to be caught and eaten again.

Finally, the many foods indigenous to North America that were transported around the world by traders and homeward-bound conquistadors permanently altered the eating habits of entire nations. Can you imagine Ireland without the potato? Or the Mediterranean without corn and tomatoes? Other foods exported from America included squash, pumpkin, okra, sweet potatoes, turkey, and peanuts, to name a few. Surely the Native Americans inhabited a bountiful and tasty piece of the world!

Native American

Apple Wild Rice Breakfast

Wild rice is not a true rice, but a grain native to North America. High in protein and carbohydrate value, it is an excellent way to start the day.

Yield: 2 servings

1/3 cup wild rice
1 1/3 cups water
salt to taste
1 unpeeled apple, cut into 1/2-inch slices
1 teaspoon butter
1 to 2 tablespoons brown sugar
1/4 teaspoon salt
1/4 teaspoon cinnamon

Variation: May drizzle cooked wild rice with honey or maple syrup and sprinkle with brown or granulated sugar; top with cream.

✤ Rinse rice; drain. Combine rice, water and salt to taste in saucepan. Bring to a boil; reduce heat. Simmer, loosely covered, for 45 to 60 minutes or until rice is tender and most of liquid has been absorbed. Let stand for 5 minutes; drain.

✤ Sauté apple in butter in skillet for 5 minutes. Sprinkle brown sugar, 1/4 teaspoon salt and cinnamon over apples. Stir in rice. Cook just until heated through, stirring frequently. Serve plain or with milk or cream.

Cornmeal Porridge

The shellfish liquid in this recipe is the direct result of the Narragansett Indians' location on the Rhode Island coastline.

Yield: 2 to 3 servings

1 cup cornmeal
1 cup cold water
3 cups shellfish liquid

Note: May serve immediately or fry at a later time.

✤ Combine cornmeal and cold water in heavy saucepan. Stir in shellfish liquid 1 cup at a time.

✤ Cook over medium heat until mixture comes to a boil, stirring constantly. Reduce heat. Simmer for 10 minutes, stirring occasionally.

Narragansett Fish Chowder

If you don't have pigweed growing in your yard, use finely chopped fresh basil or tarragon as a substitute in a quantity to suit your taste.

Yield: 15 servings

½ pound salt pork, chopped
½ cup chopped onions
6 stalks celery, chopped
1 teaspoon celery seeds
2 teaspoons wild pepper seeds
2 teaspoons pigweed seeds
2 pounds Jerusalem artichokes, peeled
1 pound hulled corn
1 pound codfish
1 pound butterfish
1 pound flatfish
1 pint oysters

✤ Sauté salt pork, onions and celery in skillet until brown. Combine sautéed mixture with celery seeds, wild pepper seeds, pigweed seeds, artichokes, corn and enough water to cover in stockpot; mix well. Cook until artichokes are tender, stirring occasionally.

✤ Stir in codfish, butterfish, flatfish and undrained oysters. Simmer for 30 minutes or until fish flakes easily. Ladle into soup bowls.

Variation: May stir in 2 cups whipping cream if desired.

Dr. Ella Sekatau, Medicine Woman of the Narragansett Indian Tribe of Charlestown, Rhode Island, remembers her mother and grandmother, as well as her father—men being as good cooks as women in Narragansett tradition—preparing this ancient recipe for fish chowder. Her father's efforts, she recalls laughingly, were in fact always "a little better than the others."

Ingredients listed here are traditional, with the exception of the salt pork, which was added with the introduction of pigs into the Narragansett community in the eighteenth century. Before this, the ancestors used many kinds of animal fats or fish oils. The addition of milk or cream was the result of European influence as well. Use either fresh or saltwater fish in Ella's recipe; the taste will vary accordingly.

Shrimp and Okra Stew

Southern influence is evident in this recipe submitted by the Mississippi Band of Choctaw Indians.

Yield: 6 to 8 servings

1 pound okra
6 tomatoes, cored
1 bay leaf, crumbled
4 peppercorns
1 cup water
1½ pounds shrimp, peeled, deveined
½ teaspoon gumbo filé
1 tablespoon cold water
1½ teaspoons salt

❦ Slice only the large okra pods into halves crosswise. Combine the okra, tomatoes, bay leaf, peppercorns and 1 cup water in stockpot; mix well. Simmer, covered, for 20 minutes or until tomatoes and okra are tender, stirring occasionally.

❦ Stir in shrimp. Simmer for 10 minutes, stirring occasionally. Add mixture of gumbo filé and 1 tablespoon cold water; mix well. Season with salt. Simmer for 10 minutes. Ladle into soup bowls.

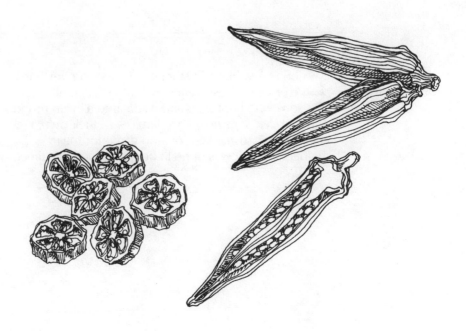

Venison Stew

Yield: 8 servings

2 pounds venison meat, cut into ½-inch pieces
8 cups water
1 teaspoon salt
½ teaspoon pepper
1 bay leaf
1 small bunch cilantro, chopped
4 cloves of garlic
1 small onion, chopped
2 tablespoons flour
1 cup sliced carrots
1 cup sliced celery
½ cup wild or brown rice

♣ Combine venison, water, salt, pepper, bay leaf, cilantro, garlic and onion in stockpot; mix well. Simmer for 3 hours, stirring occasionally.

♣ Stir in flour, carrots, celery and rice. Cook for 30 minutes or until rice is tender, stirring occasionally. Discard bay leaf. Ladle into soup bowls.

Leona "Ayashume" Dabney who lives on the Tule River Indian Reservation in central California, has four sons who hunt deer and wild game all year round. Although her sons now have families of their own, they continue to provide venison and game for their mother, just as it was done in her grandmother's time.

Duck Eggs and Oysters

Yield: 4 servings

1 pint oysters
4 duck eggs, beaten

✤ Place undrained oysters in heavy saucepan. Simmer until edges curl.
✤ Stir in eggs. Cook until eggs are fluffy, stirring constantly.
✤ Serve with bread or toast.

Roast Duck Casserole

Yield: 3 to 4 servings

1   4-pound duck
1/4 pound salt pork, cut into pieces
1/2 cup chopped onion
2 cups brown or wild rice
4 bay leaves
1 cup raisins
1 teaspoon ginger

✤ Preheat oven to 400 degrees.
✤ Rinse duck and pat dry. Brown duck on all sides in Dutch oven. Remove and set aside. Add pork, onion and rice to Dutch oven. Cook until brown, stirring constantly.
✤ Add bay leaves, raisins, ginger and enough water to cover; mix well. Arrange duck breast side down in center of Dutch oven. Cook, covered, for 1 1/2 hours or until duck is tender, adding additional water as moisture evaporates. Discard bay leaves.

Posole

Native Americans in the Southwest create their traditional hash in a highly-seasoned way.

Yield: 6 servings

1½ to 2 pounds beef or pork, cut into bite-sized
    pieces
3 cups water
2 red chili pods or 3 tablespoons chili powder
¼ teaspoon oregano
1 small onion, chopped
1 clove of garlic, finely chopped
3 cups canned hominy

✤ Combine beef or pork and water in stockpot. Cook until meat is tender, stirring occasionally.

✤ Stir in red chili pods, oregano, onion, garlic and hominy. Simmer for 30 to 60 minutes or until desired consistency, stirring occasionally.

✤ Serve with Sopaipillas, a light Mexican bread (see page 22).

Corn was one of the principal staples of both the Southeastern and Southwestern Indians, especially in the form of hominy, which was made by boiling the corn kernels with wood or corncob ashes until they swelled. The lye in the wood ashes may have assisted in dissolving the skin of each kernel of corn. Hominy supplemented the diet in a variety of ways, including being fermented into a soup, ground into bread or grits, or added to pork or venison in a hearty stew. One of the best of these stews was *posole*, which refers to the proper name of the hominy itself as well as the name of the dish. *Posole*, made with either blue, white or yellow corn in combination with meat, was served during holidays or other important celebrations. We are fortunate to have recipes for three versions of *posole* from three different tribes.

Mohawk Hash

This basic dish from upstate New York was used to cook whatever was available at the time, though this version uses pork. It makes a great buffet dish and is usually served at weddings.

Yield: 3 servings

2 pounds lean pork
4 pounds potatoes, cooked, drained, cubed
salt and pepper to taste

♣ Grind the pork twice or have your butcher do it for you. Combine pork with enough cold water to cover in stockpot. Bring to a boil; reduce heat. Simmer to 1½ to 2 hours or until pork is tender, stirring frequently so meat will not form into large clumps. Drain, reserving liquid.

♣ Combine potatoes and pork in bowl; mix well. Stir in reserved liquid if too dry. Season with salt and pepper.

Pashofa

This traditional dish is served when the ceremony for healing a sick member of the Chickasaw tribe is performed.

Yield: 15 to 20 servings

1 pound cracked corn or pearl hominy
1 gallon water
1½ pounds lean pork, cut into bite-sized pieces
salt to taste

♣ Rinse corn, removing hulls.

♣ Bring water to a boil in stockpot; add corn. Reduce heat. Simmer for 2½ hours, stirring frequently. Add pork; mix well. Cook for 1½ to 2 hours or until corn and pork are tender and mixture is thickened. Season with salt.

Wild Onion Omelet

Yield: 2 servings

4 eggs
½ cup chopped wild onions (scallions)
1 tablespoon butter
salt and pepper to taste

Note: Serve with diced tomatoes, wild coriander
and diced green chili peppers.

* Beat eggs in mixer bowl until foamy.
* Sauté onions in butter in skillet until tender.
  Pour the eggs over the onions. Cook over
  low heat until bottom is light brown. Turn
  over. Cook until light brown. Season with salt
  and pepper.

Leona "Ayashume" Dabney has fond childhood memories of walking into the mountains with her grandmother to gather wild onions. Often joined by her grandmother's friends, the two would pack a lunch and spend an enjoyable day while the women worked and gossiped. In addition to the onions, the group gathered other herbs and plants to be used for medicines and herbal teas—recipes that were handed down from one generation to another.

The wild onions always appeared in the spring on shady hillsides in the foothills of the Sierra Nevada mountains in central California's San Joaquin Valley. Some of the freshly picked onions would be used immediately, while the remainder would be dried and stored for future use. Leona remembers the onions being made into marble-sized rolls and served as a side dish; her favorite accompaniment was fried potatoes and biscuits.

Dried Corn

These traditional instructions for drying and reconstituting corn were provided by Mr. Watie Pettit, an Oklahoma Cherokee and recorded on paper in 1955.

For the dried corn:
Fresh ears of corn

For preparing the dried corn:
dried corn
water to cover
salt to taste
meat seasoning to taste

To dry the corn:

✤ Scrape top ¾ of corn kernels off cob into bowl. Spread corn on cheesecloth stretched on a frame. Place in sun to dry. Turn corn 4 times a day until all moisture has evaporated and kernels are very hard. Store corn in a bag or in a covered earthen jar in a dry place.

To prepare the corn:

✤ Combine corn and enough water to cover in heavy saucepan. Season with salt and meat seasoning. Cook until corn is tender, stirring frequently.

Note: May store dried corn indefinitely.

The Legend of Corn

The ancient ones in time of need
Discovered how to use their seed.
The hunters threw aside their bows,
And planted corn in hills and rows.

The blood drenched corn of sacrifice;
The golden song which echoes thrice,
All bow down to the great sun God,
His high priest blesses, smiles and nods.

The Spanish conquerors of old
Took home this seed, instead of gold,
To plant it in the old, old soil,
To bring new life to those who toil.

Today the grain is used for feed,
And mills refine the golden seed;
Over the world the tall corn grows,
The gift of the Indian—the tall green rows.

By Dawn
Great-great-granddaughter of
War Eagle, Sioux Chieftan

Baked Pumpkin

Yield: 6 to 8 servings

1 small pumpkin
2 tablespoons honey
2 tablespoons apple cider
2 tablespoons melted butter or margarine

♣ Preheat oven to 350 degrees.
♣ Rinse pumpkin and pat dry. Place on baking sheet. Bake for 1½ hours.
♣ Slice top from pumpkin, reserving top. Scoop out pulp and seeds. Baste inside of pumpkin with mixture of honey, cider and melted butter. Replace pumpkin top. Place on baking sheet. Bake for 35 to 40 minutes or until pumpkin is tender, basting occasionally.
♣ Serve whole at the table. Scoop out individual portions or cut into wedges. Drizzle each serving with a small amount of honey mixture.

Baked Squash and Wild Onions

Yield: 4 to 6 servings

2 pounds yellow squash or zucchini, cut into ¼-inch slices
8 scallions with tops, cut into ¼-inch slices
½ teaspoon dillseeds, crushed
salt to taste
¼ teaspoon marjoram
¼ teaspoon freshly ground pepper
3 tablespoons butter or margarine

♣ Preheat oven to 350 degrees.
♣ Arrange squash in 8x8-inch baking dish. Add scallions; mix well. Sprinkle with mixture of dillseeds, salt, marjoram and pepper. Dot with butter.
♣ Bake, covered with foil, for 1 to 2 hours or until squash is tender.

Succotash

This is one of many different versions of succotash that have been created over the years—this particular one is Cherokee in origin.

Yield: 6 to 8 servings

2 cups green beans
salt to taste
2 cups fresh corn, cut from cob
2 tablespoons butter
salt and pepper to taste

Variation: May add meat, wild onions and/or peppers.

* Combine green beans, salt and enough water to cover in saucepan. Simmer until green beans are tender, stirring occasionally; drain.

* Cook corn in saucepan just until heated through. Stir into green beans. Season with butter, salt and pepper. Bring to a boil, stirring constantly. Remove from heat.

Wild Rice, Cranberry and Mushroom Stuffing

This recipe evolved in Wisconsin where Native American wild rice dishes are common.

Yield: 6 servings

2/3 cup wild rice
2 2/3 cups water
salt to taste
1 1/2 cups finely chopped mushrooms
1/2 cup chopped onion
3 tablespoons butter or margarine
1/4 teaspoon salt
freshly ground pepper to taste
1 cup chopped fresh or frozen cranberries
1/3 cup currants or raisins (optional)

Note: May also use as stuffing for double-thick pork chops, chicken or turkey.

✦ Rinse rice; drain. Bring rice, water and salt to taste to a boil in saucepan. Reduce heat. Simmer, loosely covered, for 45 to 60 minutes or until rice is tender and most of liquid has been absorbed. Let stand for 5 minutes; drain.

✦ Sauté mushrooms and onion in butter in skillet for 10 minutes or until mushrooms and onion are tender. Stir in 1/4 teaspoon salt, pepper, cranberries, currants and rice.

✦ Preheat oven to 350 degrees. Spoon stuffing into baking dish. Bake for 30 minutes.

Sopaipillas

Yield: 48 servings

4 cups flour
1 tablespoon baking powder
1 teaspoon salt
3 tablespoons shortening
water
oil for frying

✦ Sift flour, baking powder and salt into bowl; mix well. Cut in shortening until crumbly. Stir in just enough water to make stiff dough.

✦ Roll dough 1/8 inch thick on lightly floured surface. Cut into 3-inch squares.

✦ Fry in hot oil in skillet until brown on both sides; drain.

Gitchie Gumi Fry Bread

Yield: 4 servings

1/3 cup wild rice
1 1/3 cups water
salt to taste
2 cups flour
1 cup cornmeal
1 tablespoon baking powder
3/4 teaspoon salt
1 cup milk
oil for frying
confectioners' sugar

* Rinse rice; drain. Bring rice, water and salt to taste to a boil in saucepan. Reduce heat. Simmer, covered, for 45 to 60 minutes or until rice is tender and most of liquid has been absorbed. Let stand for 5 minutes; drain. Cool.
* Combine rice, flour, 1/4 cup cornmeal, baking powder and 3/4 teaspoon salt in bowl; mix well. Stir in milk until stiff dough forms.
* Divide dough into 4 portions. Knead until smooth.
* Sprinkle remaining cornmeal on hard surface. Pat each portion into 10-inch circle.
* Heat oil in 10-inch skillet to 400 degrees. Fry dough circles 1 at a time for 45 to 60 seconds on each side or until golden brown and center is cooked through. Drain on paper towels.
* Serve hot sprinkled with confectioners' sugar. Tear apart or cut into wedges.

Indian Bread

Native Americans have an oral tradition where information is passed from one generation to another by telling stories and observing elders. This bread has been made for generations by the Cabazon Band of Mission Indians in California. It is served at holiday celebrations and family gatherings.

Yield: 8 servings

3 cups flour
1 teaspoon salt
2 teaspoons baking powder
1 to 2 cups warm water
oil for frying

* Combine flour, salt and baking powder in bowl; mix well. Stir in enough warm water to form soft dough.
* Divide dough into 8 portions. Roll each portion into a circle on lightly floured surface.
* Fry circles in hot oil in skillet until brown on both sides, turning once; drain. Blot with paper towel. Remove to warm platter.

Indian Corn Light Bread

Yield: 24 servings

2 cakes yeast
1/2 cup lukewarm water
2 cups hot water
6 cups yellow cornmeal
6 cups rye flour
3 tablespoons shortening
1 teaspoon baking soda
1 cup thick molasses

✦ Dissolve yeast in 1/2 cup lukewarm water. Pour 2 cups hot water over cornmeal in bowl. Let stand until lukewarm. Stir in yeast, rye flour, shortening, baking soda and molasses. Let rise until doubled in bulk.

✦ Knead on lightly floured surface for 10 minutes; shape into 2 loaves. Place in loaf pans. Let rise for 2 hours.

✦ Preheat oven to 450 degrees.

✦ Bake for 15 minutes. Reduce oven temperature to 350 degrees. Bake for 30 minutes longer.

Sweet Potato Bread

Yield: 8 to 10 servings

2 large sweet potatoes
1 cup cornmeal
1 cup flour
1 teaspoon baking powder
1 1/2 teaspoons salt
2 tablespoons honey
2 tablespoons melted butter
1 1/4 cups warm milk
2 eggs, lightly beaten

✦ Parboil sweet potatoes in saucepan for 50 minutes or until tender-crisp. Cool. Peel sweet potatoes; cut into 1/4-inch cubes.

✦ Preheat oven to 400 degrees.

✦ Sift cornmeal, flour, baking powder and salt into bowl; mix well. Stir in mixture of honey, melted butter, milk and eggs. Fold in sweet potatoes.

✦ Pour batter into greased 8x8-inch baking dish. Bake for 1 hour.

✦ Cut into squares; drizzle with melted butter.

Blueberry Sweet Bread

Yield: 15 servings

10 cups flour
2 tablespoons baking powder
¾ tablespoon salt
1½ cups plus 1½ tablespoons water
9½ tablespoons sugar
1   8-ounce package frozen blueberries
vegetable oil for deep frying
confectioners' sugar

✤ Combine flour, baking powder and salt in bowl. Add water; stir to mix well. Stir in sugar and blueberries; mixture will be very stiff.
✤ Preheat oil to 325 degrees in deep-fryer.
✤ Shape dough into servings the size of tennis balls. Deep-fry for 10 to 12 minutes or until deep brown. Drain on paper towel. Sprinkle with confectioners' sugar.

For the past ten years Mikki Aganstata and Sherman Paul have been offering traditional recipes like Seminole Pan Potatoes, Blueberry Sweet Bread and Strawberry Drink at Native American powwows across New England and beyond. Organized as Native American Cuisine, their Hartford-based business benefits from Cherokee recipes handed down through Mikki's family as well as other tribes. Sherman is a member of the Maliseet tribe of Northern Maine, part of the Algonquin Nation. Together they both teach us and feed us, and most importantly, keep alive time-honored traditions at up to 20 powwows each year. We are very happy to share this recipe for Blueberry Sweet Bread with you.

Indian Pudding

Yield: 6 to 8 servings

3 cups milk
1 cup (about) cornmeal
1 cup shortening
1 cup sugar
1 cup raisins
1 teaspoon salt
1 teaspoon vanilla extract

✤ Preheat oven to 300 degrees.
✤ Bring milk just to the boiling point in saucepan. Stir in enough cornmeal to make mixture consistency of mush. Add shortening, sugar, raisins, salt and vanilla; mix well. Spoon into baking dish.
✤ Bake for 45 minutes or until set.

Strawberries Poached in Honey Syrup

Yield: 4 to 6 servings

¼ cup honey
2 tablespoons sugar
⅔ cup water
1 quart strawberries, stems removed

❋ Combine honey, sugar and water in saucepan; mix well. Bring to a boil. Cook for 5 minutes, stirring frequently. Reduce heat. Stir in strawberries. Simmer for 5 minutes.

❋ Cool to room temperature. Serve warm or cold.

Pumpkin Cookies

Yield: 36 servings

½ cup shortening
1¼ cups packed brown sugar
2 eggs
1½ cups mashed cooked pumpkin
¼ teaspoon ginger
½ teaspoon nutmeg
½ teaspoon cinnamon
2½ cups less 2 teaspoons flour
4 teaspoons baking powder
½ teaspoon salt
1 cup raisins or dates
1 cup chopped nuts
1 teaspoon lemon extract

❋ Preheat oven to 400 degrees.

❋ Cream shortening and brown sugar in mixer bowl until light and fluffy. Add eggs, pumpkin, ginger, nutmeg and cinnamon; mix well.

❋ Add sifted mixture of flour, baking powder and salt; mix well. Stir in raisins, nuts and lemon extract.

❋ Drop by teaspoonfuls onto greased cookie sheet. Bake for 8 minutes or just until edges begin to brown. Remove to wire rack to cool.

Africa

The African continent is so vast and varied, and home to so many cultures, that it is no surprise that African cookery reflects this diversity and variety as well. Although native plant foods such as millet and sorghum are few, African cooking features a vast abundance of fresh fruits and vegetables introduced to its gardens and farms by the Europeans and Arabs. In fact, over ninety percent of the cultivated foods of the world are found in Africa—from the familiar yams, cabbage, and bananas to the more exotic plantains and cassavas. The relative scarcity of meats, poultry, and seafood has resulted in diet mainstays of soups and stews, classic ways to stretch small amounts of these ingredients. A thick, hearty soup or stew along with a starch of some kind is usually the basis of each of the two main meals served at noon and in the evening. Nearly constant snacking takes the place of additional meals. Recipes, always versatile with ingredient substitutions for unavailable ingredients, are traditionally passed down from generation to generation by memory, in much the same manner as oral storytelling.

Africa

Dabo Kolo
(Crunchy Appetizer Bits), 29

West African Nut
Snack, 29

North African Lemon
Salad Dressing, 30

Sweet Potato Salad, 30

Doro Wat
(Chicken Stew), 31

West African Lemon
Chicken, 32

Chicken Yassa, 32

Cheb-Ou-Jen, 33

Sesew Froe
(Shrimp and Eggplant), 34

Cabbage and Bacon, 35

Mchicha Wa Nazi
(Spinach with Coconut Milk
and Peanut Sauce), 35

Yellow Rice with
Raisins, 36

Mjdara
(Lentils with Rice), 36

Berberé
(Hot Pepper Seasoning), 37

Simpler Berberé, 37

Moroccan Bread, 38

Yam Bread, 39

Banana and Coconut
Pudding, 40

Sweet Potato Tart, 40

Dabo Kolo (Crunchy Appetizer Bits)

Yield: 4 cups

2 cups flour
2 to 2½ tablespoons Berberé (page 37)
1 tablespoon sugar
1½ teaspoons salt
¼ cup oil
⅓ to ⅔ cup water
salt to taste

✦ Preheat oven to 350 degrees. Mix flour, Berberé, sugar and 1½ teaspoons salt in bowl. Add oil and enough water to form stiff dough.

✦ Knead on unfloured surface for 5 minutes or until smooth. Let rest, covered, for 30 minutes.

✦ Pinch off a small portion of dough at a time, keeping remaining dough covered. Roll each portion into a rope ¼ inch in diameter; cut into ½-inch pieces.

✦ Place on baking sheet; sprinkle with salt to taste. Bake for 16 to 20 minutes or until crunchy, stirring several times. Cool and store in airtight container.

West African Nut Snack

Adjust the seasonings for this snack to make it as spicy as you like.

Yield: 2 cups

¼ cup peanut oil
¼ teaspoon cayenne pepper
1 teaspoon curry powder
salt to taste
2 to 3 cups mixed peanuts, cashews, sunflower seeds and pumpkin seeds

✦ Preheat oven to 250 degrees. Line shallow baking pan with parchment.

✦ Heat peanut oil in large skillet over medium heat. Stir in cayenne pepper, curry powder and salt. Add nuts and seeds, stirring to coat well. Cook until heated through. Spread in prepared baking pan.

✦ Bake for 45 minutes to 1¼ hours or until light brown. Adjust seasonings.

North African Lemon Salad Dressing

Yield: 8 servings

1/4 cup lemon juice
grated rind of 2 lemons
2 cloves of garlic, finely chopped
2/3 cup olive oil
1 teaspoon sugar
1/2 teaspoon dry mustard
1/2 teaspoon cumin
1/2 teaspoon paprika
1/2 teaspoon coriander
1/8 teaspoon red pepper or Tabasco sauce
1 1/2 teaspoons salt

✤ Combine lemon juice, lemon rind, garlic, olive oil, sugar, dry mustard, cumin, paprika, coriander, red pepper sauce and salt in covered jar. Shake to mix well. Store in refrigerator.

✤ Serve on fruit and cottage cheese salad or on vegetable salad consisting of tomatoes, onions, cucumbers and green peppers.

Sweet Potato Salad

Yield: 8 to 10 servings

3 1/2 pounds sweet potatoes
1 medium onion, thinly sliced
1 green bell pepper, cut into strips
1 cup tarragon vinegar
1/2 cup oil
1 tablespoon honey
2 cloves of garlic
2 bay leaves
1/4 teaspoon oregano
1/4 teaspoon thyme
1/2 teaspoon salt
1/4 teaspoon pepper

✤ Cook sweet potatoes in water to cover in saucepan for 20 minutes or just until fork-tender; drain. Peel; cut into halves lengthwise. Cut into 1/4-inch slices.

✤ Mix sweet potatoes, onion and green pepper together in bowl. Combine vinegar, oil, honey, garlic, bay leaves, oregano, thyme, salt and pepper in covered jar. Shake to mix well. Pour over vegetables, tossing to coat.

✤ Marinate in refrigerator for 3 hours or longer. Discard garlic cloves and bay leaves. Spoon into serving bowl.

Doro Wat (Chicken Stew)

Yield: 10 servings

¼ cup butter
2 or 3 onions, chopped
2 cloves of garlic, minced
3 heaping tablespoons Berberé (page 37)
8 ounces tomato paste
salt and pepper to taste
2 small chickens, cut up
4 hard-cooked eggs, peeled

* Melt butter in large stockpot. Add onions and garlic. Sauté for 5 minutes or until onions are translucent.
* Add Berberé, tomato paste, salt and pepper. Simmer for 15 minutes.
* Add chicken pieces, turning to coat well. Simmer, adding enough water to maintain the consistency of heavy cream.
* Pierce hard-cooked eggs all over with fork. Add to stew. Simmer, covered, for 20 to 30 minutes or until chicken is tender.
* Serve with flat bread.

In the depths of the game-filled African bush, meat is a luxury. Sheep, goats and cattle are used as forms of currency and not usually squandered on mere eating.

West African Lemon Chicken

This sauce can also be used with fish or lamb. Add sliced pimento before serving for color.

Yield: 8 servings

2 chickens, cut up
3/4 cup peanut oil
juice of 5 lemons
3 onions, thinly sliced
1/2 cup white wine vinegar
1 clove of garlic, chopped
1/2 teaspoon thyme
1 bay leaf
1/2 to 1 1/2 teaspoons chopped hot pepper
1 teaspoon salt
1/2 teaspoon pepper
1 cup water

✤ Preheat oven to 350 degrees.
✤ Rinse chicken and pat dry. Brown in 1/4 cup peanut oil in heavy skillet; remove to baking dish.
✤ Combine remaining 1/2 cup peanut oil, lemon juice, onions, vinegar, garlic, thyme, bay leaf, hot pepper, salt and pepper in saucepan. Bring to a boil. Stir in water. Pour over chicken.
✤ Bake, tightly covered, for 1 hour or until chicken is tender; discard bay leaf. Serve on hot rice.

Chicken Yassa

This and the following recipe were contributed by a staff member of the Senegal Tourist Office.

Yield: 8 servings

juice of 6 limes
salt, ground red pepper and ground black pepper
  to taste
1 bay leaf
2 chickens
6 large onions, thinly sliced
2 tablespoons oil
oil for sautéing
1 cup (or more) water

✤ Combine lime juice, salt, red pepper, black pepper and bay leaf in shallow dish. Cut each chicken into 8 pieces; rinse and pat dry. Add to marinade, coating well. Place onion slices over chicken. Add 2 tablespoons oil.
✤ Marinate chicken in refrigerator for 2 hours to overnight. Drain chicken, reserving marinade.
✤ Grill chicken lightly over charcoal or wood fire.
✤ Strain marinade, reserving onions and marinade. Sauté onions in heated oil in skillet. Add reserved marinade. Cook for 5 minutes.
✤ Add chicken and water. Simmer, covered, for 45 minutes or until tender. Serve with rice.

Cheb-Ou-Jen

This recipe uses some ingredients with which you may not be familiar. Cassava root, for example, is a tropical tree root used to make flour and tapioca pearls—a pure starch.

Yield: 15 servings

1/2 hot red pepper, chopped
chopped green onions to taste
2 cloves of garlic, minced
parsley, salt, black pepper and bay leaf to taste
3 1/2 pounds thiof or other firm white fish, cut into steaks
3 large onions, sliced
oil for sautéing
4 ounces dried fish
1/2 cup tomato purée
3 quarts water
3 large carrots
1 small cabbage, cut into quarters
1 1/2 cups chopped peeled cassava root
1   10-ounce sweet potato, peeled, cut into halves
1 to 1 1/4 cups chopped peeled pumpkin
1   10-ounce eggplant, unpeeled, cut into halves
1 3/4 cups chopped peeled turnips
1 1/2 hot red peppers
7 3/4 cups uncooked small grain rice

- Combine 1/2 red pepper, green onions, garlic, parsley, salt, black pepper and bay leaf in bowl; pound into paste. Cut a slit in each fish steak. Spoon paste into slits.
- Sauté sliced onions lightly in oil in saucepan. Add dried fish and stuffed fish steaks. Cook until stuffed steaks are golden brown. Remove steaks to plate.
- Stir mixture of tomato purée and water into saucepan. Bring to a boil. Add carrots, cabbage, cassava root, sweet potato, pumpkin, eggplant, turnips and fish steaks; float 1 1/2 hot peppers on top.
- Simmer, covered, for 20 minutes or until all ingredients are tender, removing fish and vegetables to bowl with slotted spoon as they cook; cassava root will take the longest to cook. Add a small amount of cooking liquid and keep warm.
- Cook rice in saucepan in enough remaining cooking liquid to measure approximately twice the amount of rice. Spoon rice onto large platter.
- Arrange fish and vegetables over rice. Serve with lemon quarters and any remaining cooking liquid.

Sesew Froe (Shrimp and Eggplant)

Yield: 6 servings

2 medium tomatoes
2 cups boiling water
1 bunch scallions, chopped
2 fresh hot green chili peppers, seeded
1 medium eggplant, peeled, chopped
1/2 teaspoon salt
1 pound large shrimp in the shells
1 cup water
2 tablespoons oil
2 tablespoons tomato paste
1/2 teaspoon ground ginger
1/2 teaspoon salt

Garnish:
chopped parsley

* Drop tomatoes into 2 cups boiling water in saucepan. Cook for 15 seconds; remove with slotted spoon and cool slightly. Remove skin. Combine with scallions and chili peppers in food processor container; process until smooth; set aside.

* Add eggplant and 1/2 teaspoon salt to boiling water. Cook until tender; drain and set aside.

* Peel and devein shrimp, reserving shells; chop shells. Cook shells in 1 cup water in saucepan for several minutes; strain, reserving cooking liquid.

* Sauté the tomato mixture in hot oil in large skillet for several minutes. Add the reserved shrimp stock. Bring to a boil. Add tomato paste, ginger and 1/2 teaspoon salt; mix well. Cook, covered, for 5 minutes.

* Add shrimp. Cook until pink and cooked through. Add eggplant. Cook until heated through. Serve with rice. Garnish with chopped parsley.

Cabbage and Bacon

Yield: 8 servings

2 pounds cabbage
1/3 pound bacon
3 tablespoons water
1/3 teaspoon salt
3 apples, peeled, grated

Garnish:
1 apple, cut into wedges

♣ Chop cabbage into 1½-inch pieces. Steam for 5 minutes. Rinse under cold water in colander until cool; drain.

♣ Cut bacon into 1-inch pieces. Sauté in large saucepan until crisp. Add cabbage, 3 tablespoons water and salt. Simmer, covered, over medium heat for 15 minutes. Add grated apples. Simmer for 5 minutes longer. Serve immediately. Garnish with apple wedges.

Mchicha Wa Nazi (Spinach with Coconut Milk and Peanut Sauce)

Yield: 4 to 6 servings

2 pounds fresh spinach, trimmed
1 teaspoon salt
1 cup finely chopped onion
1/4 teaspoon minced fresh hot chili peppers
2 tablespoons butter
1 cup coconut milk
1/2 cup roasted unsalted peanuts, puréed

♣ Cook spinach with salt in water in covered saucepan over medium heat for 10 minutes or until tender. Drain spinach and chop coarsely.

♣ Sauté onion and hot chili peppers in butter in heavy 10-inch skillet until tender but not brown. Stir in coconut milk and peanut purée.

♣ Bring to a simmer; reduce heat to lowest temperature. Simmer for 2 to 3 minutes, stirring constantly.

♣ Add spinach; mix gently. Cook until heated through. Serve immediately in heated dish.

Yellow Rice with Raisins

Yield: 8 servings

2¼ cups uncooked rice
¼ cup margarine
4 cups boiling water
1 cinnamon stick
1 teaspoon turmeric
1 teaspoon salt
1 bay leaf
1 cup raisins

✤ Stir rice and margarine into boiling water in saucepan. Add cinnamon stick, turmeric, salt and bay leaf.

✤ Bring to a boil; reduce heat. Simmer, covered, for 20 minutes or until rice is tender and liquid is absorbed. Discard cinnamon stick and bay leaf. Stir in raisins

Mjdara (Lentils with Rice)

Yield: 6 to 8 servings

2 cups lentils
2 teaspoons salt
¾ cup uncooked rice
½ teaspoon pepper
2 onions, chopped
¼ cup olive oil

Note: May add ham, raisins, pistachios and/or chopped tomatoes.

✤ Soak lentils in water to cover in bowl overnight; drain. Combine lentils, salt and enough water to cover in saucepan; mix well.

✤ Cook for 45 minutes, stirring occasionally. Add rice and pepper; mix well. Cook for 20 minutes or until rice is tender, adding additional water if necessary.

✤ Sauté onions in olive oil in skillet until tender. Stir into lentil mixture.

Berberé (Hot Pepper Seasoning)

Use this seasoning in sauces, dips, cheese balls or baked cheese appetizers.

Yield: 1 cup

2 teaspoons cumin seeds
4 whole cloves
6 cardamom pods
½ teaspoon whole black pepper
¼ teaspoon whole allspice
1 teaspoon whole fenugreek (optional)
½ cup dried minced onions
3 dried long red chili peppers
3 to 6 dried small hot chili peppers
½ teaspoon ground ginger
¼ teaspoon turmeric
2 teaspoons salt

♣ Toast cumin seeds, cloves, cardamom, black pepper, allspice and fenugreek in a small skillet over medium-low heat for 1 minute or until light brown. Combine with dried onions in blender or food processor container; process until finely ground.

♣ Discard stems and seeds of hot chili peppers. Process in blender or food processor until finely ground. Mixture should measure about ½ cup.

♣ Combine with toasted spices and onion mixture, ginger, turmeric and salt in bowl; mix well. Store in covered container.

Berberé is an incendiary seasoning used in Ethiopian dishes, particularly Doro Wat, a chicken stew (see page 31). A man will sometimes make subtle inquiries about the quality of a potential bride's berberé before a wedding ceremony takes place. It is the focal point of Ethiopian cuisine, a universal seasoning used by everyone, rich or poor, to season everything from a gourmet meal to a chunk of bread.

Simpler Berberé

Yield: ¼ cup

1 teaspoon ground ginger
3 tablespoons cayenne pepper
¼ teaspoon ground cloves
¼ teaspoon cinnamon

♣ Combine ginger, cayenne pepper, cloves and cinnamon in small bowl.

♣ Store in airtight container.

Moroccan Bread

In Morocco, where freshly baked bread is considered almost sacred, the dough is prepared at home and then taken to a communal oven for baking.

Yield: 16 servings

2 envelopes dry yeast
1 tablespoon sugar
1 cup 95-degree water
7 to 8 cups unbleached flour
3/4 cup milk
2 tablespoons butter
1 tablespoon salt
1 teaspoon caraway seeds (optional)
1 teaspoon anise seeds (optional)
1/4 cup cornmeal

✤ Dissolve yeast and sugar in 1 cup warm water in 2-cup measure. Stir in 1/4 to 1/2 cup flour; mixture may be slightly lumpy. Set aside.

✤ Warm milk slightly in saucepan. Stir in butter. Combine with salt, caraway seeds and anise seeds in large bowl. Stir in yeast mixture. Add flour 1 cup at a time, mixing until dough pulls from side of bowl.

✤ Knead on floured surface for 10 minutes or until smooth and elastic, adding enough remaining flour to keep dough from sticking.

✤ Place in greased bowl, turning to coat surface. Let rise for 1 hour or until doubled in bulk. Punch dough down. Shape into 2 round loaves. Place on baking sheet sprinkled with cornmeal; sprinkle tops with cornmeal. Let rise for 45 minutes or until doubled in bulk.

✤ Preheat oven to 400 degrees.

✤ Slash tops of loaves with knife. Bake for 20 minutes. Reduce oven temperature to 300 degrees. Bake for 20 to 30 minutes longer or until loaves are golden brown and sound hollow when tapped.

Yam Bread

Yield: 24 servings

1 cup boiling water
1 cup milk, scalded
1/2 cup honey
2 tablespoons sugar
3 tablespoons oil
2 teaspoons salt
2 envelopes dry yeast
1/2 cup lukewarm water
2 eggs, beaten
1   16-ounce can yams, drained, mashed
3 cups all-purpose flour
3 cups whole wheat flour

* Combine boiling water, scalded milk, honey, sugar, oil and salt in bowl; mix well. Cool to room temperature.
* Dissolve yeast in lukewarm water; mix well. Stir into cooled mixture.
* Beat eggs and yams in mixer bowl until blended. Add yeast mixture; mix well. Add all-purpose flour and whole wheat flour gradually, mixing well after each addition.
* Knead on lightly floured surface until smooth and elastic, adding additional flour as needed.
* Place dough in greased bowl, turning to coat surface. Let rise, covered, until doubled in bulk. Punch dough down. Divide into 2 portions.
* Shape into loaves. Place in 2 greased 5x9-inch loaf pans. Let rise until doubled in bulk.
* Preheat oven to 350 degrees.
* Bake for 50 to 60 minutes or until brown. Cool in pans for several minutes. Invert onto wire rack to cool completely.

Sesame seeds, cumin, peanuts, okra, rice and yams were all brought from Africa to colonial America where they were assimilated into the culinary history of the southern states. In fact, the word yam is derived from the verb *to eat* in several African languages.

Banana and Coconut Pudding

Yield: 6 servings

3 eggs
2 tablespoons sugar
1 cup half and half
1³/₄ cups grated coconut
2 bananas, mashed
¹/₂ teaspoon freshly ground nutmeg
grated coconut

✤ Preheat oven to 350 degrees. Butter baking dish.

✤ Beat eggs and sugar in mixer bowl until thickened. Add half and half, 1³/₄ cups coconut, bananas and nutmeg; mix well. Spoon into prepared dish; sprinkle with additional coconut.

✤ Place baking dish in larger pan of hot water. Bake for 35 to 45 minutes or until top is brown and knife inserted in center of pudding comes out clean. Serve warm or chilled.

Sweet Potato Tart

The Northfield Mount Herman School in Massachusetts attracts many foreign students and features international food nights using recipes the students bring from home. This is one of several you'll find sprinkled throughout the book.

Yield: 8 servings

1¹/₂ tablespoons orange marmalade
1 unbaked pie shell
¹/₂ cup margarine, softened
¹/₂ cup sugar
1¹/₂ tablespoons flour
1 cup mashed cooked sweet potatoes
3 egg yolks
¹/₂ teaspoon ground nutmeg
3 egg whites

✤ Preheat oven to 325 degrees. Brush marmalade over bottom of pie shell.

✤ Cream margarine and sugar in mixer bowl until light and fluffy. Add flour; mix well. Add sweet potatoes, egg yolks and nutmeg; mix well.

✤ Beat egg whites in mixer bowl until stiff peaks form. Fold into sweet potato filling. Spoon into prepared pie shell.

✤ Bake for 30 to 35 minutes or until set.

The Americas

*T*he New World was considered the land of opportunity by Europeans over 400 years ago, just as it was during the mass migrations to the United States in the late 1800s and early 1900s. The fertile grounds of North and South America and the islands aided the development of regional cuisines based on indigenous foods. These combined with Old World foods, using the seasoning techniques and advanced cooking utensils of the settlers. From the maple syrup of Canada to the cocoa beans further south, innumerable new taste sensations were provided to the immigrants to the American continents, including the tomato, potato, sweet potato, pineapple, pumpkin, vanilla, squash, wild rice, okra, beans, sweet and hot peppers, turkey, and corn. An unlimited repertoire resulted, with inhabitants of tropical climates developing spicy foods to help keep them cool, and those in cooler climates creating hearty, stick-to-your-ribs fare.

Outside influences, on the other hand, affected the Americas. In Canada, the influx of tradesmen and blue collar workers from Eastern and Western Europe added stews, pies, and puddings to the local culture. The Spanish and Portuguese are credited with most influencing the warmer regions. They brought beef and pork livestock, fruits, vegetables, and herbs from the Mediterranean, and spices from the East Indies.

This synergy has had a very positive effect on our food habits. It brought exposure to so many foods and techniques that the best could be selected and adapted. This is still true today as a new wave of immigrants from non-European countries arrives with their own specialties, keeping the cuisines of the Americas vital.

The Americas

Fiesta Pepitas

This is a healthy snack, with lots of protein in the seeds.

Yield: 2 cups

2 cups pumpkin seeds or a combination of
  pumpkin seeds, sunflower seeds and almonds
2 tablespoons tamari shoyu soy sauce

* Preheat oven to 350 degrees.
* Spread seeds on large baking sheet. Roast for 15 to 20 minutes or until done to taste, stirring occasionally. Spoon into bowl.
* Add tamari soy sauce gradually, mixing to coat well. Let stand until cool. Store in airtight container.

Chicken Liver Pâté

Yield: 12 servings

1 pound chicken livers
1/4 cup bacon fat
1 small onion
2 eggs
2 tablespoons butter
2 tablespoons flour
2 cups milk
1/4 teaspoon allspice
2 teaspoons salt
1/4 teaspoon pepper

* Preheat oven to 350 degrees. Grease loaf pan.
* Rinse chicken livers and pat dry. Combine with bacon fat, onion and eggs in blender container; process until smooth.
* Melt butter in saucepan. Blend in flour. Cook for several minutes. Stir in milk. Cook until thickened, stirring constantly.
* Add white sauce to liver mixture 1/2 at a time, mixing well after each addition. Add allspice, salt and pepper; mix well.
* Spoon into prepared pan. Place in larger pan of water. Bake for 1 1/2 hours or until knife inserted in center comes out clean. Cool on wire rack.
* Invert pâté onto serving plate. Serve with rounds of French bread or crackers.

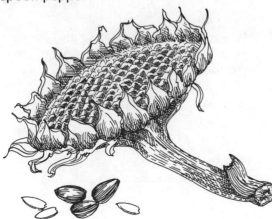

Quick Salsa

This is good to serve with tortilla chips, as topping for nachos or on tacos, burritos or omelets.

Yield: 12 servings

1   15-ounce can whole tomatoes
1   4-ounce can chopped green chilies
1 tablespoon sliced pickled jalapeño peppers
1/2 medium onion, cut into quarters
1/2 cup loosely packed fresh cilantro leaves
1/2 cup Bloody Mary mix or spicy vegetable juice
   cocktail
2 teaspoons chili powder
1 teaspoon ground cumin
1 teaspoon garlic salt

✦ Combine tomatoes, green chilies, jalapeño peppers, onion, cilantro, Bloody Mary mix, chili powder, cumin and garlic salt in food processor container; process for 30 seconds.

✦ Store in covered container for up to 2 weeks. Let stand until room temperature before serving.

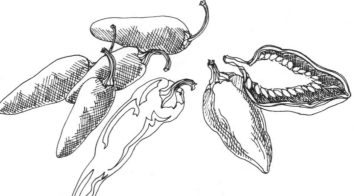

Mexican Dip

Yield: 20 to 25 servings

2   7-ounce cans bean dip
3 avocados, mashed
2 tablespoons lemon juice
1/2 teaspoon salt
1/2 teaspoon pepper
1 cup sour cream
1/2 cup mayonnaise
1 to 11/2 envelopes taco seasoning mix
3 or 4 bunches green onions, chopped
6 medium tomatoes, chopped
2   4-ounce cans chopped black olives
2 cups shredded sharp Cheddar cheese

✦ Spread bean dip in dish with 1 to 11/2-inch rim.

✦ Combine mashed avocados with lemon juice, salt and pepper in bowl; mix well. Spread over bean dip.

✦ Mix sour cream, mayonnaise and taco seasoning mix in small bowl. Spread over avocado layer.

✦ Add layers of green onions, tomatoes, olives and cheese. Chill until serving time. Serve with taco chips.

Cream of Chickpea Soup

This dish also may be made with cooked beans instead of chickpeas.

Yield: 6 servings

3 scallions, chopped
¼ cup oil
1½ 16-ounce cans chickpeas, drained, rinsed
2 medium tomatoes, roasted, peeled
1 chipotle chile (optional)
4 cups chicken stock
salt and pepper to taste
½ cup light cream

Garnish:

sliced avocado or sliced roasted red bell pepper

* Sauté scallions lightly in oil in saucepan. Add chickpeas, tomatoes and chipotle chile. Cook for several minutes. Cool slightly.
* Process with a small amount of the chicken stock in blender until smooth. Strain into earthenware cooker or heavy saucepan.
* Add remaining stock; mix well. Bring to a simmer. Add salt, pepper and cream; mix well. Bring just to a simmer; do not boil. Ladle into soup bowls. Garnish with avocado or roasted red bell pepper slices.

Curried Pumpkin Soup

Yield: 6 servings

1 large onion, chopped or sliced
2 tablespoons butter or margarine
1 16-ounce can pumpkin or 2 cups puréed pumpkin
3 cups chicken stock
1 potato, peeled, chopped
1 teaspoon curry powder
⅛ teaspoon freshly ground nutmeg
1 cup half and half
Worcestershire sauce or Tabasco sauce to taste
salt and pepper to taste

Note: May make ahead; freezes well.

* Sauté onion in butter in 2-quart saucepan until tender. Add pumpkin, chicken stock, potato, curry powder and nutmeg; mix well. Cook over low heat until potato is tender.
* Process in several batches in blender. Combine with half and half, Worcestershire sauce, salt and pepper. Simmer until heated through. Ladle into soup bowls.

Sopa de Frijol Negro (Cuban Black Bean Soup)

Black beans, often served with rice, are basic to the "soul" of traditional Cuban dishes. Now featured in many organic food menus, black beans have become Cuban "soul" transcended.

Yield: 8 servings

1 pound dried black beans
10 cups water
1 large onion, chopped
2/3 cup olive oil
1 large green bell pepper, chopped
4 cloves of garlic, chopped
1/4 teaspoon fresh oregano
1 bay leaf
2 tablespoons sugar
4 teaspoons salt
1/2 teaspoon pepper
2 tablespoons vinegar
2 tablespoons cooking sherry
2 tablespoons olive oil

> The Caribbean is truly the culinary melting pot of the Americas. Strong influences from Africa, Spain, India, South America and Latin America all converge to make the *Island Food* among the most distinctive in the world.

* Rinse and sort beans. Soak in water to cover in saucepan overnight. Drain.

* Add 10 cups water. Bring beans to a boil. Cook for 1 hour.

* Sauté onion in 2/3 cup olive oil in skillet. Add green pepper and garlic. Sauté for several minutes.

* Remove and mash 1 cup of the partially cooked beans. Stir into sautéed mixture; mix well. Add to beans in saucepan.

* Add oregano, bay leaf, sugar, salt and pepper. Simmer, covered, for 1 hour. Add vinegar and wine. Simmer, covered, for 1 hour or until desired consistency, removing cover during last 30 minutes if necessary.

* Stir in 2 tablespoons olive oil just before serving; discard bay leaf. Serve over white rice.

Note: May make ahead; freezes well.

Roasted Red Pepper Soup

Yield: 8 to 10 servings

1 or 2 dried hot peppers
4 cloves of garlic
2 tablespoons olive oil
1½ quarts canned or fresh chicken broth
3 pounds red bell peppers, roasted, seeded,
   peeled
2 tomatoes, peeled

Garnish:
salt and cayenne pepper or black pepper to taste
sour cream or sliced avocado

✤ Soak hot peppers in water until softened;
   drain. Sauté garlic in olive oil in large
   saucepan; remove garlic with slotted spoon.

✤ Reserve 1 cup chicken broth. Process garlic
   with bell peppers and remaining chicken
   broth in several batches in blender. Return
   to saucepan.

✤ Process hot peppers and tomatoes with
   reserved chicken broth in blender. Add to
   soup.

✤ Simmer over very low heat for 20 to 30
   minutes. Season with salt and cayenne pepper.
   Ladle hot soup into bowls. Serve with sour
   cream or avocado slices.

Sopa de Lima (Lime and Tortilla Soup)

Yield: 4 servings

2 corn tortillas
oil for frying tortillas
⅓ cup chopped onion
1 California chili, roasted, peeled, chopped, or
   ¼ cup canned chopped green chilies
2 teaspoons oil
4 cups chicken broth
1 cup shredded cooked chicken
salt to taste
1 tomato, chopped
1 tablespoon (or more) lime juice
4 large lime slices

✤ Cut tortillas into ½x2-inch strips. Fry in ½-inch
   365-degree oil in small skillet until brown and
   crisp; drain on paper towel.

✤ Sauté onion and chili pepper in 2 teaspoons
   oil in large saucepan until tender but not
   brown. Add chicken broth, chicken and salt.

✤ Simmer, covered, for 20 minutes. Add tomato.
   Simmer for 5 minutes. Stir in lime juice.

✤ Sprinkle tortilla strips into soup bowls; ladle
   soup into prepared bowls. Top each serving
   with slice of lime.

Avocado and Citrus Salad

This is a nice alternative to an ordinary salad, especially when served with a heavy entrée.

Yield: 4 servings

For the dressing:

1½ tablespoons red wine vinegar
1 tablespoon orange juice
salt and pepper to taste
5 tablespoons olive oil
1 clove of garlic, minced
½ teaspoon grated orange rind
1 tablespoon minced fresh basil
1 teaspoon minced fresh mint

For the salad:

1 large avocado, chopped
sections of 2 oranges
1 tablespoon crushed peanuts

To make the dressing:

✦ Combine vinegar, orange juice, salt and pepper in small bowl. Add olive oil gradually, stirring constantly until smooth. Add garlic, orange rind, basil and mint. Let stand, covered, at room temperature for 1 hour.

To make the salad:

✦ Combine avocado and oranges in salad bowl. Add dressing; mix gently. Top with peanuts.

Black and White Bean Salad

This is good served with chicken.

Yield: 10 servings

1   16-ounce can Great Northern beans, rinsed, drained
1   16-ounce can black beans, rinsed, drained
1¼ cups chopped seeded tomatoes
¾ cup chopped red bell pepper
¾ cup thinly sliced green onions
½ cup salsa
¼ cup red wine vinegar
1 tablespoon chopped cilantro (optional)
¼ teaspoon salt
⅛ teaspoon pepper
lettuce leaves

✦ Combine beans, tomatoes, bell pepper, green onions, salsa, vinegar, cilantro, salt and pepper in bowl; mix well.
✦ Spoon into lettuce-lined bowl. Serve with tortilla chips.

Pineapple Slaw

Yield: 6 servings

3 cups shredded cabbage
2 tablespoons chopped green bell pepper
1/2 cup chopped unpeeled apple
1/4 cup vinegar
1 tablespoon sugar
1 teaspoon salt
lettuce leaves
1 cup shredded carrot
6 slices pineapple

* Combine cabbage, green pepper, apple, vinegar, sugar and salt in bowl; mix well.
* Spoon into lettuce-lined salad bowl.
* Top with carrot and pineapple.

Bermuda Codfish Cakes

These are traditionally served with hot cross buns on Good Friday, when Bermudians also make homemade kites and fly them over the open places on the island.

Yield: 4 to 6 servings

2 pounds salted boneless codfish
3 pounds potatoes, peeled, chopped
1 onion, finely chopped
1/2 cup butter
2 eggs
chopped parsley, thyme, salt and pepper to taste
flour
oil

Garnish:
lemon wedges
parsley sprigs

* Soak fish in cold water to cover in bowl overnight; drain.
* Combine with fresh water to cover in saucepan. Cook for 45 minutes. Add potatoes and onion. Cook for 45 minutes longer or until vegetables are tender; drain.
* Mash with potato masher until smooth. Add butter, eggs, parsley, thyme, salt and pepper; mix well. Shape into cakes.
* Coat fish cakes with flour. Fry in a small amount of oil in skillet until golden brown. Serve with lemon wedges and parsley sprigs.

Feijoada

This hearty stew recipe, from a Brazilian newspaper, is made with canned beans, but cooked dried beans can also be used.

Yield: 8 to 10 servings

1 onion, chopped
2 cups chopped tomatoes
2 or 3 stalks celery, chopped
2 cloves of garlic, minced
2 tablespoons chopped parsley
2½ tablespoons olive oil
3   10-ounce cans black bean soup
1 cup water
2 cups mixed orange juice and red wine
3 to 5 pounds chopped or sliced cooked pork,
    beef, ham, lamb or corned beef
salt to taste

* Sauté onion, tomatoes, celery, garlic and parsley in olive oil in skillet.
* Combine with soup, water and mixture of orange juice and wine in large saucepan. Add meat and salt. Simmer for 15 to 20 minutes or until heated through.
* Mash some of the beans or add chicken stock or additional bean soup to make the mixture desired consistency.

Note: May make ahead.

Feijoada is the national dish of Brazil. It was originally developed by slaves 200 years ago as a hearty black bean soup using the scraps of left-over meat from the plantation owners' kitchens. It has since been refined and is served traditionally at noon on Saturday at most family gatherings and at restaurants, especially in Rio de Janeiro. The bean and meat mixture is served over rice with finely shredded romaine lettuce or kale and sliced peeled oranges. Brazilians also sometimes serve avocado salad, baked bananas and bread as accompaniments.

Venezuelan Bisteck

Yield: 10 servings

4 pounds beef sirloin
salt and pepper to taste
¼ cup (or less) oil
1 large onion, sliced
1 large tomato, sliced
3 cloves of garlic, minced
2 tablespoons chopped cilantro

* Cut beef into serving pieces; pound until tender. Sprinkle with salt and pepper.
* Brown beef in oil in skillet over medium heat for 10 minutes. Add onion, tomato, garlic and cilantro. Cook until onion is golden brown, stirring frequently.
* Cook for 20 to 30 minutes longer or until vegetables and beef are tender.

Mexican Pork

Yield: 10 servings

2 pounds boneless center-cut pork
oil
1 medium onion, chopped
2   4-ounce cans whole chilies
1   10-ounce can chicken broth
1   28-ounce can tomatoes, crushed
5 cloves of garlic, crushed
salt and pepper to taste

* Chop pork into small pieces. Brown in a small amount of oil in saucepan. Add onion. Sauté until pork is tender. Seed chilies and cut into long strips. Add to saucepan. Stir in chicken broth, tomatoes, garlic, salt and pepper.
* Simmer, covered, for 2 to 3 hours or until of desired consistency. Serve with refried beans, Mexican rice and flour tortillas.

Picadillo

This ground beef mixture can be used as the filling for tacos or burritos or served with refried beans.

Yield: 4 servings

2 pounds lean ground beef
2 large cloves of garlic, mashed
2 large onions, chopped
2 cups chopped canned tomatoes
2 medium potatoes, chopped
1 tablespoon chopped cilantro
1/2 teaspoon cumin
salt to taste
1/2 teaspoon pepper

✦ Brown ground beef with garlic and onions in skillet over medium heat, stirring until ground beef is crumbly; drain. Add tomatoes, potatoes, cilantro, cumin, salt and pepper; mix well.

✦ Simmer over medium-low heat for 20 to 25 minutes or until done to taste, stirring occasionally.

Pronto Mexican Casserole

Yield: 4 to 6 servings

1 pound ground beef
1/2 medium onion, chopped
1 15-ounce can ranch-style beans or chili hot beans
1 10-ounce can tomatoes
1 10-ounce can cream of mushroom soup
1 4-ounce can chopped green chilies, drained
1 teaspoon cumin
1/4 teaspoon pepper
8 to 10 corn tortillas, torn
2 cups shredded Cheddar cheese

✦ Preheat oven to 350 degrees. Grease or spray 9x13-inch baking dish with nonstick cooking spray.

✦ Brown ground beef with onion in skillet, stirring until ground beef is crumbly; drain. Add beans, tomatoes, soup, green chilies, cumin and pepper; mix well. Simmer for 10 minutes, stirring occasionally.

✦ Alternate layers of tortillas and beef mixture in prepared baking dish until all ingredients are used. Top with cheese.

✦ Bake for 30 minutes.

Tourtiere (Canadian Meat Pies)

*In French Canada, there exists an old custom at Christmas of gathering after midnight Mass to take part in festivities called the **Reveillon**. One of the traditional dishes served at the feast is the pork pie. This is made with an old pastry recipe which never fails.*

Yield: 2 pies

For the pastry:
4½ cups sifted flour
2 teaspoons salt
2 cups shortening
⅔ cup cold water

For the pies:
2 pounds lean ground pork
2 pounds lean ground beef
1 onion, chopped
3 medium potatoes, chopped
1 teaspoon salt
½ teaspoon pepper
2 cups water
¼ teaspoon each nutmeg, cinnamon and cloves
crushed unsalted saltine crackers
2 tablespoons milk

To make the pastry:

♣ Sift flour and salt into bowl. Reserve ¼ cup of the mixture. Cut shortening into remaining flour mixture until crumbly.

♣ Blend reserved flour mixture with cold water in bowl to form paste. Add to crumb mixture; mix well with fork to form dough. Shape into a ball. Chill, wrapped with waxed paper, for 30 minutes.

♣ Divide pastry into 4 portions. Roll 2 of the portions on floured surface and fit into two 9-inch pie plates. Roll remaining pastry for top crusts.

To make the pies:

♣ Preheat oven to 425 degrees.

♣ Combine ground pork, ground beef, onion, potatoes, salt, pepper and water in saucepan. Cook for 30 to 45 minutes or until vegetables are tender.

♣ Mash meat and vegetables well. Add nutmeg, cinnamon, cloves and enough cracker crumbs to thicken to desired consistency; mix well.

♣ Spoon mixture into pastry-lined pie plates; top with remaining pastry. Prick vents in top; brush with milk.

♣ Bake for 45 to 50 minutes or until golden brown.

Goat Curry

Yield: 6 to 8 servings

1²/₃ teaspoons chili powder
3¹/₃ tablespoons garam masala
1¹/₂ teaspoons aniseed
7¹/₂ teaspoons turmeric
3¹/₃ teaspoons garlic powder
6²/₃ teaspoons cumin
6²/₃ teaspoons coriander powder
7¹/₂ teaspoons ginger powder
1 leg of kid, boned, cut into bite-sized pieces
flour
salt and pepper to taste
3¹/₂ tablespoons butter
2 medium onions, chopped
3¹/₂ tablespoons tomato paste
2¹/₄ cups chicken stock
1   10-ounce can coconut milk or cream
grated rind and juice of ¹/₂ lemon
1 bay leaf
4 tomatoes, chopped

Note: To sweat the onions, place onions in heavy saucepan. Cover with buttered waxed paper or parchment paper. Sauté over medium-low heat until tender; discard waxed paper or parchment. The onions should be soft but not brown.

✤ Combine chili powder, garam masala, aniseed, turmeric, garlic powder, cumin, coriander and ginger in bowl; mix well.

✤ Toss goat in mixture of flour, salt and pepper. Brown on all sides in butter in skillet. Remove to platter.

✤ Sweat onions in heavy skillet or saucepan. Add spice mixture; mix well. Cook for 5 minutes, stirring occasionally. Add tomato paste; mix well. Cook for 5 minutes, stirring occasionally.

✤ Add chicken stock and coconut milk. Bring mixture to a boil, stirring constantly. Add goat, lemon rind, lemon juice and bay leaf.

✤ Simmer for 45 to 60 minutes or until thickened, stirring occasionally. Skim off fat frequently while simmering.

✤ Stir in chopped tomatoes; adjust seasonings. Discard bay leaf.

Tomatillos (pictured here) are green tomatoes encased in a thin "skin." Small and pungent, they are used in salsa verde and other Mexican dishes and are usually available in larger supermarkets. Unripened red tomatoes are not a substitute.

Chicken in Tomatillo Sauce

Yield: 6 servings

6 pieces chicken
2 tablespoons flour
1/2 teaspoon salt
1/2 teaspoon pepper
6 tablespoons oil
1/2 medium onion, chopped
8 cloves of garlic, chopped
6 canned or dried chipotle chilies, chopped
20 tomatillos, peeled, chopped
1 cup water
2 tablespoons chopped cilantro

✤ Rinse chicken and pat dry. Combine with flour, salt and pepper in plastic bag; shake to coat chicken well.

✤ Fry chicken in heated oil in large skillet until golden brown. Add onion and garlic. Cook for 5 minutes. Add chipotle chilies and tomatillos; mix well.

✤ Cook over medium heat for 5 minutes. Add water and cilantro. Simmer for 1 hour or until chicken is tender and tomatillos are of desired consistency for sauce. Serve with warm corn tortillas.

The first Spanish explorers found the native Arawak Indians cooking thin strips of seasoned meat and fish over open fires on a loose mat of woven green sticks called a barbacoa. Brought back to Europe, this technique immediately became popular and was known in France as barbe à queue. With some refinements, the Arawak tradition continues today as our barbecue.

One explanation of the origin of jerk suggests that the Jamaican *maroons*, escaped slaves, used jerk sauce when cooking in the wilds.

Hot Jamaican Jerk Chicken

Yield: 4 servings

1   2 1/2 to 3-pound chicken
1/2 lemon
1 small onion, chopped
2 cloves of garlic, crushed
1/2 teaspoon allspice
1/2 teaspoon salt
1 tablespoon jerk seasoning or to taste

✤ Rinse chicken and pat dry. Rub with lemon.

✤ Mix onion, garlic, allspice and salt in small bowl. Rub over chicken; sprinkle with jerk seasoning. Marinate in shallow baking dish in refrigerator for 2 hours or longer.

✤ Preheat oven to 325 degrees or preheat grill.

✤ Bake for 1 1/2 to 2 hours or grill until tender, basting with marinade; do not overcook.

✤ Serve with seasoned rice, fried plantain and green salad.

Maple Baked Carrots

Yield: 6 servings

4 large carrots, peeled, sliced
salt to taste
2 medium apples, peeled, thinly sliced
2 tablespoons maple syrup
2 tablespoons brown sugar
2 tablespoons butter

✤ Preheat oven to 375 degrees. Grease 1½-quart baking dish.
✤ Cook carrots in a small amount of salted boiling water in saucepan until tender; drain. Combine with apples in prepared baking dish.
✤ Pour maple syrup over top. Sprinkle with brown sugar; dot with butter.
✤ Bake for 30 to 40 minutes or until apples are tender, stirring once or twice.

Milho Verde com Queijo (Corn with Cheese)

Yield: 4 servings

5 large egg whites
2 large egg yolks, beaten
1 cup whipping cream
½ cup grated Parmesan cheese
freshly ground nutmeg, salt and pepper to taste
½ to 1 cup cooked small shrimp
1 to 2 cups fresh corn kernels

✤ Preheat oven to 450 degrees. Grease 4 individual ramekins.
✤ Beat egg whites in mixer bowl until stiff peaks form. Fold in egg yolks 1 at a time. Add cream; mix gently.
✤ Combine Parmesan cheese, nutmeg, salt and pepper. Fold into egg mixture with shrimp and corn. Spoon into prepared ramekins.
✤ Bake for 8 minutes or until set and golden brown.

Hopping John

Yield: 8 servings

1 onion, chopped
1 cup chopped tomato
¼ pound salt pork, chopped
5 cups water
2 cups drained, canned or frozen green lima beans
2 cups uncooked rice
salt and pepper to taste

♣ Sauté onion and tomato with salt pork in saucepan. Add water, lima beans, rice, salt and pepper.
♣ Simmer over low heat until liquid has evaporated.

Stuffed Pattypan Squash

This dish also may be made with yellow squash.

Yield: 12 servings

12   2 to 3-inch pattypan squash
¼ cup sliced green onions
1   4-ounce can chopped black olives
2 tablespoons chopped green chilies
1 tablespoon chopped jalapeño peppers
¼ cup chopped fresh cilantro leaves
¼ cup shredded Cheddar cheese
¼ cup shredded Monterey Jack cheese

Note: Does not freeze well.

♣ Preheat oven to 350 degrees.
♣ Scoop out centers of squash with melon baller, discarding pulp. Steam squash in boiling water in saucepan for 5 minutes; invert onto paper towel to drain.
♣ Combine green onions, black olives, green chilies, jalapeño peppers, cilantro, cheeses and cooked squash in bowl; mix well.
♣ Spoon stuffing into squash, mounding firmly. Place in shallow baking dish with ½ inch water.
♣ Bake for 15 minutes. Remove to serving plate. Serve stuffed squash immediately in warmed salsa or picante sauce.

Boniatos Glaseados con Ron (Rum-Glazed Boniatos)

Look in Hispanic markets for boniatos which are firm and free from soft spots. If you are unable to find boniatos, substitute sweet potatoes and decrease the brown sugar to 2 tablespoons.

Yield: 8 servings

3 pounds boniatos, scrubbed
3 tablespoons melted butter
3 tablespoons dark brown sugar
salt and pepper to taste
3 tablespoons dark spiced rum or light rum
¼ teaspoon ground coriander
1 tablespoon melted butter

* Preheat oven to 350 degrees. Grease shallow baking dish.
* Bring boniatos to a boil in water to cover in large saucepan. Cook for 15 to 20 minutes or just until tender; drain and cover with cold water. Let stand until cool enough to handle.
* Peel boniatos and slice ¼ inch thick. Arrange in overlapping layers in prepared dish. Drizzle with 3 tablespoons butter; sprinkle with brown sugar, salt and pepper.
* Bake, covered, for 20 minutes. Increase oven temperature to 425 degrees. Bake, uncovered, for 10 minutes.
* Drizzle with mixture of rum, coriander and 1 tablespoon butter. Bake for 5 minutes longer. Serve hot.

Brazilian Rice

Yield: 8 servings

1 large onion, chopped
2 tablespoons bacon drippings
2 cups uncooked rice
3 tomatoes, chopped
salt to taste
4 cups boiling water

* Brown onion in bacon drippings in saucepan. Add rice. Sauté until light brown.
* Stir in tomatoes, salt and boiling water. Cook, covered, for 20 minutes; do not remove lid.

Carrot Jam

Yield: 2 pints

5 pounds carrots
juice of 5 lemons
6 cups sugar

✤ Peel and grate carrots. Combine with lemon juice and sugar in saucepan.

✤ Simmer over low heat until thickened to desired consistency.

Strawberry-Hot Pepper Sauce

Serve sauce with pork, lamb or duck.

Yield: 12 servings

8 dried red California chilies
2 cups boiling water
½ large onion
4 cloves of garlic
1 tablespoon corn oil
1 tomato, peeled
1 to 2 tablespoons strawberry jelly
1 teaspoon salt

✤ Soak dried chilies in boiling water in bowl; drain, reserving liquid. Purée chilies with 1 cup soaking liquid in blender or food processor.

✤ Sauté onion and garlic in hot oil in medium saucepan over medium heat; remove with slotted spoon.

✤ Strain puréed peppers into saucepan, reserving seeds and skins. Cook for 8 to 10 minutes.

✤ Combine reserved seeds and skins with tomato and sautéed vegetables in same blender container. Add remaining 1 cup reserved liquid from soaking peppers; process until smooth. Strain into saucepan.

✤ Add jelly and salt; mix well. Cook over very low heat for 10 to 15 minutes or until desired consistency.

Pan de Naranja (Orange Quick Bread)

Yield: 12 servings

¹⁄₄ cup butter, softened
¹⁄₄ cup packed brown sugar
¹⁄₄ cup sugar
2 eggs
¹⁄₂ cup orange juice
¹⁄₂ teaspoon vanilla extract
2 cups flour
2 teaspoons baking powder
1 tablespoon grated orange rind
¹⁄₄ teaspoon coriander
¹⁄₂ teaspoon salt

Note: May glaze with a mixture of confectioners' sugar, milk and Grand Marnier.

* Preheat oven to 350 degrees. Grease and flour 5x9-inch loaf pan.
* Cream butter, brown sugar and sugar in mixer bowl until light and fluffy. Beat in eggs 1 at a time. Add orange juice and vanilla; mix well.
* Combine flour, baking powder, orange rind, coriander and salt in small bowl. Add to creamed mixture; mix just until moistened. Spoon into prepared pan.
* Bake for 45 to 60 minutes or just until top springs back when lightly touched. Cool in pan for 5 minutes. Loosen edges with knife and remove to wire rack to cool slightly. Serve warm.

Crispy Hot Corn Bread

Yield: 8 servings

1¹⁄₂ cups yellow cornmeal
¹⁄₄ cup flour
1 teaspoon baking soda
1 tablespoon sugar
¹⁄₂ teaspoon salt
2 cups buttermilk
1 egg, beaten
3 slices bacon, crisp-fried, crumbled
chopped seeded jalapeño pepper to taste

Variation: May pour batter into cold skillet and bake for 5 minutes longer for less crisp corn bread.

* Preheat oven to 425 degrees. Grease 9-inch cast-iron skillet and preheat in oven.
* Combine cornmeal, flour, baking soda, sugar and salt in bowl. Add buttermilk, egg, bacon and pepper; mix well.
* Pour batter into heated skillet. Bake for 20 minutes or until golden brown. Serve warm.

Flan de Mama Nena

Yield: 6 to 8 servings

1 cup sugar
2 cups milk
1 cinnamon stick
salt to taste
1 large egg
6 large egg yolks
1 teaspoon vanilla extract

Note: Can make 1 day ahead; does not freeze well.

* Preheat oven to 350 degrees.
* Heat ½ cup sugar in small heavy saucepan over medium heat until bubbly; do not stir. Cook for 6 to 8 minutes or until caramelized, stirring constantly. Pour into 2-quart ovenproof mold, swirling to coat bottom; set aside.
* Combine remaining ½ cup sugar with milk, cinnamon and salt in heavy saucepan. Cook over low heat until sugar dissolves, stirring frequently. Cool. Remove cinnamon stick.
* Combine egg and egg yolks in bowl; beat until smooth. Add to cooled milk mixture. Stir in vanilla. Pour into pan with caramelized sugar.
* Place pan in larger pan on middle oven rack. Add enough lukewarm water to reach ⅔ up side of smaller pan. Bake, covered, for 1 hour. Test with silver knife to see if flan is set. If knife does not come out clean, bake, uncovered, for 15 to 20 minutes longer.
* Cool on wire rack. Chill for 2 to 3 hours. Invert onto serving plate, spooning caramel sauce over top.

Sugar was the star of Cuba, and Cubans were brought up on intoxicatingly sweet flans and custards. Sugar was cheap, available and even patriotic, since it supported the economy. Every home, rich or poor, had its favorite traditional flan, plus a couple of adaptations, often embellished with sweetened grated coconut or grated orange peel.

Oh-So-Good Walnut Pie

Yield: 8 servings

1 cup sugar
1 tablespoon butter
2 tablespoons vinegar
2 tablespoons water
1/2 teaspoon cinnamon
1/4 teaspoon cloves
1/2 cup raisins
1/2 cup chopped walnuts
2 eggs, beaten
1 unbaked pie shell

Note: Can be made ahead; freezes well.

* Preheat oven to 450 degrees.
* Combine sugar, butter, vinegar, water, cinnamon and cloves in mixer bowl; mix well. Fold in raisins and walnuts. Add eggs; mix well.
* Spoon into pie shell. Bake for 10 minutes. Decrease oven temperature to 350 degrees. Bake for 15 to 20 minutes longer or until golden brown.

Apple Cake

Yield: 12 servings

2 cups flour
1 teaspoon baking soda
1 teaspoon cinnamon
salt to taste
3/4 cup oil
1 cup sugar
2 eggs
2 teaspoons vanilla extract
1/2 cup chopped nuts
1/2 cup chocolate chips
3 cups sliced peeled apples

* Preheat oven to 325 degrees.
* Sift flour, baking soda, cinnamon and salt together; set aside.
* Combine oil, sugar and eggs in bowl; mix well with wooden spoon.
* Stir in vanilla, nuts and chocolate chips.
* Add flour mixture; mix well. Fold in apples; batter will be very thick.
* Spoon into ungreased tube pan. Bake for 45 to 60 minutes or just until cake tests done. Cool on wire rack. Invert onto cake plate.

Coconut Layer Cake

Make this cake for a special occasion. It is well worth the effort.

Yield: 16 servings

For the cake:

1½ cups flour
2 teaspoons baking powder
¾ cup butter, softened
1 cup sugar
½ cup milk
5 egg whites, stiffly beaten
1 teaspoon almond extract
½ teaspoon vanilla extract

For the filling:

2 tablespoons butter
1 cup sugar
⅓ cup water
grated rind of 1 orange
½ cup cream
4 egg whites, beaten stiff and dry
2 cups (heaping) grated coconut

For the icing:

⅓ cup water
1 cup sugar
2 egg whites, beaten until stiff but not dry

For assembly:

dry grated coconut
coarse granulated sugar

To make the cake:

✦ Preheat oven to 350 degrees. Butter and flour 2 cake pans. Sift flour with baking powder several times.

✦ Cream butter and sugar in mixer bowl until light and fluffy. Add flour mixture and milk; mix well. Fold in egg whites and flavorings.

✦ Spoon into prepared cake pans. Bake for 20 minutes or until layers test done. Cool in pans for several minutes. Remove to wire rack to cool completely.

To make the filling:

✦ Combine butter, sugar, water and orange rind in saucepan. Cook for 10 minutes, stirring frequently. Strain into double boiler.

✦ Stir in cream. Fold in egg whites and coconut. Cook over hot water until thickened, stirring gently.

✦ Spread in shallow dish. Cool to room temperature.

To make the icing:

✦ Boil water and sugar in saucepan until mixture spins a thread when dropped from spoon. Pour very gradually over egg whites, beating constantly.

To assemble the cake:

✦ Spread filling between cake layers on serving plate. Spread icing over top and side of cake. Sprinkle with as much additional coconut as possible; sprinkle with coarse sugar.

Baked Papaya

Yield: 12 servings

4 eggs
4 cups milk
1 cup sugar
pulp, juice and grated rind of 1 orange
4 cups papaya pulp
1 cup shredded coconut

✤ Preheat oven to 350 degrees.
✤ Combine eggs, milk and sugar with orange pulp, juice and rind in saucepan; mix well. Cook until slightly thickened, stirring constantly. Place pan in larger pan of cool water; stir until cool.
✤ Place papaya and coconut in baking dish. Pour egg mixture into prepared dish. Bake until set.

Orchata (Nicaraguan Rice Drink)

Yield: 3 servings

1/4 cup uncooked rice
1/4 cup sugar
3 cups milk
1 tablespoon baking cocoa
1/8 teaspoon cinnamon
allspice to taste
1/8 teaspoon vanilla extract

✤ Soak rice in water to cover in bowl overnight; drain.
✤ Combine rice with sugar, milk, baking cocoa, cinnamon, allspice and vanilla in blender container. Process for 2 minutes.
✤ Strain liquid over ice cubes in glasses.

Sangria

Yield: 8 servings

1/4 cup honey
1/2 cup hot water
1 lime, thinly sliced
1 orange, thinly sliced
1/2 cup orange juice
juice of 1 lemon
1 liter dry red wine

✤ Stir honey into hot water in saucepan. Cook over medium heat until honey is completely dissolved and mixture comes just to a simmer; remove from heat.
✤ Add lime slices, orange slices, orange juice and lemon juice; mix well. Let stand at room temperature for 4 hours.
✤ Combine with wine in large pitcher; mix gently. Serve over ice.

Asia

In the thirteenth century, a great Buddhist city of a thousand stone temples, named Pagan, was ruled by King Narathihapate. His nickname was "Eater of Three Hundred Curries" because whenever he dined there had to be 300 dishes, "salted and spiced, sweet and sharp, bitter and hot, luscious and parching"! This is an example of how seriously food is considered in Asia and how seasonings are one way to distinguish one regional cuisine from another.

In China it is important that every dish is a harmonious blend of flavor, multiple textures, and color. The Japanese value visual appeal, as well, and greatly appreciate nature's culinary treasures. Where else would you buy the first, luscious melon of the season carefully boxed as a gift? Or hand massage beer-fed cattle to produce unparalleled beef? There is an agricultural bounty in this part of the world that is gratefully received and fully utilized. There is no word for hunger in the Thai language because of their successful farming, which reaps multiple rice crops each year and steady supplies of fresh vegetables. An abundance in the seas and rivers is also highly visible in Asian cooking. Frying, steaming, and grilling are the primary cooking methods, and in Korea, ingredients are sliced and chopped so finely that they are merely "shown" to the pan and taken out again—cooked just that quickly.

Consider the age of the ancient Chinese civilization for a moment. The area made up of Vietnam, Laos, and Kampuchea (Cambodia) is even older and domesticated rice 1,000 years before China or India. The same is true of tool developments, pottery, and language, and The University of Hanoi is older than any university in Europe! The discriminating assimilation of alien foods and food ways, exemplified in the Philippines, is just one way these cultures slowly and carefully evolve, ensuring continued longevity.

Asia

Udang Kelapa (Shrimp with Coconut)

Yield: 6 servings

1 pound cooked peeled shrimp, deveined
1 large onion, cut into quarters
juice of 3 lemons
1 cup sweetened coconut
1 small red chili pepper, fried
1/2 teaspoon coriander

* Preheat oven to 400 degrees.
* Arrange shrimp in baking dish.
* Combine onion, lemon juice, coconut, chili pepper and coriander in blender container. Process at medium speed until onion is puréed.
* Pour mixture over shrimp, tossing gently to coat. Bake, covered with foil, for 20 minutes.

Chinese Sugared Walnuts

Yield: 8 servings

1/2 pound walnut halves
1 cup water
3 tablespoons sugar
3 tablespoons brown sugar
3 cups oil

* Combine walnut halves, water, sugar and brown sugar in saucepan. Cook over moderate heat for 5 minutes, stirring frequently. Drain until dry.
* Fry walnut halves in oil in deep saucepan for 8 minutes or until crisp. Drain; cool.

Ma Ho (Galloping Horses)

Yield: 16 servings

1/2 pound hot Italian sausage
5 cloves of garlic, finely chopped
1 1/2 tablespoons fish sauce
1/8 teaspoon pepper
1 chili pepper, seeded, chopped
2 tablespoons chopped fresh cilantro
1 tablespoon oil
fresh pineapple slices, cut into bite-sized pieces
Bibb lettuce, torn into bite-sized pieces

* Brown sausage with garlic, fish sauce, pepper, chili pepper and cilantro in oil in skillet, stirring until sausage is crumbly.
* Spoon sausage mixture onto pineapple pieces; place on lettuce pieces.
* Serve with wooden picks.

Vegetarian Low-Fat Egg Rolls

Yield: 24 servings

¹/₄ cup water
1 cup chopped onion
1 tablespoon finely chopped fresh gingerroot
4 cloves of garlic, finely chopped
2 cups chopped celery
¹/₂ cup chopped fresh shiitake mushrooms
¹/₂ cup chopped white mushrooms
3 cups chopped green cabbage
1 cup chopped bamboo shoots
1 cup chopped drained water chestnuts
2 tablespoons soy sauce or tamari sauce
1 tablespoon rice wine
24 egg roll wrappers
2 tablespoons dark sesame oil, heated

✤ Preheat oven to 400 degrees.

✤ Heat water in wok until simmering. Add onion, gingerroot and garlic. Stir-fry for 5 minutes or until onion is tender. Add celery, shiitake mushrooms, white mushrooms, cabbage, bamboo shoots and water chestnuts; mix well. Stir-fry for 5 to 8 minutes or until vegetables are tender.

✤ Remove wok from heat. Stir in soy sauce and rice wine. Drain mixture in colander over bowl. Let stand for 10 minutes.

✤ Place 1 egg roll wrapper on dry work surface with corner pointing away from you. Spoon ¹/₄ cup vegetable mixture in center of egg roll wrapper. Brush edges lightly with water. Fold side corners to center, enclosing filling. Fold bottom corner to center; tuck end under filling. Roll to enclose filling; moisten edges with water and press to seal. Repeat process with remaining egg roll wrappers and filling.

✤ Place egg rolls seam side down on baking sheet. Brush with sesame oil. Bake for 15 to 20 minutes or until golden brown. Serve immediately.

Many food historians believe that what we know as *cooking* was born in Asia, probably in China. It may have started when prehistoric man discovered that fire not only could be used for warmth, but could also thaw his food in winter.

Spicy Coconut Milk and Shrimp Soup

Take a walk on the wild side with this popular Thai soup. It is a classic rich, tangy soup—spicy and slightly sweet.

Yield: 6 servings

4 cups chicken stock
1/4 cup fish sauce
1   1-inch piece galanga root, sliced or 2 dried
    pieces
2 stalks fresh lemon grass or 1 tablespoon dried
    lemon grass
1/4 cup fresh lime juice
1 small dried red chili pepper, chopped
1   8-ounce can straw mushrooms
8 ounces shrimp, peeled, deveined
2 cups coconut milk
1 teaspoon sugar
2 tablespoons chopped scallions
2 tablespoons chopped cilantro

Note: All Asian ingredients are available in specialty markets.

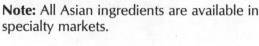

* Bring chicken stock to a boil in stockpot. Add fish sauce, galanga root, lemon grass, lime juice, chili pepper and straw mushrooms. Simmer for 15 to 20 minutes or until of desired consistency, stirring occasionally. Discard galanga root and lemon grass.

* Stir in shrimp. Cook until shrimp turn pink.

* Add coconut milk and sugar. Simmer for 5 minutes.

* Ladle into soup bowls; sprinkle with scallions and cilantro.

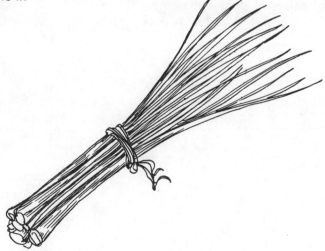

Canh Chua (Vietnamese Sour Soup)

Yield: 6 to 10 servings

1 small onion, chopped
1 tablespoon oil
1 clove of garlic, finely chopped
1   8-ounce can juice-pack crushed pineapple
1   16-ounce can tomatoes
1 small bunch celery with leaves, cut into diagonal
   slices
5 cups water or chicken broth
¼ cup fish sauce or soy sauce
1 teaspoon salt
1 teaspoon sugar
1 teaspoon crushed fresh gingerroot
2 teaspoons basil
3 ounces fresh tomatoes, cut into wedges
3 green onions with tops, chopped

Variation: May substitute fresh tomato wedges
and pineapple chunks for canned ingredients.
May add fresh bean curd at the end of the
cooking cycle, or add shrimp and cook until
shrimp turn pink.

✤ Sauté onion in oil in stockpot until brown. Add
   garlic. Sauté for 1 minute.
✤ Add pineapple, canned tomatoes, celery and
   water; mix well. Bring to a boil. Season with
   fish sauce, salt, sugar, gingerroot and basil.
   Cook for 10 to 15 minutes or until celery is
   tender-crisp, stirring frequently.
✤ Stir in fresh tomatoes and green onions.
   Remove from heat. Ladle into soup bowls.

Asians love to combine
the yin and yang of
tastes, such as sweet and
sour, salty and sour, or salty
and bitter, to add interest to
their dishes.

Thai Salad

Yield: 4 servings

1/2 cup red-skinned peanuts
2 cups shredded cabbage
1 cup shredded carrots
1 cucumber, very thinly sliced
1 scallion, thinly sliced, including greens
2 teaspoons nam pla (fish sauce)
2 teaspoons sugar
1 clove of garlic, minced
2 tablespoons lime juice
2 tablespoons rice vinegar
1/4 cup peanut oil
freshly ground pepper to taste

♣ Heat a small skillet until very hot. Add peanuts. Cook over dry heat until skins turn black, stirring constantly. Remove peanuts to colander. Let cool for several minutes. Rub peanuts between hands to remove skins. Chop peanuts and set aside.

♣ Arrange cabbage, carrots, cucumber and scallion slices on 4 salad plates.

♣ Combine nam pla, sugar, garlic, lime juice, vinegar and oil in bowl; mix well. Pour over salads. Season with pepper to taste.

Sweet and Sour Radish Salad

Yield: 3 to 4 servings

2 bunches radishes
1/2 teaspoon salt
2 tablespoons light brown sugar
2 tablespoons cider vinegar
1/2 teaspoon Oriental sesame oil

Note: Although radishes will taste better by soaking longer in brown sugar and vinegar, they will be discolored and less crisp.

♣ Trim ends from radishes; crush with side of blade of cleaver or bottom of jar. Sprinkle with salt. Let stand for 15 minutes; drain.

♣ Pour mixture of brown sugar and vinegar over radishes in bowl.

♣ Drizzle with sesame oil. Serve immediately.

Chefs in Asia look upon cooking as an art rather than a skill. Cooking is a means of personal expression, and one seldom sees an accomplished Asian cook using a cookbook.

Hawaiian Pot Roast

Yield: 8 to 10 servings

3 to 4-pound beef arm or blade pot roast
3 tablespoons bacon drippings or lard
1 cup soy sauce
1/2 cup water
1 teaspoon pepper
1 teaspoon ground ginger
1 medium onion, sliced
1   4-ounce can mushroom stems and pieces
1 to 3 cups sliced celery
1   9-ounce can pineapple chunks, drained
1/4 cup water
2 tablespoons flour

✦ Brown pot roast in bacon drippings or lard in heavy saucepan; drain. Stir in soy sauce, 1/2 cup water, pepper, ginger and onion.

✦ Cook, covered, over low heat for 3 to 31/2 hours or until pot roast is tender. Stir in mixture of mushrooms, celery and pineapple. Cook for 20 to 30 minutes or until celery is tender.

✦ Transfer roast to warm serving platter. Stir mixture of 1/4 cup water and flour into pan drippings. Cook until thickened, stirring constantly.

✦ Serve gravy with pot roast.

Beef with Snow Peas

Yield: 4 servings

1 pound sirloin steak, thinly sliced
1/4 cup cooking sherry
2 tablespoons soy sauce
2 tablespoons cornstarch
1/4 cup vegetable oil
2 teaspoons minced garlic
3/4 pound fresh snow peas, ends trimmed
1 cup beef stock

✦ Combine steak, sherry, soy sauce and cornstarch in large bowl; toss to mix well.

✦ Heat oil in wok or large skillet. Add steak mixture. Sauté until steak is cooked through, stirring constantly. Add garlic and snow peas. Sauté for several minutes.

✦ Add beef stock. Cook until a thick sauce forms, stirring constantly.

✦ Serve immediately over rice.

Honey Pork

Yield: 8 servings

1½ teaspoons soybean oil
1 tablespoon black bean sauce
1 teaspoon chopped garlic in oil
½ teaspoon salt
1¼ teaspoons ground ginger
2 tablespoons honey
¾ teaspoon Five Spice powder
2 pounds cubed pork
chopped garlic to taste
¾ teaspoon finely chopped gingerroot
1½ tablespoons oyster sauce
¾ cup chicken stock
1½ tablespoons cold water
1 tablespoon cornstarch
1½ teaspoons sesame oil
1⅛ pounds Chinese cabbage, cut into 2x2-inch
    pieces
2 tablespoons soybean oil

❦ Combine 1½ teaspoons soybean oil, black bean sauce, 1 teaspoon chopped garlic, salt, ground ginger, honey, Five Spice powder and pork in bowl; mix well. Marinate, covered, in refrigerator for 24 hours. Drain, reserving marinade.

❦ Preheat oven to 325 degrees. Place pork in baking pan. Bake for 30 minutes, stirring after 15 minutes; drain. Pour reserved marinade over pork. Bake, covered, for 15 minutes.

❦ Combine chopped garlic to taste, gingerroot, oyster sauce and chicken stock in saucepan; mix well. Cook until heated through. Stir in mixture of cold water and cornstarch. Add sesame oil; mix well. Cook until thickened, stirring constantly. Remove from heat.

❦ Sauté cabbage in 2 tablespoons soybean oil in skillet until it begins to wilt. Stir in thickened sauce. Spoon into serving dish. Top with pork and sauce.

Chinese Chicken with Cashews

Yield: 8 servings

For the marinade:

1/3 cup sesame oil
1/3 cup rice vinegar
1/4 cup dry sherry
2 cloves of garlic, finely chopped
2 pounds boned and skinned chicken pieces

For the stir-fry:

1/2 pound snow peas, trimmed
1/3 cup soy sauce
1 1/2 teaspoons cornstarch
1/3 cup hoisin sauce
1 tablespoon sugar (optional)
2 tablespoons grated fresh gingerroot
2 tablespoons vegetable oil or peanut oil
1   7-ounce can water chestnuts, drained, sliced
1/2 pound mushrooms, sliced
1 1/2 cups chopped cashews
3/4 to 1 cup sliced scallions with tops
3 cups rice, cooked

To marinate the chicken:

✤ Combine sesame oil, rice vinegar, sherry and garlic in bowl; mix well.

✤ Rinse chicken and pat dry. Cut into 1-inch pieces. Add to marinade.

✤ Marinate in refrigerator for 1 hour. Drain, reserving marinade.

To stir-fry the chicken:

✤ Blanch snow peas in boiling water in saucepan for 30 seconds; drain.

✤ Combine soy sauce and cornstarch in bowl; mix well. Stir in hoisin sauce, sugar and ginger.

✤ Heat oil in wok or heavy saucepan over high heat. Add chicken. Stir-fry for 3 to 4 minutes or until chicken is opaque and white.

✤ Stir in reserved marinade and soy sauce mixture. Add snow peas, water chestnuts, mushrooms and cashews; mix well. Cook for 5 to 6 minutes or until mixture is heated through, stirring frequently.

✤ Add scallions; mix well. Stir-fry for 1 minute. Serve on hot cooked rice.

Chicken Oriental

Yield: 6 servings

3 6-ounce boneless skinless whole chicken
   breasts
¾ cup hoisin sauce
2 tablespoons soybean oil
2 tablespoons cooking sherry
2 tablespoons soy sauce
2 tablespoons honey
1 tablespoon chopped garlic in oil
1½ teaspoons finely chopped gingerroot
1½ teaspoons cornstarch
1½ tablespoons water

Variation: May also serve as an appetizer.

* Cut chicken into bite-sized pieces; rinse chicken and pat dry. Combine hoisin sauce, soybean oil, sherry, soy sauce, honey, chopped garlic and gingerroot in bowl; mix well. Add chicken, tossing to coat. Marinate, covered, in refrigerator overnight. Drain, reserving marinade.

* Preheat oven to 375 degrees.

* Bring marinade to a boil in saucepan. Stir in mixture of cornstarch and water. Cook until thickened, stirring constantly.

* Arrange chicken on baking sheet. Bake until internal temperature reaches 165 degrees on meat thermometer, basting occasionally with thickened sauce.

Pancit

Yield: 4 servings

2 whole chicken breasts
½ pound pork roast or pork chops, cut into
   bite-sized pieces
2 cloves of garlic, finely chopped
1 tablespoon peanut oil
1 medium onion, chopped
1 cup cooked shrimp
soy sauce to taste
1 tablespoon peanut oil
1 or 2 carrots, sliced diagonally
1 or 2 stalks celery, sliced diagonally
½ head cabbage, chopped
1 10-ounce package pancit noodles

* Rinse chicken. Combine chicken and enough water to cover in saucepan. Cook for 20 minutes or until tender. Drain, reserving stock. Chop chicken, discarding skin and bones.

* Brown pork with garlic in 1 tablespoon peanut oil in wok. Stir in onion, chicken, shrimp and soy sauce. Transfer mixture to platter.

* Heat 1 tablespoon peanut oil in wok. Stir-fry carrots, celery and cabbage in batches until tender-crisp. Transfer mixture to platter.

* Cook noodles in 2 cups reserved stock in saucepan until tender; drain.

* Combine noodles, pork mixture and vegetable mixture in bowl; mix well. Serve immediately.

Cau Da (Seafood with Ginger, Tomato and Chilies)

*From **The Simple Art of Vietnamese Cooking**.*

Yield: 4 servings

2 tablespoons oil
6 cloves of garlic, pounded in mortar to a paste
1   1-inch piece of gingerroot, peeled, chopped
½ pound medium shrimp, peeled, deveined
½ pound sea scallops
½ pound flounder or sole fillets, cut into 2-inch pieces
1 tablespoon sugar
¼ cup bottled fish sauce (nuoc mam)
¼ to 1 teaspoon dried chili flakes or to taste
1 large tomato, seeds removed, chopped
2 large scallions, thinly sliced
¼ cup chopped coriander

✤ Heat oil over high heat in large skillet or wok. Add garlic and ginger. Stir-fry for 30 seconds. Arrange shrimp, scallops and flounder evenly in wok. Cook for 2 minutes or just until seafood tests done, turning once. Remove seafood to platter.

✤ Add sugar, fish sauce and chili flakes to wok. Cook for 2 minutes or until slightly thickened, stirring constantly. Stir in tomato and scallions. Stir-fry for 1 minute.

✤ Return seafood and any accumulated juices to wok; mix well. Stir-fry for 30 seconds or until heated through. Spoon onto platter; sprinkle with coriander. Serve with hot cooked rice.

For those who think the American dream is a thing of the past, consider Bihn Van Duong and his contribution of another thread in the tapestry of America. Bihn Van Duong was born in South Vietnam, the ninth of twelve children. With the fall of South Vietnam in 1975, five members of his family escaped to the Philippines, eventually to locate in Hartford, Connecticut. The family worked at various jobs to survive, which included working for other Asians in the restaurant business. After several years, they opened Truc Orient Express in Hartford and another in West Stockbridge, Massachusetts. Bihn attended the Culinary Institute of America and at age 21 took over the operation of the Hartford restaurant. He has coauthored *The Simple Art of Vietnamese Cooking*, which was nominated for the Best Ethnic Cookbook in 1992 by the International Association of Culinary Professionals. He has received many other honors and accolades in his chosen profession, for which he gives his mother credit. Says Mr. Duong, "I owe a lot to my mother for what she taught me, particularly about cooking. Culturally, it was not acceptable for a man to prepare food. My father would not have approved. I think though that he would see that the cuisine that we took for granted in Vietnam has sustained us in more than one way in our new homeland."

Asparagus Shung Tung

Yield: 10 servings

1½ pounds asparagus, trimmed
1½ quarts water
1½ teaspoons salt
1 tablespoon sugar
1 teaspoon Oriental sesame oil

Note: May store asparagus in water to cover in refrigerator for several days.

* Cut asparagus diagonally into ¼-inch pieces.
* Bring water to a boil in wok or large saucepan. Add asparagus. Cook for 1½ minutes. Drain; immerse in cold water several times to cool quickly. Drain.
* Place asparagus in bowl. Pour mixture of salt, sugar and sesame oil over asparagus, tossing to coat.

Stir-Fried Vegetable Medley

Yield: 10 servings

1½ pounds asparagus, trimmed
½ pound fresh mushrooms, sliced
4 scallions, chopped
1 tablespoon peanut oil
1½ teaspoons salt
1 tablespoon sugar
1 tablespoon Oriental sesame oil

* Cut asparagus diagonally into ¼-inch pieces.
* Stir-fry asparagus, mushrooms and scallions in peanut oil in wok or skillet until tender-crisp.
* Add salt, sugar and sesame oil; mix well.
* Serve immediately.

Indonesian Rice

Yield: 8 to 10

4 cups water
2 cups rice
1 cup sliced carrots
1 cup julienned celery
1 cup canned or fresh French-style green beans
1 cup sliced onion
1/2 cup butter, softened
1 teaspoon salt
1/2 cup sliced almonds
1/2 cup raisins
1/4 teaspoon thyme
1/4 teaspoon marjoram
1/4 teaspoon basil
1/4 teaspoon dried parsley

✦ Bring water to a boil in saucepan. Add rice. Cook, covered, until water is absorbed.

✦ Combine carrots, celery, green beans and onion with enough water to cover in saucepan. Cook until vegetables are tender; drain.

✦ Combine rice and vegetables in bowl; mix well. Stir in butter, salt, almonds, raisins, thyme, marjoram, basil and parsley.

Vegetable Lo Mein

Yield: 4 servings

2 tablespoons olive oil
1 pound mushrooms, cut into quarters
2 tablespoons olive oil
8 ounces Chinese pea pods, trimmed
4 stalks celery, cut diagonally into 1/2-inch pieces
1 small bunch scallions, cut into 1-inch slices
1 large red bell pepper, thinly sliced
1 pound bean sprouts
1/4 cup soy sauce
1 tablespoon sherry
1 teaspoon cornstarch
1 envelope vegetable or chicken bouillon
1/2 cup water
1   8-ounce package linguine, cooked, drained
1/4 cup roasted unsalted peanuts (optional)

✦ Heat 2 tablespoons olive oil in 12-inch skillet. Add mushrooms. Cook over high heat until tender and light brown, stirring constantly. Transfer to bowl.

✦ Add 2 tablespoons olive oil to skillet. Add pea pods, celery, scallions, red pepper and bean sprouts. Cook over high heat for 5 minutes or until vegetables are tender-crisp, stirring constantly.

✦ Stir in mixture of soy sauce, sherry, cornstarch, bouillon and water. Bring to a boil. Add linguine and mushrooms; mix gently. Cook until heated through, stirring frequently.

✦ Spoon mixture onto warm serving platter; sprinkle with peanuts.

Com Chay (Vietnamese Stir-Fried Vegetables)

Yield: 6 servings

8 dried black Chinese mushrooms
1/2 cup water
1 tablespoon soy sauce
1 teaspoon Oriental sesame oil
2 teaspoons sugar
1 tablespoon vegetable oil
1 clove of garlic, crushed
1/2 teaspoon finely chopped gingerroot
2 to 3 cups chopped Chinese cabbage
2 carrots, cut into 1/2-inch slices
4 green onions, sliced
3 to 4 cups bean sprouts
1/4 cup water
1 teaspoon cornstarch
1 tablespoon water
1 1/2 tablespoons soy sauce
cooked rice

Note: May substitute or add any vegetable desired including turnips and mustard greens.

✦ Soak Chinese mushrooms in enough water to cover in bowl for 30 minutes; drain and slice.
✦ Combine 1/2 cup water, 1 tablespoon soy sauce, sesame oil and sugar in saucepan. Add mushrooms. Simmer until most of liquid is absorbed, stirring occasionally.
✦ Heat vegetable oil in wok. Stir-fry garlic and gingerroot briefly. Add cabbage, carrots, green onions and bean sprouts. Stir-fry for 2 to 3 minutes or until vegetables are tender-crisp.
✦ Add mushroom mixture and 1/4 cup water; mix well. Bring to a boil. Stir in mixture of cornstarch and 1 tablespoon water. Cook until thickened, stirring constantly.
✦ Season to taste with remaining soy sauce. Serve over hot cooked rice.

Thai Peach Marinade

Yield: 1 cup

1   16-ounce can juice-pack peaches
1 clove of garlic, crushed
1 tablespoon black peppercorns, crushed
1 cup finely chopped parsley
juice of 1 lemon
2 to 3 teaspoons ground coriander

Note: Use as marinade or serve as sauce with cooked lamb or veal.

✦ Process undrained peaches in blender until smooth. Combine peach purée with garlic, peppercorns, parsley, lemon juice and coriander in bowl; mix well.
✦ Spoon marinade over lamb or veal. Marinate in refrigerator for 2 hours to overnight. Drain, reserving marinade. Heat reserved marinade in saucepan.

Chinese Almond Cookies

Yield: 36 servings

1 teaspoon almond extract
2 cups shortening
4 cups flour
1½ cups sugar
1½ teaspoons salt
¾ cup whole blanched almonds

Note: May substitute butter or margarine for shortening.

✦ Preheat oven to 300 degrees.

✦ Cream almond extract and shortening in mixer bowl until smooth. Add flour gradually, mixing well after each addition. Add sugar and salt; mix well. Knead until paste is formed.

✦ Shape dough into thick roll; cut into ½-inch slices. Place on ungreased cookie sheet. Press almond into center of each cookie.

✦ Bake for 30 minutes. Remove to wire rack to cool.

Ginger and Persimmon Ice

Yield: 6 cups

1 cup water
1 cup sugar
3 cups persimmon purée
6 tablespoons orange liqueur
¼ cup minced candied ginger
1 tablespoon minced fresh ginger
½ teaspoon cinnamon

✦ Combine water and sugar in saucepan. Cook until sugar is dissolved. Cool to room temperature. Chill for 2 hours or longer.

✦ Combine sugar syrup with remaining ingredients in bowl; mix well. Pour into ice cream freezer container.

✦ Freeze using manufacturer's directions.

The ginger used in cooking is actually the root of the ginger plant. It can be used fresh, dried or preserved or candied. Most preserved ginger comes from China. It is also valued for its medicinal uses for a stomachache or toothache.

Australia

*T*he hunting and gathering Aboriginal peoples of Australia, known as Bush Tuckers, once comprised over 500 tribes. They lived harmoniously with nature for over 40,000 years before their lands were settled by European immigrants. There were over 4,000 varieties of indigenous plants, animals, and insects that provided a surprisingly nutritious diet. Included in a list would be wichetty grubs, mangrove worms, green plum, yams, berries, goannas, kangaroos, wombats, woolly-butt grass seeds, and a multitude of fish and shellfish varieties along the coast and inland rivers. These sources of food also played an important role in the spiritual lives of the individual tribes. Plants and animals prized as delicacies by a coastal tribe of New South Wales might be the sacred "totem" of a tribe in the central plains.

With the arrival of settlers from Europe during the late 1700s, a variety of new crops and livestock, primarily cattle and sheep, was introduced to Australia. These new citizens of the "land down under" did not embrace the indigenous foods and customs of the natives and immediately set about recreating the cuisines they left behind.

Although known for large meals of heavy starches and meats, modern Australia is finally adapting the cooking techniques of Asia and Polynesia. There is a new emphasis on fruits and vegetables from the virtually pollution-free growing region of the Antipodes and the bounty of the sea.

Australia

Vegemite Pinwheels

Yield: 54 servings

1½ cups flour
1½ teaspoons salt
1½ teaspoons baking powder
cayenne pepper to taste
1 teaspoon dry mustard
2 tablespoons butter
1½ cups shredded cheese
⅓ cup water
Vegemite

♣ Preheat oven to 375 degrees.

♣ Sift flour, salt, baking powder, cayenne pepper and dry mustard in bowl; mix well. Cut in butter until crumbly. Add cheese; mix well. Add water, stirring until stiff dough forms.

♣ Knead dough on lightly floured surface. Roll into rectangle; spread with Vegemite. Roll as for jelly roll; cut into slices. Place on greased baking sheet.

♣ Bake for 15 to 20 minutes or until brown. Remove to wire rack to cool.

Vegemite Sticks

Yield: 72 servings

12 slices bread
2 tablespoons butter, softened
¼ 4-ounce jar Vegemite
2 cups shredded Cheddar cheese

♣ Preheat oven to 375 degrees.

♣ Spread bread slices with butter and Vegemite. Sprinkle with cheese. Cut each bread slice into 6 strips. Place on nonstick baking sheet.

♣ Bake for 15 to 20 minutes or until crisp. Remove to wire rack to cool. Store in airtight container.

A uniquely Australian food product is something called Vegemite. It's a concentrated yeast extract that Australians spread on toast instead of jam. It's packed with vitamins and other nutrients and is an Australian staple. In the U.S. it's available from The Australian Catalogue Company, 7412 Wingfoot Drive, Raleigh, NC 27615 as well as some health food stores. You may also substitute any non-meat-based yeast extract for Vegemite, such as Bovril.

New Zealand Fish Soup

Yield: 4 servings

1 large onion, chopped
3 cloves of garlic, finely chopped
2 tablespoons olive oil
2 cups chopped fresh tomatoes
2   14-ounce cans chicken broth
1 pound white fish, cut into 1-inch pieces
3 cups chopped spinach
3 kiwifruit, peeled, chopped
½ cup chopped fresh basil

♣ Sauté onion and garlic in olive oil in skillet until soft. Stir in tomatoes and chicken broth. Simmer for 10 minutes, stirring occasionally.

♣ Add fish and spinach; mix well. Simmer for 5 minutes or until fish flakes easily, stirring occasionally. Stir in kiwifruit and basil just before serving.

Queensland Blue Pumpkin Soup

Queensland Blue is a variety of pumpkin noted for its flavor and keeping qualities. If this variety is not available to you, use whatever pumpkin variety you can find.

Yield: 6 servings

½ cup butter
4½ cups chopped peeled pumpkin
½ cup chopped onion
2 cups water
1 cup milk
¼ cup butter
3 tablespoons flour
1 egg yolk, beaten
salt to taste

♣ Melt ½ cup butter in heavy saucepan. Add pumpkin and onion; mix well. Cook, covered, for 10 minutes, stirring occasionally. Stir in water. Cook until pumpkin is tender, stirring occasionally.

♣ Pour pumpkin mixture and some milk in blender container. Process until puréed.

♣ Melt ¼ cup butter in heavy saucepan. Stir in flour gradually until blended. Add pumpkin purée and remaining milk; mix well. Simmer for 20 minutes, stirring constantly.

♣ Stir a small amount of pumpkin soup into egg yolk; stir egg yolk into pumpkin soup. Season with salt. Ladle into soup bowls.

Melon Salad with Prawns

Prawns are actually extra-large shrimp.

Yield: 6 servings

½ head endive, torn
1 pound prawns, cooked, peeled
½ honeydew melon, chopped
½ cantaloupe, chopped
1 tablespoon tomato sauce
2 teaspoons Worcestershire sauce
½ cup mayonnaise
1 tablespoon lemon juice
2 teaspoons castor (superfine) sugar
2 tablespoons chopped fresh parsley

♣ Arrange endive on serving platter. Top with prawns, honeydew melon and cantaloupe.
♣ Combine tomato sauce, Worcestershire sauce, mayonnaise, lemon juice, sugar and parsley in bowl; mix well.
♣ Spoon over salad.

Pumpkin Salad

Yield: 6 servings

4 slices bacon, chopped
2¼ pounds pumpkin, peeled, cut into cubes
¾ cup chopped walnuts
1 apple, chopped
3 shallots, chopped
1 stalk celery, chopped
½ cup mayonnaise
½ teaspoon nutmeg

♣ Fry bacon in skillet until crisp; drain. Cool.
♣ Combine pumpkin and enough water to cover in saucepan. Cook over medium heat until tender; drain. Cool.
♣ Combine bacon, pumpkin, walnuts, apple, shallots, celery, mayonnaise and nutmeg in bowl; mix well.

Orange-Ginger Roast Beef

Yield: 6 servings

1¾ pounds lean topside or eye of round, trimmed
freshly ground pepper
2 cloves of garlic, cut into slivers
1   1-inch piece gingerroot, cut into slivers
2 thin strips orange rind
⅓ cup orange juice
1 tablespoon honey
12 new potatoes
¾ pound broccoli flowerets
2 medium carrots, julienned
1 teaspoon cornstarch or cornflour
cold water

✦ Rub roast with pepper. Make slits in roast with a sharp knife. Insert garlic and ½ of the ginger slivers into slits. Place on an upturned microwave-safe saucer in microwave-safe dish.

✦ Combine orange rind, orange juice, honey and remaining ginger in bowl; mix well. Brush roast with orange mixture.

✦ Microwave on High for 5 minutes. Microwave on Medium for 8 minutes; turn roast. Brush with remaining orange mixture. Microwave on Medium for 8 minutes.

✦ Steam potatoes in steamer basket in saucepan for 8 minutes. Add broccoli and carrots. Steam for 5 minutes.

✦ Remove roast to platter; wrap in foil. Let stand for 10 minutes. Strain pan drippings into microwave-safe dish. Stir in mixture of cornstarch and a small amount of cold water. Microwave on High for 2 minutes. Serve with roast and vegetables.

Barbecued Leg of Lamb

Yield: 8 servings

1/2 bottle of dry white wine
2 tablespoons virgin olive oil
3 cloves of garlic, crushed
6 basil leaves
1 small carrot, chopped
1 small onion, chopped
5 black peppercorns
1 3-pound leg of lamb, trimmed, butterflied
vegetable oil
salt and pepper to taste

* Combine white wine, olive oil, garlic, basil, carrot, onion and peppercorns in shallow dish; mix well. Add lamb; mix well.
* Marinate, covered, in refrigerator for 4 hours or longer. Drain; brush lamb with vegetable oil.
* Preheat grill.
* Grill lamb over hot coals for 7 minutes on each side. Season with salt and pepper. Grill for 20 minutes longer or until desired degree of doneness, turning once. Let stand, wrapped in foil, for 10 minutes before slicing.

Spicy Vindaloo Paste

Brush mixture over beef or lamb while cooking on grill.

Yield: 7 tablespoons

1 teaspoon ground cardamom
1 teaspoon chili powder
1 teaspoon ground cinnamon
1/4 cup white vinegar
2 teaspoons ground cumin
2 teaspoons turmeric
2 teaspoons dry mustard

* Combine cardamom, chili powder, cinnamon, vinegar, cumin, turmeric and dry mustard in bowl; mix well.

Jolly Jumpbuck in a Tuckerbag

This is a spectacular-looking entrée. The pastry forms a pouch enclosing the herbed lamb filling. The bone extending out of the top of the pouch looks like the stem coming off a piece of fruit.

Yield: 4 servings

1   1-pound lamb loin, trimmed, cut into 1-inch
    pieces
2 mint leaves
1 sprig of rosemary
1 sprig of marjoram
1 sprig of parsley
½ onion
1 egg
salt and pepper to taste
4 sheets puff pastry
4 cutlet bones, cleaned (optional)
8 to 12 long cooked spaghetti strands or chives
1 egg, beaten
1 tablespoon water
2 tablespoons butter
1 cup sliced mushrooms (optional)
4 teaspoons flour
1 cup beef broth
1 tablespoon minced chives
3 tablespoons sweet Madeira wine

✤ Preheat oven to 350 degrees.

✤ Grind lamb, mint leaves, rosemary, marjoram, parsley and onion in meat grinder. Combine mixture with 1 egg in bowl; mix well. Season with salt and pepper. Let stand, covered, in refrigerator while preparing pastry.

✤ Cut 8-inch circle in each puff pastry sheet. Shape lamb mixture into 4 patties. Place lamb patty in center of each puff pastry circle. Place cutlet bone vertically in each patty. Draw up sides; squeeze end pieces between forefinger and thumb around cutlet bone. Tie tops with spaghetti. Place on lightly greased baking sheet. Brush with mixture of remaining 1 egg and water. Bake for 15 to 20 minutes or until golden brown.

✤ Melt butter in saucepan. Add mushrooms. Sauté for 3 minutes or until golden. Sprinkle with flour. Stir in broth. Cook until thickened, stirring frequently. Add chives and Madeira. Cook for 3 minutes longer.

✤ Serve immediately with hot Madeira sauce and vegetable.

> Until fairly recently, Australians were recognized as the greatest meat eaters of the world. Until the postwar migration years, Australians rarely ate fruit or salads and virtually ignored the large variety of seafood that surrounded them.

Dinner Loaf

This is an unusual stuffed bread that is a meal in itself!

Yield: 6 servings

1 round loaf whole wheat or white bread
1 onion, chopped
2 cloves of garlic, crushed
2 medium zucchini, sliced
1 teaspoon oil
1⅓ pounds ground round
1 tablespoon flour
¼ cup beef broth
2 teaspoons Worcestershire sauce
2 tablespoons chopped parsley
salt and pepper to taste
4 lettuce leaves, torn into bite-sized pieces
2 medium tomatoes, cut into wedges
1 small cucumber, thinly sliced

Note: Store leftover bread crumbs in freezer.

✤ Preheat oven to 350 degrees.
✤ Cut top from bread loaf, reserving top. Remove center carefully, leaving ¾-inch shell. Cut bread from center into cubes; make into bread crumbs, reserving ¾ cup.
✤ Sauté onion, garlic and zucchini in oil in skillet for 5 minutes. Add meat; mix well. Cook for 5 minutes, stirring frequently; drain.
✤ Stir in flour, beef broth, Worcestershire sauce and parsley. Simmer until thickened, stirring constantly. Season with salt and pepper. Stir in reserved bread crumbs.
✤ Spoon mixture into bread shell, replacing bread top. Wrap in foil. Place on baking sheet.
✤ Bake for 15 minutes; open foil. Bake for 5 minutes longer; cut into wedges. Serve with a lettuce, tomato and cucumber salad.

Lobster Medallions with Curry Sauce

Yield: 4 servings

1¼ cups sour cream
⅓ cup white wine
1 teaspoon curry powder
2 teaspoons lemon juice
2 teaspoons chopped fresh coriander
1 tablespoon chopped fresh chives
4 lobster tails

✤ Combine sour cream, wine and curry powder in saucepan. Cook over low heat until thickened. Stir in lemon juice, coriander and chives. Cook just until heated through.
✤ Remove lobster meat from shell. Cut into 1-inch slices. Grill over hot coals until tender. Serve with warm curry sauce.

Mushrooms with Cilantro Butter

Yield: 4 servings

¹/₂ cup butter
1 clove of garlic, crushed
2 teaspoons grated lime rind
¹/₃ cup chopped fresh cilantro
1 pound mushrooms, stems removed

✤ Combine butter, garlic, lime rind and cilantro in bowl; mix well.
✤ Spread underside of mushroom caps with butter mixture. Place on baking sheet.
✤ Bake until mushrooms are tender.

Sugar-Crusted Parsnips

Yield: 4 servings

1 pound parsnips, peeled, cut into julienne strips
2 tablespoons butter
1 tablespoon brown sugar
nutmeg to taste
¹/₄ teaspoon salt
¹/₈ teaspoon pepper

✤ Cook parsnips in enough water to cover for 5 minutes; drain.
✤ Melt butter in saucepan. Stir in brown sugar, nutmeg, salt and pepper. Add parsnips; mix well. Cook for 2 minutes, stirring occasionally.

Oddly enough, the United States is largely responsible for the settlement of Australia. The American Revolution made it impossible for England to use America as its prison. The settlement of Australia started after 1770 when the British started using it as a dumping ground for its convicts. Between 1788 and 1856, 157,000 convicts were sent to Australia. This is only ¹/₃ of the total number previously sent to the United States. Today's Australians are quite proud of their past and the independent spirit it has fostered in their national character.

Potato and Pumpkin Casserole

Yield: 6 servings

2 large potatoes, sliced
1/2 pound pumpkin, peeled, sliced
1 large onion, sliced
1/2 cup half and half
2 tablespoons white wine
1 cup shredded Cheddar cheese
1/4 cup margarine, softened

* Preheat oven to 350 degrees.
* Arrange potatoes, pumpkin and onion in greased baking dish.
* Combine half and half, wine, cheese and margarine in bowl; mix well. Spoon mixture over vegetables.
* Bake, covered, for 30 to 40 minutes or until vegetables are tender.

Potatoes Stuffed with Crab Meat

Yield: 6 servings.

6 baking potatoes, baked
2 tablespoons margarine, softened
1   6-ounce can crab meat, drained, flaked
2 tablespoons chopped fresh chives
1/2 cup sour cream
1/4 cup mayonnaise
1 tablespoon chopped fresh parsley
2 tablespoons corn and chili relish
1 tablespoon lemon juice

* Preheat oven to 350 degrees.
* Slice tops off potatoes, reserving tops. Scoop out pulp carefully, leaving 1-inch shell. Mash potato pulp with margarine in bowl.
* Stir in crab meat, chives, sour cream, mayonnaise, parsley, relish and lemon juice. Spoon mixture into shells; replace reserved tops. Place on baking sheet.
* Bake for 20 to 30 minutes or until heated through.

Creamy Paprika Sauce

Yield: 4 servings

1 tablespoon butter or margarine
1 onion, finely chopped
1 1/2 tablespoons paprika
1 cup light sour cream
1 tablespoon tomato paste
freshly ground pepper

* Melt butter or margarine in saucepan. Add onion. Cook until tender.
* Add paprika. Cook for 1 minute.
* Stir in sour cream, tomato paste and pepper. Heat just to serving temperature. Serve with veal.

Best Barbie Sauce

Serve with beef or lamb.

Yield: 4 servings

1 onion, finely chopped
1 clove of garlic, crushed
1/4 cup tomato sauce
1/2 cup red wine
1 tablespoon olive oil
1 tablespoon soy sauce
1/2 teaspoon chili powder
freshly ground pepper

* Combine onion, garlic, tomato sauce, red wine, olive oil, soy sauce, chili powder and pepper in saucepan.
* Bring to a boil, stirring frequently. Cook for 10 minutes, stirring frequently.

Mint and Onion Sauce

Serve with lamb.

Yield: 4 servings

2 tablespoons butter or margarine
2 large onions, finely chopped
1/2 cup water
1/4 chopped mint
freshly ground pepper
1 to 2 drops of green food coloring

* Melt butter in saucepan. Add onions and water; mix well. Cook, covered, over low heat for 15 minutes or until onions are tender, stirring occasionally.
* Spoon into blender or food processor container. Process until puréed. Stir in mint, pepper and food coloring.

Peach Sauce

Serve with lamb or veal.

Yield: 4 servings

1 cup peach nectar
1/4 teaspoon cinnamon
2 teaspoons cornstarch or cornflour

* Bring peach nectar, cinnamon and cornstarch to a boil in saucepan, stirring constantly.

Bushman's Tucker

Damper is a bread known in Australia as "Bushman's Tucker." Traditionally made by bushmen, damper can be cooked in the hot ashes of a fire. The outside will be burnt, and when the damper is broken open, only the center is eaten. If you bake this bread in an oven, you may eat the whole thing!

Yield: 12 servings

3 cups flour
3½ teaspoons salt
3 teaspoons baking powder
1 tablespoon sugar
½ cup butter
1 cup water or skim milk

✤ Preheat oven to 400 degrees.
✤ Combine flour, salt, baking powder and sugar in bowl; mix well. Cut in butter until crumbly. Add water; mix well.
✤ Shape dough into 8-inch round loaf. Place on nonstick baking sheet. Bake for 10 minutes. Reduce oven temperature to 350 degrees. Bake for 15 to 20 minutes longer or until loaf sounds hollow when tapped.

Drover's Damper

This is a more sophisticated version of the basic damper recipe above.

Yield: 8 servings

2 cups flour
2½ teaspoons salt
2 teaspoons baking powder
2 teaspoons sugar
1 tablespoon butter
1 cup shredded cheese
1 cup beer
milk

✤ Preheat oven to 400 degrees.
✤ Sift flour, salt and baking powder into bowl; mix well. Stir in sugar. Cut in butter until crumbly. Stir in cheese. Add beer. Mix until medium-soft dough forms.
✤ Knead lightly on floured surface until smooth. Shape into round loaf. Place in round bread pan; brush with milk.
✤ Bake for 10 minutes. Reduce oven temperature to 350 degrees. Bake for 10 minutes longer or until light brown. Wrap damper in tea towel. Let stand until cool. Serve with butter and golden syrup or jam.

Pikelets

Yield: 6 servings

2 eggs, beaten
milk
2 cups flour
1 teaspoon baking soda
1½ teaspoons cream of tartar
salt to taste
2 tablespoons sugar

✦ Preheat griddle. Combine eggs with enough milk to measure 1 cup; mix well.
✦ Sift flour, baking soda, cream of tartar, salt and sugar in mixer bowl; mix well. Add egg mixture, beating in as much air as possible.
✦ Drop by tablespoonfuls onto hot buttered griddle. Bake until brown on both sides.
✦ Serve with whipped cream and strawberry jam.

Anzac Biscuits

These were often sent to Australian soldiers at Gallipoli in Turkey during World War I by loving families.

Yield: 60 servings

1 cup rolled oats
1 cup desiccated coconut
1 cup flour
1 cup packed brown sugar
2 teaspoons ginger
½ cup butter
1 tablespoon golden or corn syrup
½ teaspoon baking soda
2 tablespoons boiling water

✦ Preheat oven to 350 degrees. Mix oats, coconut, flour, brown sugar and ginger in bowl.
✦ Combine butter and golden syrup in saucepan. Cook over low heat until butter melts, stirring constantly. Add mixture of baking soda and boiling water; mix well.
✦ Pour butter mixture into center of oat mixture, stirring until a moist and firm dough forms.
✦ Drop by teaspoonfuls onto cold greased baking sheet. Bake for 15 minutes. Remove to wire rack to cool.

Peach Melba

This dessert was named for the famous singer, Dame Nellie Melba.

Yield: 6 servings

3 large peaches, peeled
1½ cups vanilla ice cream
whipped cream
raspberry syrup

✦ Combine peaches and enough water to cover in saucepan. Cook until tender; drain. Cut peaches into halves, discarding pits. Chill.
✦ Place peaches cut side up on individual plates. Fill with ice cream; top with whipped cream. Spoon raspberry syrup around peaches.

Famous Cornflour Sponge Cake

Yield: 16 servings

2/3 cup cornflour
1 tablespoon (heaping) all-purpose flour
1 teaspoon baking powder
3 egg whites
salt to taste
1/2 cup castor (superfine) sugar
3 egg yolks
1/4 teaspoon vanilla extract

♣ Preheat oven to 375 degrees.
♣ Sift cornflour, all-purpose flour and baking powder together 3 times.
♣ Beat egg whites and salt in mixer bowl until soft peaks form. Add sugar gradually, beating constantly until stiff peaks form. Beat in egg yolks and vanilla until blended.
♣ Fold dry ingredients into egg mixture. Spoon into 2 greased and floured 8-inch round cake pans. Bake for 18 to 20 minutes or until layers test done. Remove to wire rack to cool completely.

Pavlova

The Pavlova was created in 1935 by Chef Bert Sachse while he was working at Perth's Esplanade Hotel. He made it in honor of the hotel's most distinguished guest of previous years, the great prima ballerina, Anna Matveena Pavlova. It is now considered a national dish.

Yield: 12 servings

oil
4 egg whites
salt to taste
1 1/4 cups castor (superfine) sugar
1 teaspoon vinegar
2 teaspoons cornstarch of cornflour
whipped cream
strawberries
sliced kiwifruit
sliced passion fruit
sliced bananas

♣ Preheat oven to 350 degrees. Draw 8-inch circle on parchment; brush with oil. Place on greased baking sheet.
♣ Beat egg whites and salt in mixer bowl until stiff but not dry. Add sugar 1 tablespoon at a time, beating until meringue is smooth and glossy. Sprinkle vinegar and cornflour over meringue; fold into mixture.
♣ Spread meringue evenly over greased butcher paper circle, making depression in middle with back of spoon. Place on rack in bottom half of oven. Reduce heat to 250 degrees. Bake for 1 1/2 hours. Turn off heat. Let stand in oven with door closed until cooled.
♣ Remove shell from butcher paper; place on serving plate. Fill shell with whipped cream. Arrange strawberries, kiwifruit, passion fruit and bananas over top.

Lamingtons

These small cakes were popularized by Queenslanders in the early 1900s.

Yield: 36 servings

For the lamingtons:

2¹/₂ cups flour
2¹/₂ teaspoons salt
2¹/₂ teaspoons baking powder
10 tablespoons butter, softened
10 tablespoons sugar
2 eggs, beaten
¹/₄ cup milk
vanilla extract to taste

For the chocolate icing:

1 pound dark chocolate, melted
¹/₄ cup butter
2 tablespoons baking cocoa
vanilla extract to taste
toasted coconut

Note: To toast coconut, spread in shallow baking pan. Bake in 250-degree oven until brown.

To make the lamingtons:

+ Preheat oven to 350 degrees.
+ Sift flour, salt and baking powder several times.
+ Cream butter and sugar in mixer bowl until light and fluffy. Add eggs, milk and vanilla; mix well. Beat in flour.
+ Spoon batter into buttered 9x13-inch baking pan. Bake for 30 minutes. Invert onto wire rack. Cool overnight.

To make the chocolate icing:

+ Combine chocolate with mixture of butter, baking cocoa and vanilla in bowl; mix well.

To assemble the lamingtons:

+ Cut lamingtons into squares. Frost all sides with chocolate icing; roll in coconut.

Billy Tea

To be had where old mates yarn. Some old-timers swing the billy of boiling tea around their heads. This is a sure way of making a good brew.

Yield: variable

fresh stream water
1 handful of tea leaves
1 to 2 green gum leaves

+ Bring a billycan of fresh stream water to a boil over hot coals of a fire. Add 1 handful of tea leaves. Boil for 1 minute. Add 1 to 2 green gum leaves. Let stand by the fire for 2 minutes.
+ Tap sides of can with a stick to settle the tea leaves. Pour tea into mugs.

Eastern Europe & Russia

*T*his chapter represents an amazing amount of ground—literally and figuratively! In the fifteen former Soviet Republics and Eastern Europe there is an amazing range of languages, climate, religions, and cultures. These countries do share physical proximity and some common foods, but more importantly, they have shared common experiences. Despite religious repression, political upheavals, natural disasters, sieges, purges, occupations, and the horrors of wars, there is an optimism in these people known only by true survivors. You can see it in their love of fresh flowers, the folklore, the multitude of feasts celebrated with gusto, and religious and ethnic traditions that somehow survived.

There is a remarkable sense of community. It is evident in Schumata, Bulgaria, where once a year townspeople together produce their famous plum brandy, slivova. In Sofia, Romania, St. Nicholas festival dishes are baked overnight in the town baker's ovens. In Daghestan, an old dating-dance ritual brings together young people whose social interactions are hindered by the extreme mountainous terrain.

The cuisines have been affected over the centuries by Middle Eastern, Asian, and European influence, but traditional foods are distinctive, hearty fare designed to satisfy your soul. In the Caucasus region of Armenia, Azerbaijan, and Georgia, the delicious, healthy diet affects body and soul. It often is credited with the longevity of the citizens of the region, where many work until they are 100, and some live to see 130 birthdays!

The resurgence of interest in ethnic foods in America, coupled with free travel into this exotic part of the world, will spark an explosive demand for these unheralded foods.

Note: For the sake of brevity only, in our chapter titles we have "named" the fifteen former Soviet Republics "Russia," a word that traditionally represented the entire region to Americans. It was not our intention to slight the recently formed fourteen independent states in any way.

Eastern Europe & Russia

Mushrooms in Sour Cream

Yield: 4 servings

1½ pounds mushrooms
salt to taste
butter for sautéing
1 cup sour cream
herbs to taste such as dill, basil or parsley

✤ Remove mushroom stems and slice caps. Add salt. Sauté in butter in skillet until liquid has evaporated.

✤ Stir in sour cream and herbs. Bring just to a simmer.

Fleischküchla (Little Meat Cakes)

Yield: 6 to 8 servings

For the filling:
2 pounds lean ground beef
¾ pound finely ground pork
1 cup finely chopped onion
1 cup warm water
salt and pepper to taste

For the pastry dough:
4 cups wheat flour
1 teaspoon salt
1 cup milk
1 cup (about) water
vegetable or canola oil for deep frying

To make the filling:

✤ Brown ground beef and pork with onion in skillet, stirring until meat is crumbly; drain. Stir in warm water, salt and pepper. Cook until heated through.

This dish was originally brought to the Crimean Peninsula by the Mongolian people in the 13th century; they probably made it with mutton. The dish was adapted by the German-Russians in the area and was prepared after the autumn slaughter of pigs and deep-fried in the lard rendered at that time. German-Russian immigrants from the Crimea brought the recipe to their settlements in North Dakota, where it is still served. A Russian variation, called Pelmeni, uses egg in the pastry dough and instead of deep frying, the dumplings are simmered in boiling water. These are traditionally served with butter or sour cream and small glasses of vodka.

To make the meat cakes:

✤ Mix flour and salt in bowl. Add milk and enough water to form a soft dough; mix well. Let rest, covered, for 10 to 15 minutes. Roll dough on floured surface. Cut into 3 to 4-inch squares. Place 1½ tablespoons filling on each square. Fold dough over to enclose filling, sealing edges.

✤ Deep-fry in 375-degree oil until golden brown.

Hot Borscht

This recipe is from Chef Paul Ingenito of the renowned Russian Tea Room in New York City.

Yield: 6 servings

¹/₂ cup sliced onion
3 tablespoons bacon drippings
2 tablespoons clarified butter
1 cup shredded cabbage
¹/₂ cup julienned carrots
4 cups beef consommé
1 tablespoon tomato purée
2 cups julienned beets
3 cups water
¹/₄ cup red wine vinegar
2 tablespoons potato starch or cornstarch
salt and pepper to taste
¹/₂ cup sour cream, warmed

Garnish:
¹/₄ cup chopped fresh dill

* Sauté onion in bacon drippings and clarified butter in large saucepan until tender. Add cabbage. Sauté until tender. Add carrots. Sauté until tender.

* Stir in beef consommé and tomato purée; reduce heat. Bring to a simmer, skimming surface.

* Cook beets in 3 cups water in small saucepan over medium heat until tender. Reserve ¹/₄ cup beet cooking liquid. Add beets and 2 cups of beet cooking liquid to soup. Add vinegar and bring to a simmer.

* Stir in mixture of potato starch dissolved in reserved beet liquid. Cook for 2 minutes or until thickened, stirring constantly. Season with salt and pepper.

* Ladle into soup bowls. Serve with heated sour cream. Garnish with chopped dill.

There are many recipes for this Russian and Polish soup. It can be thick or thin, with meat or meatless, hot or cold. It can also be made with *kvas*, which is a liquid fermented from rye bread, water, sugar, yeast and flour. A garnish of grated fresh beets adds an appetizing touch of color.

Sweet and Sour Cabbage Soup

This is an adaptation of a traditional soup originally made with short ribs or brisket and served with potato pancakes (page 114). It can also be made with chopped chicken or meatballs. The ratio of sweet and sour can be tailored to individual tastes by adjusting the sauerkraut and sugar or by adding lemon juice.

Yield: 4 to 6 servings

1/2 pound ground beef
1 1/2 to 2 pounds cabbage, shredded
1 large onion, chopped
2 medium carrots, chopped
1 28-ounce can stewed tomatoes
1 10-ounce can tomato soup
1 8-ounce can sauerkraut
2 large potatoes, cut into eighths
1/4 to 1/3 cup sugar
1/4 cup packed brown sugar
4 cups water
salt and pepper to taste

Note: May make ahead; flavor improves with reheating. Freezes well.

* Brown ground beef in skillet, stirring until crumbly; drain.
* Combine beef with cabbage, onion, carrots, tomatoes, soup, undrained sauerkraut, potatoes, sugar, brown sugar and water in saucepan. Season with salt and pepper.
* Simmer, covered, for 2 1/2 to 3 hours; adjust seasoning. Ladle into soup bowls. Serve with sour cream and dark pumpernickel bread.

Potato Soup

Yield: 14 servings

16 medium potatoes
3 1/2 quarts beef stock
5 tablespoons flour
2 cups sour cream
3 tablespoons dried parsley flakes
1 tablespoon dried dillweed
white pepper to taste

Garnish:
garlic and Cheddar croutons or
   Cheddar and Romano croutons

* Peel potatoes and cut into 3/4-inch cubes. Soak in cold water to cover in bowl for 20 minutes; drain.
* Add potatoes to beef stock in large soup pot. Bring to a boil; reduce heat. Simmer for 20 to 30 minutes or until tender.
* Blend flour with a small amount of water in small bowl. Add to soup; mix well. Cook until thickened, stirring constantly; remove from heat.
* Stir in sour cream, parsley flakes, dillweed and white pepper. Ladle into soup bowls. Garnish with croutons.

Ciorba de Prisoare (Meatball Soup)

*This is the most popular soup in Romania. It can be made without the meat, but it is always soured. In Moldavia or Mantania, **borsch** (produced by fermenting the flour or the grain) is used. This recipe uses lemon juice instead.*

Yield: 10 servings

For the meatballs:

2 onions, chopped
oil for sautéing
2 pounds ground veal, pork, chicken, turkey or
    beef, or a mixture of these
2 tomatoes, chopped
3 eggs
1 cup bread crumbs
1/2 teaspoon chicken base
chopped fresh dill to taste
salt to taste
1/2 teaspoon pepper

For the soup:

1 pound veal or beef bones
1 bunch celery, chopped
5 carrots, chopped
salt to taste
16 cups boiling water
2 onions, chopped
2 green bell peppers, chopped
2 cups uncooked rice
1/2 cup (or less) lemon juice
1 onion, chopped
4 tomatoes, chopped
1 cup sour cream, yogurt or milk
1 egg yolk
3 tablespoons cold water

Garnish:

chopped parsley and dill

To make the meatballs:

♣ Sauté onions in oil in skillet. Combine with ground meats and tomatoes; mix for 5 minutes. Add eggs, bread crumbs, chicken base, dill, salt and pepper; mix well. Shape into small balls.

To make the soup:

♣ Add veal or beef bones, celery, carrots and salt to 16 cups boiling water in large saucepan. Cook for 30 minutes; remove bones.

♣ Add 2 onions, green peppers, rice and lemon juice. Cook over medium heat for 10 minutes. Add meatballs. Cook for 20 minutes.

♣ Sauté 1 onion with tomatoes in nonstick skillet for 5 minutes. Add to soup. Cook until meatballs rise to top of soup; remove from heat.

♣ Mix sour cream, egg yolk and 3 tablespoons water in small bowl. Stir into soup. Ladle into soup bowls. Garnish with chopped parsley and dill.

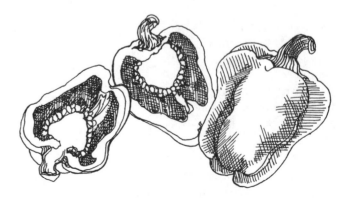

Rosolje (Beet and Potato Salad)

The beets give this traditional Estonian potato salad a rosy color.

Yield: 10 servings

For the dressing:
1 cup sour cream
2 tablespoons vinegar
1 teaspoon mustard
1/2 teaspoon sugar
1/4 teaspoon pepper

For the salad:
3 beets
6 potatoes
1 salted herring or prepared pickled herring
2 cups chopped roast beef
4 dill pickles, chopped
2 apples, chopped
1/2 onion, minced
2 hard-boiled eggs, chopped

To make the dressing:
* Combine sour cream, vinegar, mustard, sugar and pepper in bowl; mix well and set aside.

To make the salad:
* Cook unpeeled beets and potatoes separately in water to cover in saucepans until tender. Drain and chop into 1/2-inch pieces.
* Soak, clean and chop salted herring.
* Combine beets, potatoes, herring, roast beef, pickles, apples, onion and eggs in bowl. Add dressing; mix gently.
* Serve immediately or chill overnight.

Red Cabbage Salad

Yield: 12 servings

1   8-inch head red cabbage, coarsely shredded
3   16-ounce cans beets, drained, julienned
2 medium carrots, coarsely grated
1 red onion, sliced lengthwise
1 teaspoon oregano
2 teaspoons sweet basil
1 tablespoon parsley flakes
garlic powder, salt and coarsely ground pepper
   to taste
1/4 cup olive oil
1/4 cup red wine vinegar

* Combine cabbage, beets, carrots and onion in bowl; mix well. Add oregano, basil, parsley, garlic powder, salt and pepper to taste.
* Stir in olive oil and vinegar. Chill overnight.

Golabki (Cabbage Rolls)

Yield: 12 servings

For the filling:

3 slices bacon, chopped
1 large onion, chopped
1 large green bell pepper, chopped
3 stalks celery, chopped
1 tablespoon flour
1   8-ounce can tomato sauce
¼ cup (about) water
salt and pepper to taste
4 pounds ground beef
1 pound ground pork
½ cup rice, cooked

For the cabbage rolls:

1 large head cabbage
½ cup catsup
1 cup water

To make the filling:

✤ Sauté bacon, onion, green pepper and celery in skillet until vegetables are tender. Sprinkle with flour.

✤ Stir in tomato sauce and water. Bring to a boil; remove from heat. Season with salt and pepper. Cool slightly.

✤ Add ground beef, ground pork and rice; mix well.

To make the cabbage rolls:

✤ Preheat oven to 350 degrees.

✤ Cook cabbage in boiling water in large stockpot, removing leaves as they become tender. Cut out thick ribs with sharp knife.

✤ Spoon filling onto cabbage leaves. Amount of filling will depend on size of cabbage leaves. Roll leaves to enclose filling, tucking in ends. Place in large shallow baking pan. Mix together catsup and water and pour over rolls.

✤ Bake, covered with foil, for 2 hours.

Golabki means *little pigeons* and is a category of food that refers to packets of meat or vegetable fillings enclosed in cabbage, grape, spinach or beet leaves. Other names such as *dolmas* and *holubtsi* refer to the same thing. Golabki can be served hot or cold.

Polish Lasagna

This is an adaptation of Polish golabki. The filling, with the addition of garlic powder, can also be used to stuff peppers.

Yield: 12 servings

2 medium heads cabbage
¾ pound salt pork
2   28-ounce cans tomatoes
3 eggs
3 tablespoons parsley flakes
pepper to taste
3 pounds ground beef
3 cups white rice, cooked

Note: Serve with rye or pumpernickel bread, hot cherry peppers and a green salad.

* Preheat oven to 325 degrees.
* Remove cores from cabbages. Steam until leaves can be removed. Cut out thick ribs; drain.
* Cut salt pork into ¼-inch pieces. Render in saucepan; drain, reserving pork and 3 to 4 tablespoons drippings.
* Combine reserved pork and drippings with tomatoes; mix well. Spread half the mixture in 10x15-inch baking pan.
* Beat eggs in bowl. Add parsley, pepper, ground beef and rice; mix well.
* Layer half the cabbage leaves, ground beef mixture, remaining cabbage leaves and remaining tomato mixture in prepared baking pan.
* Place on foil in oven. Bake for 1 hour or until bubbly.

Fasouli (Lamb with Green Beans)

Yield: 4 servings

1 pound lamb stew meat
salt and pepper to taste
1 pound green beans
1 large onion, sliced
1 small can tomatoes
sugar to taste

* Sprinkle lamb with salt and pepper. Cook in water to cover in saucepan for 45 minutes.
* Cut beans into 2-inch pieces. Add to lamb with onion and tomatoes; sprinkle with sugar.
* Simmer for 45 minutes, stirring occasionally. Serve with rice pilaf.

Sweet and Sour Meatballs

Yield: 8 servings

2 pounds ground beef
1/3 cup cracker crumbs or matzo meal
1 egg
garlic salt and pepper to taste
2 tablespoons oil
2 8-ounce cans tomato sauce
3/4 cup red wine
4 to 6 tablespoons brown sugar
3 tablespoons chopped fresh parsley
3 onions, sliced
2 large lemons, sliced

Note: Must make ahead; freezes well.

* Combine ground beef, cracker crumbs, egg, garlic salt and pepper in bowl; mix well. Shape into 1-inch balls.
* Brown meatballs in oil in 10-inch skillet; drain.
* Add tomato sauce, wine, brown sugar, parsley, onions and lemons; mix gently. Simmer for 30 minutes, stirring occasionally. Cool to room temperature. Refrigerate overnight.
* Reheat meatballs in sauce for 15 minutes.

Pork Chop Casserole

This is a hearty stick-to-the-ribs pork dish.

Yield: 6 servings

1 medium onion, thinly sliced
2 cloves of garlic, sliced
1/4 cup olive oil
1 large can tomatoes or 2 pounds fresh tomatoes, peeled, seeded, chopped
12 green olives, cut into halves
2 tablespoons capers
1 hot pepper, cut into strips
1 large bay leaf
1/2 teaspoon oregano
salt to taste
6 pork chops

* Preheat oven to 325 degrees.
* Sauté onion and garlic lightly in olive oil in skillet until tender but not brown. Add tomatoes, olives, capers, hot pepper, bay leaf, oregano and salt. Cook for 10 minutes.
* Cover bottom of 9x13-inch baking dish with half the tomato sauce. Arrange pork chops in single layer in prepared dish; top with remaining sauce.
* Bake for 40 minutes; discard bay leaf. Serve over rice.

Paprikash

This dish can be made with chicken, veal, pork, lamb, turkey, rabbit or beef. Serve it with salad or pickles.

Yield: 8 servings

4 onions, chopped
1/2 cup oil
2 pounds meat, cubed
1 teaspoon paprika
4 tomatoes, chopped
2 cups water
3 green bell peppers, chopped
2 cups chopped mushrooms
4 cloves of garlic, minced
2 teaspoons chopped parsley
2 teaspoons chicken base
2 teaspoons dill
salt to taste
1/2 teaspoon pepper
1   16-ounce package pasta shells or bows or
    noodles

✤ Sauté onions in oil in saucepan until tender. Add meat, paprika, tomatoes and water. Cook for 30 minutes.

✤ Add green peppers, mushrooms, garlic, parsley, chicken base, dill, salt and pepper; mix well. Simmer for 1 1/2 hours or until meat is very tender.

✤ Add pasta. Simmer for 5 minutes.

Note: May prepare in advance and add pasta at serving time.

Variation: May substitute potatoes or dumplings for pasta or serve over noodles.

Silvia Salvari, a native of the Transylvania area of Romania, has succeeded in bringing old-world cooking to all of us lucky enough to visit her delightful restaurant in Enfield, Connecticut. Silvia's culinary interests were piqued as a child growing up in her father's bakery in Lespezi, a town with many Jewish Russians, where his adoptive Jewish parents had taught him the secrets of baking wonderful breads. She pursued these interests, studying culinary arts in Romania and eventually publishing her own cookbook, which today is being translated into English.

Following her immigration to America in 1984, she opened Silvia's Gourmet Kitchen to the delight of her customers, some of whom are recent immigrants themselves, willing to drive an hour to be greeted at the door by the familiar aromas of home. Not content to be just a Romanian restaurant, Silvia's extensive menu touts its selections as *European cooking*, with Hungarian, Polish, Greek, German, Russian and Italian cuisines represented. And, as a bow to her new country, she has included a few American favorites as well.

Also try Silvia's recipe for Ciorba de Prisoare (page 102), a traditional Romanian meatball soup.

Pierogi

There are probably as many pierogi recipes as there are Polish cooks. Pierogi can be filled with vegetable or fruit fillings. Try the prune filling, potato and cheese filling or cabbage filling on page 109.

Yield: 6 servings

For the pierogi:

2 cups flour
1 teaspoon salt
1 egg, slightly beaten
1/2 cup water
salt to taste
pierogi fillings (page 109)

To make the pierogi:

✤ Place flour in bowl; make well in center. Add 1 teaspoon salt, egg and water; mix well. Knead on floured surface for 5 minutes or until no longer sticky, kneading in additional flour if needed. Let rest, covered with small bowl, for 10 minutes.

✤ Divide into 2 portions. Roll 1 portion at a time into circle on floured surface, leaving remaining portion covered. Cut into small circles or 2-inch squares.

✤ Spoon chilled filling onto each circle or square. Fold dough over to enclose filling; press edges to seal.

✤ Drop pierogi into saucepan of salted boiling water. Cook for 2 to 5 minutes or until pierogi float to surface. Remove to colander with slotted spoon; rinse with cold water.

For the past 30 years the good parishioners of St. Michael's Church in Binghamton, New York, have been mass producing pierogi during Lent. According to Father James Dutko, the efforts of roughly 100 men and women organized by his father, Stephen Dutko, create a major fund-raising event each year. Every Friday during Lent those lucky enough to live close by purchase traditional cheese, potato or cabbage pierogi by calling (607) 729-0261. (See the following page for the St. Michael's Pierogi recipe.)

Pierogi Fillings

Vegetable-filled pierogi can be topped with onion sautéed in butter. Fruit-filled pierogi can be served with sour cream.

Yield: 3 fillings

R ecipe for St. Michael's Church Pierogi:

6,425 pounds of flour
5,420 eggs
1,836 pounds butter and margarine
12,500 pounds of potatoes
6,200 pounds of cabbage
660 pounds sauerkraut
764 pounds of extra-sharp cheese
1,000 pounds onions

Add unlimited amounts of tireless devotion and good sense of humor, and perhaps most important of all, an abundance of volunteers joyful with a living and loving faith.

If you'd like to make a smaller batch, try our recipe on these pages.

For the prune filling:
large pitted prunes

✤ Cook prunes using package directions; drain and cool. Use 1 prune for each pierogi.

For the potato and cheese filling:
2 or 3 large potatoes, peeled, cubed
1 slice onion, finely chopped
5 to 8 slices Cheddar cheese, chopped
salt and pepper to taste

✤ Cook potatoes in boiling water in saucepan until tender; drain. Add onion, cheese, salt and pepper; mash until smooth. Cool completely.

For the cabbage filling:
1 small head cabbage, chopped
1 small can sauerkraut, drained, rinsed
1 bay leaf
1 large onion, finely chopped
2 tablespoons oil
¼ cup melted butter
1   4-ounce can mushrooms pieces, drained
salt and pepper to taste

✤ Cook cabbage with sauerkraut and bay leaf in water to cover in saucepan for 15 to 20 minutes or until cabbage is tender; drain. Sauté onion in mixture of oil and butter in large skillet over medium heat. Add cabbage mixture and mushrooms. Simmer for 30 minutes. Season with salt and pepper; discard bay leaf. Cool completely.

Pita di Spinaku
(Vlach Spinach Pie)

Caryn Balamaci is descended from a small Romance-speaking Balkan ethnic group known as Vlachs or Arumanians. As members of an oral culture, the Vlachs have no shared alphabet or literary tradition, and so this pita recipe has been handed down verbally through many generations. It is different than the middle-eastern pitas you may already be familiar with.

Caryn's "Maia," or maternal grandmother, left Albania in 1916 and never returned; today, at 90, she still regales her family with vivid stories of the old country. Last year, after a 76-year separation, Maia was visited by the "baby sister" she left behind in Albania. Though Maia and her sister disagree on the finer points of making a good pita, they both agree on one thing—theirs is the best!

Maia has a few do's and don'ts regarding the art of pita making:

* **Never** cook pita on a humid day.
* **Always** make pita first thing in the morning.
* **Never** let the dough get tough; roll it until it is light and fluffy.
* **Always** remember Maia's special secret about pita dough.
* **Never** reveal Maia's special secret about pita dough.

Don't worry—a great pita can be made even without Maia's secret, and after a few tries, you'll discover your own secret ways to improve it.

Yield: 18 servings

For the spinach filling:
2   10-ounce packages frozen spinach
4 eggs
1 pound cottage cheese, farmer cheese or crumbled feta cheese
salt to taste
1 tablespoon melted butter

To make the spinach filling:
* Cook spinach using package directions. Combine with eggs, cottage cheese, salt and butter in bowl; mix well. Set aside.

Pita di Spinaku (continued)

For the pita dough:

4½ to 5 cups unbleached flour
2 teaspoons salt
2 to 2½ cups water
1 cup melted butter

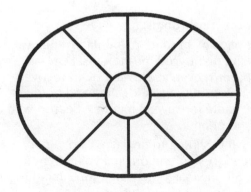

For the assembly:

1 tablespoon melted butter

To make the pita dough:

♣ Sift flour into large bowl. Stir in salt with fork. Add water gradually, working with fingers to form smooth dough.

♣ Knead on floured surface for 10 minutes, adding additional flour or water if needed. Do not let dough become tough. Let stand, covered, for 15 minutes.

♣ Divide dough into 2 portions. Roll 1 portion to 12x14-inch oval. Brush with melted butter. Draw a small circle in the center with a knife. Cut from center to outer edge to form 8 wedges.

♣ Turn 1 wedge over onto center; brush with butter. Repeat with remaining wedges, layering in center, and leaving the last wedge unbuttered. Repeat with remaining dough portion. Chill in refrigerator.

To assemble spinach pie:

♣ Preheat oven to 450 degrees. Butter 12x14-inch baking pan.

♣ Roll both portions of chilled dough 1 inch bigger than baking pan; fit 1 portion into pan. Spread with spinach filling. Top with remaining portion; tuck edge under bottom to form thick rim. Brush with butter.

♣ Bake for 15 minutes. Reduce oven temperature to 400 degrees. Bake for 15 minutes longer or until crisp and golden brown. Cut into squares.

Seared Marinated Mushrooms with Chèvre Croutons

No Russian buffet table seems complete without a mushroom dish. This one includes three mushroom varieties; their subtle tastes are underlined by a combination of contrasting flavors.

Yield: 4 to 6 servings

For the vinaigrette:

1/2 cup peanut oil
1/2 cup olive oil
1 tablespoon balsamic vinegar
1 tablespoon cider vinegar
3/4 tablespoon white wine vinegar
salt and pepper to taste

For the mushrooms:

2 ounces olive oil
1/4 pound shiitake mushroom caps
1/4 pound oyster mushrooms
1/4 pound button mushrooms
2 cloves of garlic, crushed
bouquet garni of 1/4 bunch fresh thyme and 2
    sprigs fresh rosemary
salt and freshly ground pepper to taste
2 ounces dry white wine

For the croutons:

1 baguette or French bread
olive oil
1 clove of garlic, crushed (optional)
chèvre

Garnish:

seasonal greens and frisée
1 chopped tomato

To make the vinaigrette:

✤ Combine peanut oil, olive oil, vinegars, salt and pepper in bowl; beat until smooth. Adjust seasonings.

To cook the mushrooms:

✤ Heat olive oil in sauté pan until just below smoking point. Add mushrooms. Sear mushrooms evenly, allowing oil to recover heat before stirring. Add garlic and *bouquet garni*. Sauté for several minutes. Season with salt and pepper.

✤ Add wine, stirring to deglaze. Cook until reduced to 1/4 of the original volume; reduce heat. Stir in vinaigrette. Cook for 2 minutes. Cool to room temperature.

To make the croutons:

✤ Preheat oven to 350 degrees.

✤ Slice the bread into 1/4-inch rounds. Brush with olive oil; sprinkle with garlic.

✤ Place on baking sheet. Bake until toasted and crisp.

✤ Spread with cheese. Bake just until cheese is heated.

To assemble the dish:

✤ Drain mushrooms, reserving vinaigrette; arrange randomly on plate lined with seasonal greens and frisée. Place croutons in center of plate; garnish with tomato. Drizzle with warm vinaigrette.

Eggplant Oriental

Another dish from The Russian Tea Room in New York City, this is often called Beggar's Caviar. It originated in the Caucasus and has been popular in Russia for more than a century.

Yield: 8 servings

For the sauce:

1 medium onion, sliced
2 ounces peanut oil
1 tablespoon minced garlic
12 ounces whole canned tomatoes, drained
12 ounces tomato purée
8 ounces chili sauce
½ teaspoon Tabasco sauce
salt and pepper to taste

For the eggplant:

2   1-pound eggplant, peeled, cut into 1-inch cubes
¼ cup (about) olive oil
1 tablespoon lemon juice
Tabasco sauce to taste
salt and pepper to taste
1 tablespoon fresh dill

To make the sauce:

✤ Sauté onion in peanut oil in large sauté pan until tender. Add garlic. Sauté for 2 minutes, stirring constantly. Add tomatoes, tomato purée, chili sauce, Tabasco sauce, salt and pepper; mix well. Simmer over medium heat for 1 hour, stirring frequently.

To make the eggplant:

✤ Preheat the oven to 350 degrees.

✤ Combine eggplant with olive oil and lemon juice in large baking pan; mix to coat well.

✤ Bake for 30 minutes, stirring several times. Stir in tomato sauce. Bake for 30 minutes longer or until eggplant is tender. Cool.

✤ Process in food processor until smooth or chop very fine. Add Tabasco sauce, salt and pepper. Adjust seasonings. Chill until serving time. Fold in dill. Serve slightly chilled.

Houskové Knedlécky (Bread Dumplings)

Serve these dumplings with roast pork, sauerkraut, applesauce and gravy.

Yield: 8 to 10 servings

2 large eggs
1 cup milk
2 teaspoons baking powder
¾ teaspoon salt
3 cups flour, sifted
7 or 8 slices day-old bread, cut into ½-inch cubes

✤ Beat eggs with milk, baking powder and salt in large mixer bowl. Add flour gradually, mixing well with large spoon until smooth. Stir in bread cubes.

✤ Shape into 4 balls. Drop into boiling water in saucepan. Boil for 30 minutes, turning after 15 minutes. Remove with strainer and drain.

✤ Cut into ½-inch slices immediately. Serve hot.

Kugel (Noodle Pudding)

Noodle pudding is used as a side dish, not a dessert.

Yield: 12 servings

1 16-ounce package wide egg noodles
2 cups sour cream
16 ounces cottage cheese
1 cup milk
6 tablespoons melted butter
salt to taste
1/2 cup crushed cornflakes
2 tablespoons butter

Note: May prepare in advance and chill until baking time.

* Preheat oven to 375 degrees. Grease 9x13-inch baking dish.
* Cook noodles using package directions; rinse with cold water and drain.
* Combine noodles with sour cream, cottage cheese, milk, melted butter and salt in bowl; mix well.
* Spoon into prepared baking dish. Sprinkle with cornflakes; dot with 2 tablespoons butter. Bake for 1 1/2 hours.

Holiday Potato Pancakes

These are good served with applesauce and/or sour cream.

Yield: 4 servings

2 medium-large potatoes, peeled
1 small onion, grated
1 egg, beaten, or 2 egg whites
1 1/2 tablespoons flour
1/4 teaspoon baking powder
1/2 teaspoon salt
pepper to taste
2 tablespoons (about) canola oil

Note: Pancakes freeze well; reheat in preheated 450-degree oven.

Variation: May double recipe.

* Grate potatoes into strainer. Rinse with cold water to remove starch; drain.
* Process potatoes with onion in food processor until well mixed. Combine with egg, flour, baking powder, salt and pepper in bowl; mix well.
* Drop by tablespoonfuls into hot oil in skillet. Fry until golden brown and crisp on both sides; drain.

Alla's Pickles

Yield: variable

4 cups water
1 tablespoon sugar
2 tablespoons salt
fresh dill
1 bay leaf
1 horseradish leaf
1 small carrot, peeled, chopped
5 cloves of garlic, peeled
5 peppercorns
pickling cucumbers
oak or cherry tree leaves

♣ Bring water, sugar and salt to a boil in saucepan. Add dill, bay leaf, horseradish leaf, carrot, garlic and peppercorns; remove from heat.

♣ Pour over cucumbers in large bowl or small crock. Let stand at room temperature for 1 day. Add oak or cherry tree leaves to help keep pickles crunchy.

♣ Spoon into jars, leaving ½ inch headspace; seal with 2-piece lids.

Pickles of all kinds reflect the need at one time to preserve for year-round consumption the farmer's peak-of-season bounty. The whole rhythm of the household was disrupted as every woman dropped what she was doing to join the race against time and spoilage.

Pots and funnels were brought from the cupboards, spices and herbs were sorted into cheesecloth bags and fruits and vegetables were readied to take their place among the sparkling jars lining the shelves in the preserve closet.

Blini

This traditional treat is enjoyed at Maslenitsa, The Butter Festival, which is the Russian equivalent of Mardi Gras.

Yield: 8 servings (32 blini)

2 ounces dry yeast
2½ cups lukewarm water
6¼ cups sifted flour
¼ cup melted butter
3 egg yolks, beaten
1 teaspoon salt
2 tablespoons sugar
2 cups milk, heated
3 egg whites, stiffly beaten
butter or oil for frying

Note: Blini should be very thin when cooked and full of holes like lace.

Variation: May also make blini with mixture of buckwheat flour and all-purpose flour. Add 1 pound sifted buckwheat flour in the first stage and 2¼ cups sifted all-purpose flour in the second stage.

✦ Combine yeast with just enough lukewarm water to form smooth paste in bowl. Add remaining lukewarm water and ½ of the flour; mix well. Let rise, covered, in warm place for 30 minutes or until doubled in bulk and bubbly.

✦ Stir in remaining flour gradually, beating until batter is smooth. Add melted butter, egg yolks, salt and sugar; mix well. Stir in heated milk until blended. Let rise in warm place until doubled in bulk. Fold in egg whites. Let rise in warm place until doubled in bulk and bubbly.

✦ Heat 2 small skillets. Brush bottoms with butter or oil. Pour 1 tablespoonful of batter into each skillet, tilting pan to coat bottom. Cook until brown on both sides. Remove to warm dish. Repeat process with remaining batter. May add additional heated milk if batter is too thick.

Paska (Sweet Easter Bread)

This recipe is from Marvin Eckman. His maternal grandparents immigrated to America in 1905 from the Odessa area of Russia. Farming was a long-standing family tradition brought to Wishek, North Dakota, where they also raised twelve children. To this day, Easter isn't Easter without this special bread.

Yield: 2 loaves

1 package dry yeast
½ cup lukewarm water
1 cup lard
3 cups lukewarm milk
1 teaspoon salt
2 cups sugar
1 cup lukewarm cream
6 eggs, beaten
13 to 14 cups flour
1 cup raisins

Variation: May also shape dough into buns.

- Dissolve yeast in lukewarm water; mix well.
- Combine lard, lukewarm milk, salt, sugar and lukewarm cream in 13-quart bowl; mix well. Stir in eggs and 2 cups flour. Add yeast, remaining flour and raisins, stirring until soft dough forms. Knead until dough no longer clings to side of bowl.
- Grease side and bottom of bowl. Turn dough to coat surface. Let rise, covered, in warm place until doubled in bulk. Punch dough down. Let rise, covered, until doubled in bulk.
- Shape dough into 2 loaves; place in loaf pans. Let rise, covered, until doubled in bulk.
- Preheat oven to 350 degrees.
- Bake for 20 to 30 minutes or until loaves sound hollow when tapped and are golden brown.

The ability of Ukranian women to manipulate bread dough into interesting shapes and patterns reaches its artistic peak in the traditional *Paska*. It may have colored uncooked eggs inserted into the braid before baking or be decorated with birds and rosettes, with a cross for the central motif.

Rottermann Factory, 1912

Butter Barrels, Rottermann Factory

Hardu Keck has fond memories of playing in the Rottermann Factory as a young boy in Tallinn, Estonia, where his father was CEO. Forced to flee Estonia, Hardu and his mother first lived in a displaced persons' camp in Germany after World War II. The American soldiers at the camp influenced Hardu more than they could have imagined by giving the children Hershey's candy bars. These candy bars and a friend's penchant for drawing cowboys were major factors in their selection of the United States for their new home. After migrating to California when he was 11, he quickly mastered English and learned that cowboys were no longer commonplace.

Though the family left most of their possessions behind, they somehow managed to preserve their family photographs, many of which show the workings of the Rottermann Factory in detail. The business exported flour, butter and cheese, imported machinery and automobiles, and, as these pictures show, produced bread in enormous quantities—enough to provide one fourth of the entire city's bread requirements each day.

Hardu Keck is today the Provost of the Rhode Island School of Design; ironically, the former Rottermann Factory is an art museum.

Peenleib (Nana's Black Rye Bread)

This is Lydia Keck's recipe for a hearty bread with a mild sweet and sour taste. Still baked and eaten daily throughout Estonia, it is traditionally served with barley blood sausage on Christmas Eve.

Yield: 2 or 3 loaves

For the leavening:

½ cup lukewarm milk
½ cup rye flour

For the bread:

6 cups water
2½ pounds rye flour
1 pound refined flour
1 cup sugar
1 tablespoon salt

To make the leavening:

✤ Combine lukewarm milk and rye flour in bowl; mix well. Let stand in warm place until mixture begins to bubble and sour.

To make the bread:

✤ Bring water to a boil in saucepan. Add ½ of the rye flour, stirring until dough resembles thick porridge. Sprinkle with some of the refined flour. Let stand in a warm place for 24 hours.

✤ Dissolve the bread leavening in a small amount of lukewarm water in bowl; mix well. Stir the leavening into the dough mixture. Sprinkle the dough with some of the refined flour. Let stand for 12 hours. Beat with mixer for 10 minutes. Add ½ cup sugar; mix well. Let stand overnight.

Keck Family, Tallinn, Estonia

✤ Beat the dough with mixer for 10 minutes. Add ½ cup sugar and salt; mix well. Stir in remaining rye flour and refined flour. Knead until smooth and elastic. Let rise in warm place until doubled in bulk.

✤ Shape dough into 2 or 3 loaves. Place on baking sheet sprinkled heavily with flour. Let loaves rise for 15 minutes.

✤ Preheat oven to 300 degrees. Bake for 1 hour and 45 minutes. Brush loaves with lukewarm water; cover with cloth.

Bulka

Traditionally, this Russian bread is served at the end of the evening meal with butter and cream cheese. Toasted, with butter, it also makes an enjoyable breakfast food.

Yield: 16 servings

For the bulka:

1 package dry yeast
1 teaspoon sugar
1/4 cup lukewarm water
1/2 cup butter
1/2 cup sugar
1 cup milk
salt to taste
1 teaspoon almond extract
4 eggs
4 to 5 cups flour, sifted
2 tablespoons butter, softened
1/2 cup sugar
2 tablespoons cinnamon
golden raisins (optional)

For the confectioners' sugar icing:

confectioners' sugar
water
1/4 teaspoon almond extract

Variation: May sprinkle soft icing with multi-colored sugar sprinkles.

To make the bulka:

* Dissolve yeast and 1 teaspoon sugar in lukewarm water in bowl; mix well.
* Combine 1/2 cup butter, 1/2 cup sugar, milk, salt and almond extract in saucepan; mix well. Cook until butter melts and sugar dissolves, stirring constantly. Cool to room temperature.
* Beat eggs in mixer bowl until foamy. Stir in 1 cup flour and yeast. Add 3 to 4 cups flour alternately with butter mixture, mixing well after each addition. Let rise, covered, until doubled in bulk.
* Knead dough on lightly floured surface. Place in bowl. Let rise until doubled in bulk. Knead on lightly floured surface. Roll dough into 1/2-inch thick rectangle. Brush with softened butter; sprinkle with 1/2 cup sugar, cinnamon and raisins. Roll as for jelly roll; cut into 6 pieces. Overlap sections in greased tube pan.
* Preheat oven to 350 degrees.
* Bake for 50 to 60 minutes or until light brown. Remove from oven. Let stand in pan for 10 minutes. Invert onto wire rack. Drizzle with confectioners' sugar icing.

To make the confectioners' sugar icing:

* Combine confectioners' sugar with enough water in bowl to make of spreading consistency. Stir in almond extract.

Russian Black Bread

Yield: 24 servings

4 cups rye flour
2 cups whole bran cereal
2 envelopes dry yeast
2 tablespoons caraway seeds, crushed
2 teaspoons instant coffee granules
2 teaspoons salt
1 teaspoon sugar
1/2 teaspoon fennel seeds, crushed
2 1/2 cups water
1/4 cup butter
1/4 cup white vinegar
1/4 cup dark molasses
1 ounce unsweetened chocolate
2 1/2 to 3 cups unbleached all-purpose flour
1/2 cup water
1 teaspoon cornstarch

✤ Combine rye flour, cereal, yeast, caraway seeds, coffee granules, salt, sugar and fennel seeds in bowl; mix well.

✤ Combine 2 1/2 cups water, butter, vinegar, molasses and chocolate in saucepan; mix well. Cook over medium heat until chocolate is soft and mixture is lukewarm, stirring frequently. Beat into rye flour mixture. Add enough all-purpose flour 1/2 cup at a time to make soft dough. Beat for 3 minutes.

✤ Turn dough onto lightly floured surface. Let rest, covered with bowl, for 10 to 15 minutes. Knead dough for 10 to 15 minutes or until smooth and elastic, adding additional flour as needed. Place in greased bowl, turning to coat surface. Let rise, covered with plastic wrap and hot damp cloth, in warm place until doubled in bulk. Punch dough down. Divide into 2 portions. Shape into round loaves. Place in two 8-inch round bread pans. Let rise, covered with plastic wrap, in warm place until doubled in bulk.

✤ Preheat oven to 350 degrees. Bake for 40 minutes.

✤ Bring 1/2 cup water and cornstarch to a boil in saucepan. Boil for 1 minute, stirring frequently. Brush loaves with mixture. Bake for 5 minutes.

Safran Isai (Estonian Saffron Bread)

Yield: variable

½ teaspoon saffron, crushed
½ cup warm water
2 envelopes dry yeast
½ cup warm half and half
½ teaspoon sugar
⅔ cup melted butter
½ teaspoon salt
1¾ cups sugar
6½ cups flour
2 cups half and half
1 egg, beaten
½ cup slivered almonds
⅔ cup raisins (optional)

✤ Bring saffron and warm water to a boil in saucepan. Remove from heat.

✤ Dissolve yeast in ½ cup warm half and half. Stir in ½ teaspoon sugar. Let stand in warm place for 10 to 15 minutes or until bubbles appear.

✤ Combine saffron, butter, salt, 1¾ cups sugar, ½ of the flour and 2 cups half and half in bowl; mix well. Stir in yeast mixture and remaining flour. Knead until smooth and elastic.

✤ Place dough in greased bowl, turning to coat surface. Let rise, covered, for 2 hours or until doubled in bulk.

✤ Shape the dough into a wreath, buns or crescents. Place on greased baking sheet. Let rise until doubled in bulk. Brush with egg. Sprinkle with almonds and raisins.

✤ Preheat oven to 350 degrees.

✤ Bake wreath for 45 minutes. Bake buns or crescents for 20 to 30 minutes or until brown.

Saffron is one of the world's most expensive spices. It is actually the dried stigma of the purple crocus flower. The reddish-yellow stigmas grow just three to each flower and are hand-harvested. It takes about 225,000 stigmas to produce one pound of saffron, which accounts for its high price. It only requires a pinch, however, to impart a yellow color and distinct taste to breads, cakes and rice dishes.

Haruschee

This pastry is traditionally served at weddings, funerals and other special occasions in Russia. It was brought to this country by immigrants from Onufrovichi, near Minsk.

Yield: 16 servings

3 eggs
1/3 cup sugar
2 cups (about) flour
1/2 teaspoon almond extract
oil for deep frying
confectioners' sugar

Note: The thinner the dough is rolled, the crisper the pastries will be.

♣ Beat eggs and sugar in mixer bowl until thick and lemon-colored. Add flour and almond flavoring; mix well.

♣ Roll as thin as possible on floured surface. Cut into 1 1/2x5-inch pieces. Cut a 2-inch slit lengthwise in center of each strip. Pull 1 end of each strip through slit to form bow ties.

♣ Deep-fry a few at a time in medium-hot oil until bow ties float to top. Turn and fry until golden brown; drain well. Sprinkle on both sides with confectioners' sugar.

Victoria Seitz' grandmother, Tatiana Pesarik, immigrated to America at age 16, where her brother, Feodor, arranged for her to marry Michael Bychok, another Russian immigrant. The Bychoks are pictured here in the second row, far right, at a family wedding. According to Tatiana, the crisp Russian pastries called Haruschee would have been served at just such an occasion.

Aleksandrikook (Alexander Torte)

This pastry was originally named for Czar Alexander of Russia.

Yield: 8 servings

For the torte:

1 cup unsalted butter, chilled
3 tablespoons sugar
3 cups flour
1 egg
2 tablespoons butter, softened
1/2 cup flour

For the glaze:

2 1/2 cups confectioners' sugar
2 teaspoons lemon juice
1/4 cup (scant) cold water
1/2 to 1 cup homemade raspberry jam

To make the torte:

✤ Combine 1 cup butter, sugar and 3 cups flour in large bowl; rub with fingertips until mixture has consistency of coarse meal. Beat in egg; shape into a ball. Chill for 1 hour.

✤ Preheat oven to 250 degrees. Spread softened butter on 2 baking sheets; sprinkle with 1/2 cup flour, shaking off excess.

✤ Divide pastry into 2 portions. Roll each portion into circles on floured surface. Place on prepared baking sheet.

✤ Bake for 40 minutes or until golden brown. Cool on wire rack.

To make the glaze:

✤ Combine confectioners' sugar, lemon juice and water in bowl; mix until smooth.

To assemble the torte:

✤ Place 1 circle on serving plate. Spread with jam; top with remaining pastry. Spread with glaze. Let stand until cool.

Paczki (Polish Bismarcks)

Yield: 30 servings

1 envelope dry yeast
1 cup 105 to 115-degree milk
3½ cups flour
⅓ cup sugar
½ teaspoon salt
⅓ cup melted margarine or butter
2 eggs, slightly beaten
1 teaspoon vanilla extract
½ teaspoon grated orange rind
oil for frying
confectioners' sugar

✤ Dissolve yeast in warm milk. Mix flour, sugar and salt in large bowl. Add yeast and margarine; mix well. Add eggs, vanilla and orange rind; mix to form dough.

✤ Let rise, loosely covered with plastic wrap and towel, in warm place for 1 hour or until doubled in bulk.

✤ Toss lightly on floured surface until no longer sticky. Shape into 30 balls. Place on lightly floured tray. Let rise, covered, for 20 minutes.

✤ Fry in 3 to 4 inches hot oil in skillet for 1 minute on each side or until golden brown; drain. Sprinkle with confectioners' sugar while warm.

Czechoslovakian Bar Cookies

Yield: 24 to 36 bars

1 cup butter, softened
1 cup sugar
2 egg yolks
½ teaspoon almond extract
2 cups flour
1 cup chopped walnuts
½ cup apricot, raspberry or strawberry jam or preserves

✤ Preheat oven to 325 degrees. Grease 8x8 or 7x11-inch baking pan lightly.

✤ Cream butter and sugar in mixer bowl until light and fluffy. Blend in egg yolks and almond flavoring. Add flour gradually, mixing well. Fold in walnuts.

✤ Spread half the dough in prepared baking pan. Spoon jam evenly over batter to within ¼ inch of edges.

✤ Press remaining dough into rectangle on waxed paper the size of baking pan; place over jam.

✤ Bake for 1¼ hours or until very light brown. Cool slightly on wire rack. Cut into small bars while warm.

Strudels

This recipe was taught to descendants of a Russian great-great-grandmother who lived to be 108 years old. The ingredients were measured as she worked in order to determine the amounts. The dough was rolled out on a special tablecloth and was considered thin enough when the design could be seen through the dough. She passed the tablecloth down with the recipe.

Yield: 24 servings

For the pastry:

1/4 cup oil
3/4 cup water
1 egg white
1 teaspoon sugar
1/4 teaspoon salt
4 cups (or more) flour

For the filling:

8 ounces walnuts, chopped
1   15-ounce package golden raisins
1 cup crushed cornflakes
1   32-ounce jar strawberry preserves
3/4 cup sugar
1 cup orange marmalade
1 teaspoon grated lemon rind
1 tablespoon cinnamon-sugar
oil for brushing pastry
confectioners' sugar

To make the pastry:

✦ Blend oil and water in bowl. Add egg white, sugar and salt; mix well. Stir in enough flour to form dough. Knead several times on floured surface. Place in greased bowl, turning to coat surface. Let stand overnight.

To make the filling:

✦ Combine walnuts, raisins, cornflake crumbs, preserves, sugar, marmalade, lemon rind and cinnamon-sugar in bowl; mix well.

To bake the strudels:

✦ Preheat oven to 350 degrees. Oil baking sheet.

✦ Divide the pastry dough into several easily-handled portions. Roll each portion paper thin on floured surface; brush with oil.

✦ Spread filling to within 1 inch of edges. Roll to enclose filling. Place on baking sheet.

✦ Bake for 45 minutes or until light brown. Cool on rack. Sprinkle with confectioners' sugar.

Russian Spiced Tea

Yield: 8 servings

2 tea bags
8 each whole cloves and whole allspice
2 quarts water
1 cup sugar
1/4 cup lemon juice
1/2 cup orange juice

✦ Remove staples from tea bags. Transfer tea to 1 bag. Add spices to empty bag. Restaple.

✦ Bring water to a boil in saucepan. Add sugar and spice bag. Boil for 10 minutes. Remove from heat. Add tea bag. Let steep until desired strength and color is reached. Cool. Stir in lemon juice and orange juice. Chill until serving time.

India

Indian cuisine exhibits both a diversity and a startling commonality. This nation is comprised partly of meat and bread-eaters, as is typical in the North, and vegetarian rice-eaters in the South. Dietary habits are further influenced by religion. Muslims and Hindus who don't eat pork prefer Vindaloo Lamb, Chicken, or Duck, while Catholics, on the other hand, prefer Pork Vindaloo.

A single thread unites all Indian cooks in the preparation of food, however—the use of spices. If asked to name a familiar Indian spice, most Americans would probably name curry. They would most likely also be surprised to discover that curry powder, as we know it, doesn't exist in India.

Instead, Indian cooks create a blend of hot and sweet spices, or masala, as the base from which each dish derives its character; all recipes have their own special masala as their defining ingredient, as in Rogan Josh and Vindaloo dishes, and Tandoori baking. To highlight the importance of spices, Indians have devoted more than two million acres of prime farmland to their cultivation.

India

Tandoori Lamb Kabobs

Tandoori paste gives this dish its typical reddish color.

Yield: 4 servings

1½ cups quick-cooking brown rice
1 1-inch piece of gingerroot, peeled
2 cloves of garlic
1 or 2 red chilies, seeded
20 mint leaves
1 teaspoon ground cumin
⅓ cup fresh lime or lemon juice
1¾ pounds lean lamb, cut into strips
2 tablespoons tandoori paste
1 cup plain nonfat yogurt

Note: Tandoori paste is a mixture of plain yogurt, red food coloring and ground hot red peppers.

* Cook rice according to package directions.
* Preheat grill. Grease skewers.
* Process gingerroot, garlic, chilies, mint leaves, cumin and lime juice in food processor until smooth. Reserve half the mixture.
* Combine remaining mixture with lamb and tandoori paste in bowl; mix well.
* Thread lamb strips on prepared skewers. Grill for 6 to 8 minutes over hot coals or until done to taste, turning occasionally.
* Serve lamb with mixture of yogurt and reserved lime mixture for dipping, rice and a vegetable salad.

Seven-Boy Appetizer

"Boy" is a term for an ingredient or accompaniment in Indian cooking.

Yield: 20 servings

16 ounces cream cheese, softened
2 cups cottage cheese
½ cup yogurt
4 teaspoons curry powder

Toppings:
1 10-ounce jar chutney
⅔ cup chopped green onions
⅔ cup raisins
⅔ cup flaked coconut
2 cups chopped cooked turkey
1 cup chopped salted peanuts
¼ cup chopped green pepper

* Beat cream cheese, cottage cheese, yogurt and curry powder in mixer bowl until smooth. Spread in 9x13-inch dish.
* Spoon chutney over top; sprinkle with mixture of green onions, raisins and coconut. Top with turkey, peanuts and green pepper.
* Serve with assorted crackers.

Avocado Koyamboo (Cold Avocado and Coconut Soup)

Yield: 4 to 6 servings

1 large ripe avocado
1 cup fresh or unsweetened coconut, flaked
1 clove of garlic
2 green chili peppers, seeded
1/2 teaspoon cumin
1/4 teaspoon cardamom
2 tablespoons lemon juice
1/2 teaspoon salt
2 cups water
1 1/2 cups plain yogurt
1/2 cup water
2 tablespoons chopped cilantro

* Peel avocado; cut 6 thin slices. Wrap slices in plastic wrap, reserving for garnish.
* Combine remaining avocado, coconut, garlic, chili peppers, cumin, cardamom, lemon juice, salt and 1 cup water in blender or food processor container. Process until smooth. Add 1 cup water and yogurt. Process until blended.
* Spoon mixture into soup tureen. Stir in 1/2 cup water. Chill for 1 hour. Ladle into soup bowls. Garnish with reserved avocado slices and cilantro.

Mulligatawny Soup

Yield: 4 to 6 servings

1/2 cup chopped onion
1 medium carrot, chopped
2 stalks celery, chopped
1/4 cup butter or margarine
1 1/2 tablespoons flour
2 teaspoons curry powder
4 cups chicken broth
1/2 cup chopped cooked chicken
1 Granny Smith apple, peeled, chopped
1/2 cup cooked rice
1/8 teaspoon thyme
1/4 teaspoon pepper
1/2 cup hot cream

* Sauté onion, carrot and celery in butter in saucepan until tender. Stir in flour and curry powder. Cook for several minutes, stirring constantly.
* Add chicken broth to vegetable mixture; mix well. Simmer for 30 minutes, stirring occasionally. Stir in chicken, apple, rice, thyme and pepper. Simmer for 15 minutes, stirring occasionally.
* Stir in hot cream just before ladling into bowls to serve.

Cucumber Raita (Vegetable in Yogurt)

Raita is a combination of yogurt and vegetables served as a side dish with spicy entrées, rice or as part of a basic Indian meal with flat bread, vegetables and Indian lentils.

Yield: 2 to 3 servings

1¼ cups grated peeled cucumber
1 teaspoon salt
1 cup yogurt
¾ teaspoon crushed green chilies
¼ teaspoon paprika (optional)
¼ cup chopped fresh cilantro

Variation: May be prepared in advance and chilled. May substitute finely chopped tomatoes, carrots and bananas for cucumber.

✤ Combine cucumber and salt in bowl; mix well. Let stand for 5 minutes. Squeeze moisture from grated cucumber.
✤ Combine cucumber with mixture of yogurt, green chilies and paprika in bowl; mix well. Stir in cilantro.

Lamb with Apricots

Yield: 4 servings

12 dried apricots
2 tablespoons fresh curry powder
2 tablespoons oil
2 medium golden onions, chopped
2 teaspoons finely chopped green ginger
2 teaspoons chopped garlic
2 teaspoons chili powder
½ teaspoon turmeric
2 teaspoons ground coriander
1 pound tomato concasse
1 pound fresh Australian Range lamb shoulder or
    leg, trimmed, cut into 1-inch pieces
juice of 1 lemon
1 teaspoon sugar

Variation: May substitute one 15-ounce can chopped tomatoes and 2 tablespoons tomato paste for tomato concasse.

✤ Soak apricots in warm water in bowl until soft; drain.
✤ Sauté curry powder in oil in skillet until fragrant. Add onions; mix well. Cook until tender, stirring constantly. Stir in ginger and garlic. Cook for 2 minutes, stirring constantly. Add chili powder, turmeric, coriander and tomatoes. Cook until thickened, stirring constantly.
✤ Add lamb to mixture. Cook over low heat for 45 minutes or until lamb is tender. Stir in lemon juice, sugar and apricots. Cook for 5 minutes, stirring frequently. Serve with hot cooked long grain rice and poppadums, an Indian bread similar to crackers.

Lamb Curry

Yield: 4 servings

2 large onions, chopped
1 large apple, chopped
2 or 3 cloves of garlic, crushed
1   1-inch piece of gingerroot, crushed
2 to 4 tablespoons oil
1/2 teaspoon turmeric
4 teaspoons ground coriander
2 teaspoons ground cumin
1/2 teaspoon cardamom
1/2 to 3/4 teaspoon cinnamon
1/2 to 3/4 teaspoon ground cloves
1 to 1 1/2 teaspoons chili powder
1 pound cubed lamb
2 to 3 tablespoons plain yogurt
salt to taste
1/2 to 1 cup water
8 to 10 cashews, roasted, ground

Garnish:
cilantro, parsley or onion rings

♣ Sauté onions, apple, garlic and gingerroot in oil in skillet until onions are light brown. Stir in turmeric, coriander, cumin, cardamom, cinnamon, cloves and chili powder. Cook for several minutes, stirring constantly.

♣ Add lamb; mix well. Cook until lamb is light brown, stirring frequently. Stir in yogurt, salt and water. Cook over medium heat until lamb is tender, stirring frequently. Add additional water if necessary.

♣ Stir in cashews. Cook until heated through. Garnish with cilantro, parsley or onion rings. Serve with side dishes of sliced boiled eggs, or your favorite fruits and vegetables.

Curry powder, or *Garam Masala*, is actually a mixture of spices which, in India, is made fresh by the cook and can be of varying degrees of spiciness. The blend frequently includes the basic ingredients of roasted peppercorns, cumin seeds, cloves, cinnamon, coriander seeds, cardamom, turmeric and cayenne or chili pepper, as well as up to twenty additional ingredients.

Pork Vindaloo

Yield: 12 servings

2 tablespoons red pepper flakes
2½ cinnamon sticks
2½ tablespoons coriander seeds
1¼ tablespoons cumin seeds
1½ teaspoons cardamom
1½ teaspoons peppercorns
1 teaspoon cloves
5 tablespoons lime juice
5½ tablespoons finely chopped gingerroot
5½ tablespoons finely chopped garlic
2¼ cups cider vinegar
2½ pounds onions, sliced
9½ tablespoons ghee
5 pounds cubed pork
3½ cups water
salt and pepper to taste

Garnish:
chili peppers

Variation: May substitute clarified butter for ghee. Clarified butter is created when it has been heated gently until the milky solids separate. The solids are discarded, leaving the clear liquid. This is also called drawn butter.

* Preheat oven to 350 degrees.
* Sprinkle red pepper flakes, cinnamon sticks, coriander seeds, cumin seeds, cardamom, peppercorns and cloves on baking sheet. Toast for 3 to 4 minutes or until cumin seeds pop. Cool; grind.
* Purée lime juice, gingerroot, garlic and vinegar in blender. Combine with toasted spices in bowl; mix well.
* Sauté onions in ghee in saucepan until brown. Stir in spice mixture. Cook until liquid evaporates and ghee separates, stirring frequently. Add pork; mix well. Cook for 5 minutes, stirring constantly.
* Add water; mix well. Bring to a boil; reduce heat. Simmer for 45 minutes or until pork is tender, stirring occasionally. Season with salt and pepper. Garnish with chili peppers. Serve with hot cooked rice.

Goa is a small state in the middle of the Malabar coast of India noted for its Vindaloo seasoning. After 4½ centuries of Portuguese rule, control of Goa was returned to India in 1961.

Chicken and Apricots

Yield: 12 servings

4 pounds chicken pieces
3/4 pound onions, chopped
1/2 cup oil
1 tablespoon fresh crushed garlic
2 tablespoons ground ginger
3 pods of cardamom
2 tablespoons cinnamon
1/2 pound tomatoes, chopped
1/2 pound dried apricots
3/4 teaspoon turmeric
3/4 cup milk
1 tablespoon cornstarch
1 teaspoon water

* Rinse chicken and pat dry.
* Sauté onions in oil in skillet until light brown. Add garlic and ginger; mix well. Cook until garlic is brown, stirring constantly.
* Add chicken pieces, cardamom, cinnamon and enough water to cover.
* Simmer, covered, for 1 hour or until chicken is tender. Stir in tomatoes, apricots, turmeric and milk. Simmer, covered, until apricots are tender.
* Stir in mixture of cornstarch and water. Cook until slightly thickened, stirring constantly.

Ginger Chicken

Yield: 4 servings

1 to 1 1/2 pounds boneless chicken breasts
2 onions, finely chopped
2 cloves of garlic, finely chopped
1   1 1/2-inch piece of gingerroot, peeled, finely chopped
3 tablespoons oil
1/2 cup chicken stock
1 1/2 teaspoons pepper
1/2 teaspoon salt
2 or 3 medium tomatoes, cut into wedges
3 tablespoons vinegar

* Rinse chicken and pat dry. Sauté onions, garlic and gingerroot in oil in skillet for 5 minutes or until onions are tender. Push onion mixture to side of skillet, tilting pan so oil accumulates in open space.
* Sauté chicken in skillet for 2 minutes on each side. Redistribute onion mixture around chicken. Stir in stock, pepper, salt, tomatoes and vinegar.
* Cook, covered, over low heat for 15 to 20 minutes or until chicken is tender.
* Transfer chicken to warm platter. Cook liquid over medium-high heat until slightly reduced in volume, stirring constantly. Pour sauce over chicken. Serve with hot cooked rice.

Chicken Tikka Masala

Yield: 6 servings

4 boneless chicken breasts
1 tablespoon tomato paste
1 tablespoon fresh chopped cilantro
3 cloves of garlic, finely chopped
1 2-inch piece of gingerroot, finely chopped
1 hot green chili pepper, chopped
1/2 teaspoon cumin seeds
1/2 teaspoon cumin powder
1 cup yogurt
3 tablespoons oil
1/2 teaspoon cumin seeds
1 medium onion, finely chopped
1/2 teaspoon finely chopped gingerroot
1 clove of garlic, finely chopped
hot green chilies to taste
1/4 teaspoon salt
1/4 teaspoon turmeric
1/2 teaspoon cumin powder
2 teaspoons tomato paste
1/2 tomato, chopped
1/2 green bell pepper, chopped
juice of 1/2 lemon
2 teaspoons white vinegar
1/2 cup whipping cream
2 tablespoons butter

Garnish:

lemon slices
green bell pepper slices
chopped cilantro
chopped tomatoes
chopped onion

❖ Rinse chicken and pat dry. Combine 1 tablespoon tomato paste, cilantro, 3 cloves of garlic, 2-inch piece of gingerroot, 1 chili pepper, 1/2 teaspoon cumin seeds, 1/2 teaspoon cumin powder and yogurt in bowl; mix well. Add chicken, tossing to coat. Marinate, covered, in refrigerator overnight.

❖ Preheat oven to 350 degrees.

❖ Place chicken in baking pan. Bake, covered, for 20 minutes. Cut chicken breasts into 12 pieces.

❖ Heat oil in large saucepan. Add 1/2 teaspoon cumin seeds and onion. Sauté for 2 minutes. Add 1/2 teaspoon gingerroot, 1 clove of garlic, green chilies, salt, turmeric and 1/2 teaspoon cumin powder; mix well. Stir in chicken, 2 teaspoons tomato paste, tomato, green pepper, lemon juice and vinegar. Add cream and butter.

❖ Cook until oil rises to top and mixture is light orange.

❖ Garnish with lemon slices, green pepper, cilantro, tomatoes and chopped onion. Serve with rice.

Shrimp Curry

Yield: 12 to 15 servings

5 pounds onions, chopped
bacon drippings
2 green bell peppers, chopped
1   3-ounce can curry powder
1 cup (or less) lemon juice
4 cups chicken stock
1 or 2 potatoes, chopped
5 pounds shrimp, peeled, deveined
lemon juice

* Sauté onions in bacon drippings in stockpot over very low heat for 1 hour or until golden brown, stirring frequently. Add green pepper. Cook until mixture is dark brown in color, stirring frequently.

* Dissolve curry powder in lemon juice in bowl. Add curry powder mixture and chicken stock to stockpot. Simmer for several hours or until of desired consistency, stirring occasionally. Add potatoes to thicken mixture.

* Marinate shrimp in a small amount of cooked sauce in bowl in refrigerator for 8 hours. Chill remaining sauce. Heat chilled sauce in stockpot. Add undrained marinated shrimp. Simmer until shrimp turn pink. Stir in lemon juice.

* Serve with rice. Pass bowls of green olives, chopped pickles, sliced hard-boiled eggs, raisins, crumbled bacon, chopped peanuts, toasted coconut, fried onion rings, chutney and pappadums.

Phyllis Crosby's mother-in-law, whose father served in the British Army and whose grandfather was the first harbormaster of Bombay, was born in India and lived there until she was 11. As a child, she would sneak into the kitchen to eat curry with the servants, preferring curry to the British fare available in the dining room.

When the family returned home to England, a favorite aunt missed the curry so much that she "invented" her own version in an effort to recapture her Indian experience. Phyllis says it is unlike any curry served in India, but it always makes a hit with guests. She considers it "an Indian curry that came by way of Great Britain."

Chole (Quick Spicy Garbanzo Beans)

Chole is a North Indian fast-food-style recipe popular throughout India. This easy-to-prepare recipe calls for mixing garbanzo beans into a spicy mixture of onions and tomatoes that smother the beans with gravy. It is marvelous as the main course served with tortillas, flat bread or rice dishes.

Yield: 2 to 3 servings

1 cup chopped onions
1 tablespoon oil
1 teaspoon finely chopped garlic
1/2 cup chopped tomatoes
1 teaspoon salt
1/2 teaspoon turmeric
1/2 teaspoon chili powder
1/2 teaspoon cumin powder
1 1/2 teaspoons coriander powder
3/4 teaspoon garam masala or curry powder
1/4 cup water
1   16-ounce can garbanzo beans, rinsed, drained
1 1/4 cups water
2 tablespoons chopped cilantro (optional)

Variation: May use other types of beans such as black-eyed peas or kidney beans. May substitute dried garbanzo beans for canned.

- Sauté onions in oil in skillet over medium-low heat for 5 minutes. Stir in garlic. Sauté for 2 minutes. Add tomatoes. Cook, covered, for 5 minutes or until tomatoes are tender.

- Stir in salt, turmeric, chili powder, cumin powder, coriander powder and garam masala. Sauté for 1 minute.

- Add 1/4 cup water; mix well. Cook, covered, for 3 to 5 minutes or until heated through, stirring frequently. Add beans and remaining water. Bring to a boil; reduce heat. Simmer for 5 minutes, stirring occasionally. Stir in cilantro; mix well. Add additional water if desired. Cook until heated through.

This recipe was submitted by Jessica Shah, who learned Indian cooking while growing up in Bombay. She teaches cooking classes and owns a catering business in Boulder, Colorado, specializing in authentic vegetarian cuisine in Gujarati style from western India. Be sure to try her recipes for Spicy Potato-Cabbage Casserole and Cucumber Raita also in this chapter.

Bayngan Bhurta (Eggplant Casserole)

Yield: 3 to 4 servings

1   16-ounce eggplant
½ teaspoon cumin seeds
1 medium onion, chopped
1 tablespoon oil
1 green chili pepper, chopped
1   1-inch piece of gingerroot, peeled, chopped
2 cloves of garlic, chopped
½ teaspoon each salt, chili powder, turmeric,
   cumin and ground coriander
½ cup thawed frozen peas
1 medium tomato, chopped
1 tablespoon butter
2 or 3 tablespoons whipping cream

Garnish:

chopped cilantro, chopped onions, chopped
   tomatoes, minced gingerroot, Kasoori Methi

♣ Preheat oven to 350 degrees.

♣ Prick eggplant with fork. Place in baking pan. Cook, covered, for 30 to 40 minutes or until soft. Cut eggplant into 1-inch pieces; scoop out pulp.

♣ Sauté cumin seeds and onion in oil in skillet until mixture is light red. Add chili pepper, gingerroot and garlic. Sauté for 2 to 3 minutes. Add salt, chili powder, turmeric, cumin, and coriander; mix well. Stir in peas and tomato. Cook over medium heat for 2 minutes, stirring constantly.

♣ Add eggplant to mixture; mix well. Cook until heated through, stirring constantly. Add butter and cream; mix well. Cook until oil rises to top, stirring constantly. Garnish with cilantro, onions, tomatoes, gingerroot and a dash of Kasoori Methi (an Indian herb similar to dried cilantro).

In March, 1992, Puspa Bokhiria and Sunil Kumar gathered family and friends to open India Mahal, a tandoori Indian restaurant in Groton, Connecticut. The restaurant's appeal lies in its extensive menu of traditional tandoori recipes—various breads, spicy chicken dishes and marinated lamb entrées—along with more nontraditional fish and shrimp tandoori offerings.

The tandoor, a type of clay oven common to northern India, is shaped like a large jar, either sunk into the ground or encased in plaster for insulation. Fired by charcoal, the temperature of the tandoor is scorchingly hot up to the midpoint, with the heat gradually diminishing as it approaches the neck. Skewered meats are lowered into the preheated tandoor and removed frequently for basting; breads are shaped and attached to the higher inside edges, cooking within a few minutes. The tandoor must be lit at least two hours prior to use to achieve the proper heat distribution. This is such a specialized way to cook that a tandoori chef is on staff working with Sunil.

Spicy Potato-Cabbage Casserole

This recipe uses a technique of cooking vegetables commonly used in India. Whole spice seeds are browned in heated oil and added to vegetables to impart a unique flavor.

Yield: 2 to 3 servings

2 teaspoons cumin seeds or mustard seeds
3 tablespoons oil
2½ cups chopped potatoes
2 cups shredded cabbage
½ teaspoon cumin powder
1½ teaspoons coriander powder
½ teaspoon turmeric
½ teaspoon chili powder
¾ teaspoon lemon or lime juice

Garnish:
2 tablespoons chopped fresh cilantro

Note: Other vegetable combinations may be used.

* Cook cumin seeds or mustard seeds in oil in skillet over medium-high heat for 1 minute or until brown. Stir in potatoes. Cook, covered, over low heat for 15 minutes, stirring occasionally.
* Add cabbage. Cook for 5 minutes, stirring frequently. Stir in cumin powder, coriander powder, turmeric, chili powder and lemon or lime juice. Cook, covered, until heated through.
* Garnish with cilantro.

Winter Squash Curry

Yield: 6 servings

5 tablespoons grated coconut
1½ teaspoons ground mustard
1 cup yogurt
¼ cup lentils, soaked, drained
1 tablespoon curry powder
4½ teaspoons oil
1½ pounds winter squash, cooked, chopped

* Preheat oven to 325 degrees.
* Grind coconut and mustard in food processor. Add yogurt; mix well.
* Fry lentils and curry powder in oil in skillet until lentils are crisp; drain. Stir in coconut mixture.
* Arrange squash in baking pan. Spoon coconut mixture over squash. Bake for 15 minutes or until brown.

Carrot-Rice Pilau

Yield: 4 servings

3 tablespoons oil
1 tablespoon ghee or butter
3 or 4 cloves of garlic, finely chopped
1 cup basmati rice, rinsed, drained
1/4 to 1/2 teaspoon turmeric
2 cups grated carrots
2 cups water
salt to taste
1 cup frozen peas
1/2 cup roasted cashews

✤ Heat oil and ghee or butter in skillet. Sauté garlic in skillet until light brown. Add rice; mix well. Cook for 5 to 8 minutes or until brown, stirring frequently. Stir in turmeric and carrots. Sauté over medium heat for 5 minutes.

✤ Add water and salt to mixture. Bring to a boil; reduce heat. Cook, covered, for 15 to 20 minutes or until rice is almost tender. Stir in peas. Cook until rice is tender, stirring occasionally. Sprinkle with cashews. Serve hot.

Peela Chaaval (Cardamom Rice)

Yield: 8 servings

1 medium onion, finely chopped
2 tablespoons oil
8 cardamom seed pods
3 cups chicken stock
2 teaspoons cumin seeds
1/4 teaspoon turmeric
2 cups rice
1/2 cup (or less) water

✤ Sauté onion in oil in skillet over medium-low heat until brown. Add cardamom, stirring until coated with oil. Sauté for 2 minutes.

✤ Stir in stock. Bring to a boil. Add cumin seeds, turmeric and rice; mix well. Simmer for 10 minutes. Add up to 1/2 cup water; mix well. Cook for 5 minutes or until rice is tender.

Chatni Annanaas (Sweet Pineapple Chutney)

Yield: 32 servings

1 medium pineapple, peeled, cored, finely
  chopped
1½ teaspoons ground cumin
1 teaspoon ground fennel
¼ teaspoon ground cinnamon
¼ teaspoon ground coriander
¼ teaspoon cayenne pepper
¼ teaspoon black pepper
juice of 1 lemon
1 teaspoon salt
1½ cups sugar

Note: Flavor improves if stored for 2 to 3 days
before serving. Store in refrigerator after opening.

* Bring pineapple, cumin, fennel, cinnamon,
  coriander, cayenne pepper, black pepper,
  lemon juice, salt and sugar to a boil in
  non-aluminum saucepan, stirring frequently;
  reduce heat. Simmer for 30 minutes or until
  consistency of jam, stirring frequently.
* Spoon into two ½-pint sterilized jars; seal with
  2-piece lids.

Onion Relish

Yield: 6 servings

1 teaspoon salt
¼ teaspoon black pepper
¼ teaspoon cayenne pepper
¼ cup red wine vinegar
2 medium onions, cut into ¼ to ½-inch pieces

* Combine salt, black pepper and cayenne
  pepper in bowl; mix well. Stir in vinegar and
  onions.
* Chill, covered, for 1 hour. Serve with Indian
  dishes.

Paratha

Yield: 6 servings

2 cups chapati flour
1/2 teaspoon salt
1 tablespoon oil
1/2 cup water
5 tablespoons clarified butter

Variation: May substitute mixture of 1 cup unbleached flour and 1 cup whole wheat flour for chapati flour.

✤ Combine 1 1/2 cups flour and salt in bowl; mix well. Pour oil over mixture. Add water gradually, stirring until mixture forms a ball. Add additional water if needed.

✤ Knead dough for 8 to 10 minutes. Let rest, covered with damp cloth, for 30 minutes.

✤ Knead dough for 1 to 2 minutes. Divide into 6 portions; cover with damp cloth.

✤ Roll each portion into 7-inch circle on surface sprinkled with remaining 1/2 cup flour. Brush with clarified butter; fold in half. Brush with clarified butter.

✤ Roll on lightly floured surface until sides are about 7 inches long. Repeat process for each portion.

✤ Fry dough in buttered skillet until golden brown and spotty on both sides; wrap in foil. Reheat bread in foil in 300-degree oven for 10 minutes before serving.

Poori (Fried Bread)

Yield: 48 servings

2 2/3 cups sifted all-purpose flour
1 2/3 cups whole wheat flour
2 teaspoons salt
2 tablespoons shortening
1 1/4 cups water
oil for frying

✤ Combine flour, whole wheat flour and salt in bowl; mix well. Mix in shortening until blended. Stir in water with fork until mixture forms dough.

✤ Shape dough into a ball. Let rest for 30 minutes. Knead on lightly floured surface for 5 minutes or until smooth. Roll 1/8 inch thick; cut into 3-inch circles.

✤ Fry in 365-degree oil in heavy skillet for 30 seconds or until puffed. Turn bread. Fry for 1 minute; drain.

Indian Halwax

Yield: 8 servings

1/2 cup butter
3/4 cup sifted flour
3/4 cup salted nuts
1/2 cup flaked coconut
1/4 teaspoon salt
1/2 teaspoon ground cardamom
1/2 cup sugar
2 cups milk
1/2 teaspoon almond extract
whipped cream

Note: To serve cold, chill in 8x8-inch mold; cut into squares.

✤ Melt butter in heavy deep skillet. Stir in flour, nuts, coconut, salt and cardamom. Cook over low heat until mixture is golden brown, stirring constantly. Remove from heat.

✤ Stir in sugar. Cool for a few minutes. Add mixture of milk and almond extract gradually, mixing well after each addition. Cook over medium heat for 10 minutes or until thickened and glossy, stirring constantly.

✤ Serve hot or cold with whipped cream.

Coriander Cookies

Yield: 48 servings

2 eggs
1/4 cup butter, softened
1 1/2 cups sugar
3 1/2 cups sifted flour
1 tablespoon baking powder
1/2 teaspoon salt
2 teaspoons ground coriander
1 teaspoon ground cardamom
grated rind of 1 lemon
currant jelly
1 egg, beaten
1/2 cup sugar
1/2 cup finely chopped almonds

✤ Beat 2 eggs, butter and 1 1/2 cups sugar in mixer bowl until light and fluffy. Add flour, baking powder, salt, coriander, cardamom and lemon rind; mix well. Chill, covered, for 1 hour.

✤ Preheat oven to 350 degrees.

✤ Roll dough 1/2 inch thick on lightly floured surface; cut into 1 1/2-inch strips. Make indentation down middle of strips. Place on greased cookie sheet. Pipe currant jelly in indentation.

✤ Bake for 15 minutes. Brush with mixture of 1 egg and 1/2 cup sugar. Sprinkle with almonds. Bake for 5 minutes. Cut into 1/2-inch diagonal strips.

Nerrupa Vaghai (Baked Bananas)

Yield: 6 servings

6 bananas, peeled, cut lengthwise into quarters
2 tablespoons melted butter
½ cup honey
2 tablespoons lemon juice

❖ Preheat oven to 350 degrees.

❖ Place bananas in greased baking dish. Pour mixture of butter, honey and lemon juice over bananas.

❖ Bake for 15 minutes.

Jalebis

Yield: 60 servings

3 cups all-purpose flour
¼ cup rice flour
¼ teaspoon double-acting baking powder
2 cups 110 to 115-degree water
4 cups sugar
3 cups cold water
⅛ teaspoon cream of tartar
1 teaspoon rose water
⅛ teaspoon red food coloring
2 teaspoons yellow food coloring
oil for deep frying

❖ Combine all-purpose flour, rice flour, baking powder and lukewarm water in bowl; mix well. Let stand, uncovered, at room temperature for 12 hours.

❖ Combine sugar, cold water and cream of tartar in saucepan. Cook over medium heat until sugar dissolves, stirring constantly.

❖ Bring sugar mixture to a boil over high heat. Boil for 5 minutes or until mixture reaches temperature of 220 degrees on candy thermometer; do not stir. Add rose water, red food coloring and yellow food coloring; mix well.

❖ Heat 2 to 3 inches oil to 350 degrees in a 10-inch karhai or 12-inch wok.

❖ Spoon batter into pastry bag fitted with ³/₁₆-inch tip. Squeeze batter directly into hot oil into a pretzel formed of alternating figure 8's and circles and measuring 2x3 inches.

❖ Fry for 2 minutes or until golden brown on both sides; drain. Let stand in warm syrup for 1 minute. Transfer to platter. Serve warm or at room temperature.

> Plantains and mangos are so popular and so strongly associated with Island cooking that it is easy to forget that they were brought from India.

The Mediterranean

The foundation of Western cuisine was laid by Greek and Roman chefs a full millennium before Christ. Food was of great importance to the Romans, who were responsible for many innovations we still employ today, such as the raised hearth "cook top" and public health inspectors. The competitive gluttony of ancient Rome often caused bankruptcy among the aristocracy, and the prospect of a reduced standard of living led to suicide for some, including Apicius, a first century cookbook author. We can thank Greek chefs for the introduction of delicate white wine sauces, goose liver delicacies, fish fillets, and cocktail appetizers. The great Greek philosophers were formidable gourmands as well, spreading an appreciation of fine foods among the masses. Spain's forte has always been fine sherries, and because the Phoenicians planted olive trees here more than 3,000 years ago, Spain can now boast of producing 65% of the world's olive oil.

Due to the extreme diversity of the region, it is impossible to describe "a" typical Mediterranean cuisine. We may say, however, that regional wines and liquors accompany virtually every lunch and dinner. Meals usually end with fruits and cheese, as sugary "desserts" are more often an afternoon snack. The backbone of the Mediterranean diet includes olive oil, herbs, garlic, and the tomato, a New World treasure introduced to these sunny kitchens in the sixteenth century.

Isn't it ironic that while sophisticated Greeks and Romans vitally influenced the ancient roots of Western cuisine, it was the simple American tomato that permanently altered it 300 years ago?

The Mediterranean

Loukanika (Greek Sausage Balls)

Yield: 24 servings

2 pounds ground pork
1 pound ground beef
1/2 cup dry wine
2 tablespoons chopped parsley
1/2 cup shredded cheese
2 tablespoons grated orange rind
anise flavoring, hot pepper flakes, salt and black
    pepper to taste

Variation: May serve with a tomato sauce if desired.

* Preheat broiler.
* Combine ground pork, ground beef, wine, parsley, cheese, orange rind, anise flavoring, pepper flakes, salt and black pepper in bowl; mix well. Shape into small balls.
* Arrange on rack in broiler pan. Broil for 5 minutes on each side or until cooked through. Serve hot.

Snails in Bread Crumbs

Yield: 12 servings

1 1/2 cups seasoned Italian bread crumbs
chopped shallots or scallions to taste
1/4 cup chopped fresh parsley
3 cloves of garlic, crushed
1 cup melted butter
12 snails, rinsed, drained

* Preheat oven to 350 degrees.
* Mix bread crumbs, shallots, parsley, garlic and butter in baking dish. Bake for 20 minutes.
* Add snails to mixture; mix well. Bake for 20 minutes longer.
* Serve warm with crackers or Italian bread.

Trancetti agli Spinaci (Spinach Pinwheels)

After visiting her mother's cousins in Trino, Italy, Elaine Pelliccio was pleased to receive this recipe clipped from an Italian newspaper. It was marked with her cousin's seal of approval, "Che buono!" Here is the translation.

Yield: 6 servings

For the filling:

3 pounds spinach
salt to taste
2 tablespoons butter
1 clove of garlic
7 ounces mascarpone cheese

For the dough:

1¼ cups flour
3 eggs

For the pinwheels:

7 ounces grated Parmesan cheese
salt to taste
6 tablespoons melted butter

Note: For a stromboli-like dish, place uncooked roll on baking sheet and bake at 325 degrees for 30 to 40 minutes or until brown.

To make the filling:

✤ Cook spinach in boiling salted water in saucepan until tender. Rinse in cold water and drain, pressing out excess water.

✤ Chop spinach. Combine with 2 tablespoons butter, garlic, mascarpone cheese and salt in bowl; mix well.

To make the dough:

✤ Combine flour and eggs in bowl; mix to form dough. Roll into circle on floured surface.

To prepare and cook the pinwheels:

✤ Discard garlic clove from filling. Spread filling over dough; sprinkle with Parmesan cheese. Roll dough to enclose filling, pressing ends and edges to seal. Wrap roll in towel; secure ends.

✤ Place roll in boiling salted water in saucepan. Cook for 15 minutes; drain and remove towel.

✤ Cut roll into ½-inch slices. Arrange slices on serving plate. Drizzle with 6 tablespoons melted butter. Serve with additional Parmesan cheese.

Pasta y Fagioli

This is an adaptation of the dish which all Italian mothers make to feed as many hungry people as possible with the ingredients at hand. If more people come at meal time, they simply add another cup of water. It is nourishing and strengthening, but very economical.

Yield: 10 to 12 servings

1 cup finely chopped onions or scallions
3 tablespoons olive oil
1   16-ounce can pork and beans
1   19-ounce can cannellini or white kidney beans
1   46-ounce can chicken broth
1   16-ounce package ditalini or elbow pasta
1 teaspoon salt
½ teaspoon each garlic powder, rosemary,
    oregano, Italian seasoning, parsley and pepper
grated Parmesan or Romano cheese

Note: Flavor improves if soup is made ahead and reheated; freezes well.

* Sauté onions in olive oil in 6-quart saucepan over medium heat for 5 minutes or until tender. Add beans and chicken broth; mix well.
* Cook pasta using package directions; drain. Add to soup with salt, garlic powder, rosemary, oregano, Italian seasoning, parsley and pepper.
* Simmer for 1 hour. Ladle into soup bowls. Serve with cheese.

Italian Lentil Soup

Yield: 4 to 6 servings

6 cups water
1 cup dried lentils
2 carrots, peeled, sliced
1 large stalk celery, chopped
1 small onion, chopped
1 tablespoon olive oil
1 teaspoon aniseed
1 teaspoon salt
¼ teaspoon pepper
⅓ pound uncooked thin spaghetti, broken into
    1-inch pieces
grated Parmesan cheese

* Bring water to a boil in 3-quart saucepan. Add lentils, carrots, celery, onion, olive oil, aniseed, salt and pepper. Simmer for 30 minutes or until lentils are tender.
* Cook spaghetti using package directions; drain. Add to soup. Cook until heated through. Ladle into soup bowls. Serve with grated Parmesan cheese.

Caldo Verde (Green Soup)

Caldo Verde is to Portugal what onion soup is to France. It is often served with flour-dusted Portuguese rolls and a dish of sliced tomatoes.

Yield: 12 servings

8 to 10 large collard leaves, shredded
4 quarts water
3 medium potatoes, peeled
1 onion, chopped
salt to taste
3 tablespoons olive oil
¼ cup uncooked rice
¼ teaspoon baking soda

* Trim and shred the stems of the collard leaves. Roll each leaf lengthwise and chop into small bits rather than long slivers.

* Bring water to a boil in large saucepan. Add potatoes, onion and salt. Simmer until potatoes are tender.

* Remove potatoes from saucepan with slotted spoon and mash in bowl.

* Return potatoes to saucepan with collard leaves, olive oil, rice and baking soda; mix well. Simmer for 30 minutes. Ladle into soup bowls.

Caldo Verde is frequently accompanied by codfish cakes (see page 49). Codfish is a favorite Portuguese food. The dried codfish is soaked overnight, changing the water several times. It is then cooked with chopped potatoes and onions, mashed with parsley and eggs, shaped into patties and browned in olive oil.

The cod were actually caught on the Grand Banks near Newfoundland, thousands of miles from Portugal. The fishermen worked from small rowboats called dories, and then hauled the fish back to the "mother ship" to be salted and stored. After six months on the Grand Banks, the fishermen headed home and the fish were air dried and turned into many of Portugal's best dishes. It is said, in fact, that the Portuguese know 365 ways to prepare dried codfish.

The Caldo Verde recipe is contributed by Gail Gaspar. It is from the kitchen of her mother-in-law, Maria Nunes Gaspar. It originated in Portugal where Senhora Maria worked as a young maid in the early 1920s before emigrating to the United States in 1935. Gail wrote the poem below to celebrate the kitchen and the very life of Senhora Maria and to demonstrate the care with which she handled the soup and its accompanying codfish cakes.

safe passage

she seals the soup in mason jars
wraps the codfish cakes in cloth/on thursdays at three

we arrive bearing *beijos*
one *beijo*, each cheek/for the green soup and
the parsley-spotted/codfish cakes

from the porch/papa's portable radio plays;
the old metal blinds slice the sunlight
we stand on a throw mat and wait

from the kitchen, sãm paio
a crucifix over the stove/where the salt and
the olive oil/flavor the food
of the land and the language/and the husband she grieves,
all the while turning the fish cakes
and cutting the coarse green leaves

she comes to the curb/in a thick black dress
we will, we repeat, *save the jar*

the orange lard/rises to the top of the soup
in the box at the back of our van

the codfish/makes its passage
in the cradle of my hand

g. gaspar
Published in *Pivot*, Volume 42, Martin Mitchell, editor, NY

Sopa Portuguese

Yield: 10 to 12 servings

1 beef shank
salt
1 cup dried navy beans
1 pound linguica or chorizo, sliced
1½ large onions, chopped
¼ cup olive oil
1 pound kale, trimmed, chopped
1 small head cabbage, chopped
4 cups (about) chicken stock
2 cups sliced carrots
8 potatoes, chopped
2 teaspoons minced garlic
salt and pepper to taste

❖ Combine beef shank with salted water to cover in bowl. Let stand in refrigerator overnight. Combine beans with water to cover in bowl. Let stand overnight. Drain beef shank and beans.

❖ Sauté sausage with onions in olive oil in large stockpot for several minutes. Add beef shank. Sauté until beef shank is browned.

❖ Add beans, kale and cabbage. Add enough chicken stock to cover. Simmer for 1 hour. Add carrots, potatoes, garlic, salt and pepper. Simmer until beans and vegetables are tender, adding additional chicken stock if necessary for desired consistency. Serve hot.

The picturesque village of Stonington is located five miles from Mystic Seaport. The abundant fishing in Stonington's harbor attracted the first Portuguese from the Azores in the mid 1800s. They found the soil and climate here similar to home, allowing them to grow their favorite foods.

The immigrants founded the Holy Ghost Society in 1914 to celebrate the Feast of the Holy Ghost, a day commemorating the alleviation of the 16th century famine in Portugal by Queen Isabella. The queen prayed to the Holy Ghost to stop the rains and flooding. The rains ended, but the land was barren, and the queen sold her crown jewels to feed her desperate people. The *festa* is celebrated with a procession and a traditional meal, which would include a hearty soup such as this one.

Alzira Souza's father was a founding member of the Holy Ghost Society, and her family has lived here for most of the last century. When Alzira makes her variation of this soup, some of the potatoes are left whole and are served with the beef as a separate course, following the soup.

Uvarlakia Soupa

Serve this Greek soup with green salad, feta cheese and crusty bread.

Yield: 8 servings

½ cup chopped onion
1 tablespoon margarine
1   46-ounce can chicken broth
1 pound lean ground beef
2 tablespoons water
salt and pepper to taste
⅓ cup uncooked rice
2 eggs
juice of ½ lemon
¼ cup water

Garnish:

minced parsley

* Sauté onion lightly in margarine in saucepan. Add chicken broth. Bring to a simmer.
* Combine ground beef, 2 tablespoons water, salt and pepper in bowl; mix well. Shape into small balls. Add to broth in saucepan.
* Simmer for 10 minutes. Stir in rice. Simmer for 20 minutes or until rice is tender and meatballs are cooked through; remove from heat.
* Beat eggs with lemon juice and ¼ cup water in bowl. Pour gradually into soup, stirring constantly. Ladle into soup bowls. Sprinkle servings with parsley.

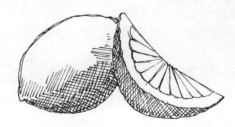

Carrot Salad

Yield: 4 servings

2 tablespoons olive oil or other oil
1½ tablespoons vinegar or lemon juice
crushed fresh garlic to taste
1 teaspoon cumin
1 teaspoon paprika
½ teaspoon salt
½ teaspoon pepper or to taste
2 cups blanched sliced carrots

Garnish:

fresh parsley

* Combine olive oil, vinegar, garlic, cumin, paprika, salt and pepper in bowl; mix well.
* Add carrots; mix well. Spoon into serving bowl; garnish with parsley.

Insalata Caprese (Tomato and Mozzarella Salad)

A traditional salad of the island of Capri, Italy, and of the Naples region, Insalata Caprese is very Mediterranean in that it has no lettuce. The main ingredient is usually a cheese, and the salad may be eaten before or after the main meal.

Yield: variable

large tomatoes
fresh mozzarella cheese
fresh basil leaves
olive oil
red wine vinegar (optional)

Garnish:
olives
parsley
fresh basil (optional)
fresh spinach leaves

✦ Slice tomatoes and mozzarella cheese ¼ inch thick. Arrange with basil in overlapping layers on serving plate.

✦ Drizzle with olive oil and vinegar. Garnish as desired with olives, parsley, basil and/or fresh spinach leaves.

Tossed Antipasto Salad

Yield: 8 servings

1 cup sliced carrots
1 cup cauliflowerets
2 medium tomatoes, cut into wedges
1 cup pitted black olives
1   8-ounce bottle of Italian salad dressing
4 cups chopped iceberg lettuce

Variation: May add chopped salami if desired.

✦ Cook carrots and cauliflower in a small amount of water in saucepan just until tender-crisp; drain. Combine with tomatoes and olives in bowl.

✦ Add salad dressing to vegetable mixture; mix gently. Marinate, covered, in refrigerator for several hours to overnight. Drain, reserving marinade.

✦ Combine vegetables with lettuce in bowl. Serve with reserved marinade.

Pastitsio (Greek Baked Macaroni and Meat)

Yield: 6 servings

For the cream topping:

½ cup margarine
¾ cup flour
2 cups warm milk
4 eggs
½ teaspoon salt

For the pastitsio:

1 cup chopped onion
6 tablespoons margarine
2 pounds ground beef
1 teaspoon salt
½ teaspoon pepper
½ teaspoon ground cinnamon
2 tablespoons tomato paste
1 pound macaroni, cooked
½ cup grated Romano or Parmesan cheese
2 eggs

To make the cream topping:

* Melt margarine in saucepan. Stir in flour. Cook for several minutes; remove from heat.
* Stir in milk gradually. Add eggs and salt; mix well. Cook until thickened, stirring constantly.

To make the pastitsio:

* Preheat oven to 375 degrees. Grease 9x13-inch baking dish.
* Sauté onion in margarine in skillet for 5 minutes. Add ground beef. Cook until ground beef is brown and crumbly; drain. Add salt, pepper, cinnamon and tomato paste. Simmer for 10 minutes.
* Add macaroni, cheese and eggs; mix well. Spoon into prepared baking dish. Top with cream topping.
* Bake for 30 minutes or until topping is set. Cut into serving pieces.

Italian Ham Pie

This is an Italian dish traditionally served at Easter.

Yield: 12 servings

14 eggs
1 pound ham, cubed
1 pound pepperoni, cubed
10 ounces Muenster cheese, cubed
10 ounces Cheddar cheese, cubed
1 cup milk
1 cup flour
1 tablespoon baking powder

* Preheat oven to 350 degrees. Grease 9x13-inch baking dish.
* Combine eggs, ham, pepperoni and cheeses in bowl; mix well. Combine milk, flour and baking powder in small bowl; mix well. Add to ham mixture; mix well.
* Spoon into prepared baking dish. Bake for 45 to 60 minutes or until set and golden brown.

Casalinga

Fortuna's Deli of Westerly, Rhode Island, shared this delicious recipe featuring soupy, a traditional Italian sausage.

Yield: 4 to 6 servings

1/2 pound fresh Italian sausage, skinned
1/4 pound each soupy (soppresatta), prosciutto
  and homemade pepperoni, sliced 1/4 inch thick
2 cloves of garlic, chopped
2   28-ounce cans whole plum tomatoes
1 scallion, chopped
pinch each of basil, oregano and red pepper
1 small jar artichoke hearts in water
1/4 cup fresh or frozen tiny green peas
1 pound fresh fettucini
grated Romano cheese to taste

* Brown Italian sausage, soupy, prosciutto and pepperoni with garlic in saucepan, stirring frequently. Add tomatoes, scallion, basil, oregano and red pepper.

* Simmer for 30 minutes. Add artichokes and peas. Simmer until heated through.

* Serve over hot cooked fettucini; sprinkle with cheese.

Sausage was first made in 1500 B.C. and had to be consumed quickly because of a lack of preservatives and refrigeration. By 500 B.C., the concept of dry-curing was being used in Salamis, Cyprus, which had large salt lagoons—the only preservative for meats known at the time. Romans later perfected sausage making and had guilds to protect the secrets of the trade. In the Middle Ages, dry-cured meats grew in popularity, as they could be stored at room temperature. Individual cities were known for specific varieties such as Salamis and Genoa in Italy and Frankfurt in Germany.

When Italian immigrants came to Rhode Island around the turn of the century, they brought their old-world recipes. Those who settled in Westerly, Rhode Island, were mostly from Calabria, Italy, and brought with them recipes for "Soupy" or soppresatta, a peppery sausage, spicy and hot. To this day it is made the same way it was hundreds of years ago and the pride of the sausage makers sparks some friendly debate and competition.

The *Los Angeles Times* has praised the efforts of Paul and Patti Stannard of Westerly as America's best and most authentic soupy. They began making the sausage in small batches for themselves and were encouraged to produce it commercially. It is now available at Fortuna's Deli in Westerly and by mail order at 1-800-42-SOUPY.

Fettucini Andrea

Named in honor of an Italian exchange student living here, Andrea Ceroni, of Tredozio, Italy, it is a fine example of Northern Italian cooking.

Yield: 6 servings

1 medium red onion, chopped
2 tablespoons olive oil
1/4 pound bacon, finely chopped
1/4 pound ham, finely chopped
1/4 pound prosciutto, finely chopped
2 cups white wine
1 tablespoon catsup
3/4 cup chopped parsley
24 ounces fettucini, cooked
grated Parmesan cheese

* Sauté onion in olive oil in large saucepan until tender. Add bacon, ham and prosciutto. Cook over medium heat for 10 minutes or until bacon is crisp.
* Stir in wine and catsup. Simmer for 30 minutes. Add parsley.
* Place hot fettucini in serving dish. Spoon sauce over top; sprinkle with Parmesan cheese.

Zucchini and Sausage Pasta

This is an adaptation of a recipe brought to this country by immigrants from a little farming village near Naples in Italy. It uses the fresh vegetables they continued to grow when they came to this country, but substitutes turkey sausage for the original Italian sweet pork sausage to reduce the fat and cholesterol.

Yield: 6 servings

4 medium zucchini
1 package Italian turkey sausage, sliced 1/2 inch thick
2 cloves of garlic, minced
2 tablespoons olive oil
10 plum tomatoes, chopped
1 pound rigatoni, cooked
1 cup grated Parmesan cheese

Note: May prepare in advance and reheat in microwave.

* Peel zucchini and cut into halves lengthwise; cut into slices.
* Sauté sausage and garlic in heated olive oil in 12-inch skillet until light brown. Remove sausage with slotted spoon.
* Add zucchini and tomatoes to skillet. Sauté for several minutes.
* Simmer, covered, for 15 minutes. Stir in sausage. Simmer, covered, for 20 minutes.
* Combine with hot pasta in serving bowl. Add Parmesan cheese; toss to mix well.

Coq au Vin (Chicken with Wine)

The herbs for this traditional Provençal dish are a mix of savory, rosemary, thyme, oregano and marjoram in proportions to suit your tastes.

Yield: 4 servings

1 chicken, cut up
2 to 3 tablespoons olive oil
3 cloves of garlic, crushed
10 shallots, chopped
3 carrots, chopped
1/2 pound mushrooms, sliced
2 cups chicken stock
1/2 bottle of Beaujolais
1 teaspoon *herbs de Provence*
sage, salt and pepper to taste

* Rinse chicken and pat dry. Brown in 2 tablespoons olive oil in large skillet.
* Sauté garlic, shallots, carrots and mushrooms in a small amount of olive oil in small nonstick skillet for 3 minutes. Add to chicken.
* Add chicken stock, wine, herbs, sage, salt and pepper; mix well. Simmer, covered, for 2 hours.
* Serve with pasta, rice or potatoes.

Lithrini me Elies (Red Snapper with Olives)

This recipe is from the family of Eric Moscahlaidis, President of the Greek Food and Wine Institute in New York. He says that the original recipe called for Greek black olives from his father's native Amtissa, the olive capital of Greece. It was adapted by his mother's family, which came from the area of the Black Sea where there was a considerable Greek population. They substituted kalamata olives, Greece's most famous variety, loved for their smooth oval shape, firm meat and pungent flavor. So, in a way, this dish represents a cross-cultural heritage.

Yield: 4 servings

1   2 1/2-pound red snapper or 2 smaller red snappers
salt and pepper to taste
2 large onions, thinly sliced
2 large tomatoes, peeled, seeded, chopped
1 green bell pepper, cut into strips
4 small cloves of garlic, thinly sliced
3 tablespoons finely chopped parsley
1 teaspoon fresh oregano
20 to 25 kalamata olives, pitted
1 cup dry white wine
1/2 cup olive oil

* Preheat oven to 380 degrees. Oil baking dish large enough to hold fish.
* Rinse fish inside and out and pat dry. Sprinkle inside and out with salt and pepper.
* Combine onions, tomatoes, green pepper, garlic, parsley and oregano in bowl; mix well. Spread half the mixture in prepared baking dish.
* Place fish in baking dish; top with remaining tomato mixture. Sprinkle with olives. Drizzle with wine and olive oil.
* Bake for 30 minutes or until fish flakes easily, basting several times.

Paella

Yield: 8 servings

½ cup thinly sliced onion
¼ cup olive oil
2 cups uncooked rice
4 cups hot chicken stock
Saffron to taste
2 cloves of garlic, pressed
2 red bell peppers, sliced
1 teaspoon paprika
¼ teaspoon oregano
salt and pepper to taste
8 pieces chicken
½ cup thinly sliced chorizo or hard Spanish
   sausage
½ pound uncooked shrimp
8 small or little neck-sized clams in the shell,
   scrubbed

❦ Preheat oven to 350 degrees.

❦ Sauté onion in olive oil in paellero until golden brown. Add rice. Sauté until rice is lightly browned.

❦ Add mixture of chicken stock and saffron; mix well. Stir in garlic, red peppers, paprika, oregano, salt and pepper; mix well.

❦ Rinse chicken and pat dry. Arrange chicken and sausage over rice mixture. Bake, covered, for 45 minutes.

❦ Arrange shrimp and clams around chicken. Bake, covered, for 10 to 15 minutes longer or until chicken is tender, shrimp turn pink and clam shells open. Discard any clams that do not open.

One of Spain's most famous and favorite dishes is paella. It takes its name from the paellero, or dish in which it is cooked. The only ingredients that are always used in a paella are olive oil, rice and saffron. The rest of the ingredients are left to the imagination of the cook and the availability of the vegetables and seafood. It can include shellfish, squid, chorizo, chicken and whatever vegetables happen to be fresh and inexpensive at the local market.

Mediterranean Rice

Pigeon peas, or gandules, and bijol may be found in ethnic food stores.

Yield: 4 to 5 servings

1 medium onion, finely chopped
1 green bell pepper, finely chopped
3 cloves of garlic, finely chopped
2 tablespoons extra-virgin olive oil
1 can pigeon peas
3 tablespoons pimento-stuffed green olives
1 tablespoon bijol
1   8-ounce can tomato sauce
2 pinches saffron
1/2 teaspoon oregano
2 tablespoons capers
1/4 teaspoon Tabasco sauce
1 teaspoon salt
1/2 teaspoon pepper
2 cups uncooked white rice
3 cups (about) water

♣ Sauté onion, green pepper and garlic in olive oil in heavy saucepan until tender. Add undrained peas, olives, bijol, tomato sauce, saffron, oregano, capers, Tabasco sauce, salt and pepper; mix well.

♣ Bring to a boil. Cook for 2 minutes, stirring frequently. Stir in rice and about 3 cups water or enough to cover ingredients by 1/8 inch.

♣ Reduce heat. Simmer, covered, for 15 minutes. Stir, mixing ingredients from bottom of pan to top. Simmer, covered, for 15 minutes longer or until rice is tender.

Spinach Squares

Yield: 8 servings

2   10-ounce packages frozen chopped spinach
2 cups cooked rice
2 cups shredded American cheese
1 cup crumbled feta cheese
4 eggs
2/3 cup milk
1/4 cup melted butter
1/2 cup minced onion
2 tablespoons parsley flakes
1 teaspoon Worcestershire sauce
1/2 teaspoon thyme
1/2 teaspoon nutmeg
1 1/2 teaspoons salt

♣ Preheat oven to 325 degrees. Grease shallow 2-quart baking dish.

♣ Cook spinach using package directions; drain well. Combine with rice and cheeses in bowl; mix well.

♣ Beat eggs in bowl. Add milk, butter, onion, parsley flakes, Worcestershire sauce, thyme, nutmeg and salt; mix well.

♣ Add to spinach mixture; mix well. Spoon into prepared dish.

♣ Bake for 1 hour. Cut into squares to serve.

Imam Bayaldi (Baked Stuffed Eggplant)

Yield: 6 servings

3 medium eggplant
salt to taste
2 cloves of garlic, minced
4 large onions, chopped
1/2 cup olive oil
4 large tomatoes, peeled, seeded, chopped
1 teaspoon sugar
salt and pepper to taste
1/2 cup soft white bread crumbs
1 tablespoon tomato paste
1 tablespoon chopped parsley
3 tablespoon chopped pine nuts (optional)
3 tablespoons dry bread crumbs

* Cook eggplant in salted boiling water in saucepan for 10 to 15 minutes or until tender; rinse with cold water and drain. Cut into halves lengthwise. Scoop out pulp, reserving pulp and shells. Rub shells lightly inside and out with olive oil; arrange in oiled baking dish.

* Sauté garlic and onions in heated olive oil in large skillet until tender. Add reserved eggplant pulp, tomatoes, sugar, salt and pepper; mix well. Simmer for 20 minutes.

* Add soft bread crumbs and tomato paste; mix well. Cook for 2 to 3 minutes, stirring constantly. Stir in parsley and pine nuts.

* Preheat oven to 350 degrees.

* Spoon stuffing into eggplant shells; top with dry bread crumbs. Bake, covered, for 20 minutes. Bake, uncovered, for 10 minutes longer. Serve hot.

Kolokithokeftaides (Fried Zucchini Cakes)

These are good served with garlic sauce.

Yield: 6 servings

1 1/2 pounds zucchini
salt
3 tablespoons fresh parsley
1 cup crushed butter crackers
2 to 3 tablespoons shredded sharp Cheddar cheese
2 eggs, beaten
1 medium onion, grated
salt and pepper to taste
flour
olive oil, vegetable oil or mixture of oil and butter for frying

* Scrape zucchini to remove skin. Grate coarsely into colander; sprinkle with salt. Let stand for 30 minutes. Press to remove excess moisture.

* Combine zucchini with parsley, cracker crumbs, cheese, eggs, onion, salt and pepper in bowl; mix well. Shape by tablespoonfuls into balls. Coat with flour; press into flat cakes.

* Fry in oil in skillet over low to medium heat until golden brown.

Italian Baked Rice

Yield: 12 servings

1 16-ounce package rice
1/2 stick pepperoni, chopped
1/2 pound mozzarella cheese, cubed
1 tablespoon parsley flakes
7 eggs
2 tablespoons grated Parmesan cheese
1 teaspoon parsley flakes
salt and pepper to taste
1/2 cup seasoned bread crumbs

✤ Preheat oven to 350 degrees. Butter baking dish.

✤ Cook rice using package directions. Combine hot rice with pepperoni, mozzarella cheese and 1 tablespoon parsley flakes in bowl; mix well. Cool for 15 to 20 minutes.

✤ Beat eggs with Parmesan cheese, 1 teaspoon parsley flakes, salt and pepper in bowl. Add to rice mixture; mix well.

✤ Spoon into baking dish; top with bread crumbs. Bake for 1 1/4 hours or until set.

Pasta with Pesto Genovese

This is best served as a separate course before the entrée, as it has a distinctive taste that should stand on its own.

Yield: 6 to 8 servings

6 cloves of garlic
15 large fresh basil leaves
6 tablespoons freshly grated Parmesan cheese
1/3 cup pine nuts
2 sprigs fresh parsley
1/2 teaspoon salt
1/2 cup olive oil
1 16-ounce package spaghetti or linguine
2 tablespoons butter
Parmesan cheese to taste

✤ Combine garlic, basil, Parmesan cheese, pine nuts, parsley and salt in food processor container; process until smooth. Add olive oil gradually, processing constantly to a smooth sauce.

✤ Cook pasta using package directions; drain. Combine with pesto sauce and butter in serving bowl; toss to mix well. Serve with additional Parmesan cheese.

Polenta

An original Italian "fun food," polenta was often served poured on a big board in the center of the table. The cook would sometimes pour it into an artistic shape, such as the boot shape of Italy. Family members served themselves from the portion of the polenta nearest them, often reshaping it to the amusement of all.

Yield: 8 to 10 servings

4 cups water
1 teaspoon salt
1½ cups finely ground cornmeal
spaghetti sauce or tomato sauce
grated Parmesan or Romano cheese

✤ Bring water to a boil in saucepan. Stir in salt and cornmeal gradually, stirring constantly to prevent lumps. Cook for 20 to 30 minutes or until mixture thickens and pulls from side of pan, stirring constantly.

✤ Pour polenta onto platter. Press indentations with back of spoon. Spoon heated sauce into indentations. Serve with cheese.

Italian Fraselle

These pepper biscuits are served in Italy for company, holidays and parties.

Yield: 4 dozen

3½ cups flour
2 tablespoons baking powder
¾ cup oil
1 cup cold water
¾ tablespoon salt
¾ tablespoon pepper

✤ Preheat oven to 400 degrees.

✤ Combine flour, baking powder, oil, cold water, salt and pepper in bowl; mix well to form dough.

✤ Roll into long ropes about ½ inch in diameter on floured surface. Slice on the diagonal.

✤ Place on ungreased baking sheet. Bake for 20 to 25 minutes or until golden brown.

Tsoureki (Greek Bread)

Yield: 6 or 7 loaves

whole cloves
1 cinnamon stick
1 bay leaf
1/2 cup water
3 envelopes dry yeast
2 cups warm water
1 cup milk
1/2 cup melted margarine
3/4 cup melted butter
5 eggs
5 pounds flour
1/2 teaspoon salt
1 egg yolk, beaten
sesame seeds

- Combine cloves, cinnamon, bay leaf and 1/2 cup water in saucepan. Bring to a boil; reduce heat. Simmer for several minutes. Strain and reserve liquid.
- Dissolve yeast in warm water in bowl.
- Combine milk, margarine and butter in bowl; mix well. Beat in eggs.
- Mix flour and salt in bowl. Add yeast and milk mixture; mix well. Add reserved liquid; mix well.
- Knead dough on floured surface; dough will be sticky. Place in oiled bowl, turning to oil surface. Let rise for 1 1/2 hours.
- Shape dough into loaves or braids. Place on baking sheet. Brush with egg yolk; sprinkle with sesame seeds. Let rise for 45 minutes.
- Preheat oven to 325 degrees. Bake bread for 1 hour. Remove to wire rack to cool.

Italian Rice Cake

Yield: 12 servings

1 cup uncooked rice
4 cups milk
1 teaspoon shortening
1/4 to 1/2 cup bread crumbs
3/4 cup sugar
1 tablespoon shortening
5 egg yolks
juice and grated rind of 1 lemon
1 teaspoon salt
5 egg whites, stiffly beaten

- Cook rice in milk in saucepan until milk is absorbed and rice is tender. Cool to room temperature for 30 to 40 minutes.
- Preheat oven to 325 degrees. Grease springform pan with 1 teaspoon shortening. Sprinkle bread crumbs into greased pan, pressing over bottom and side.
- Combine rice with sugar, 1 tablespoon shortening, egg yolks, lemon juice, grated lemon rind and salt; mix well. Fold in egg whites.
- Spoon into prepared pan. Bake for 1 hour or until brown. Cool on wire rack. Place on serving plate; remove side of pan.

Zuppa Inglese (Italian Rum Cake with Custard)

Yield: 16 servings

For the filling:

¹/₂ cup sugar
¹/₄ cup cornstarch
¹/₂ teaspoon salt
2¹/₂ cups milk
2 eggs, slightly beaten
1 tablespoon rum
several drops of red food coloring
1 teaspoon vanilla extract
¹/₂ ounce unsweetened chocolate, melted

For the cake:

6 egg yolks
1¹/₂ teaspoons lemon juice
6 egg whites
¹/₂ teaspoon cream of tartar
¹/₈ teaspoon salt
³/₄ cup sugar
1¹/₄ cups sifted cake flour
¹/₂ cup sugar

For assembling the cake:

¹/₂ cup sherry
¹/₄ cup light rum
1 cup whipping cream, whipped

To make the filling:

♣ Mix sugar, cornstarch and salt in double boiler. Stir in ¹/₂ cup milk until smooth. Add remaining 2 cups milk; mix well.

♣ Cook over hot water until thickened, stirring constantly. Stir a small amount of the hot mixture into eggs; stir eggs into hot mixture. Cook for 5 minutes longer, stirring constantly.

♣ Divide filling into 3 bowls. Add rum and food coloring to 1 bowl. Add vanilla to second bowl. Add melted chocolate to third bowl.

To make the cake:

♣ Preheat oven to 325 degrees.

♣ Beat egg yolks in mixer bowl until thick and lemon-colored. Add lemon juice; mix well.

♣ Beat egg whites in mixer bowl until foamy. Add cream of tartar and salt, beating constantly until stiff but not dry. Beat in ³/₄ cup sugar gradually.

♣ Fold egg yolk mixture gently into beaten egg whites. Fold in cake flour and ¹/₂ cup sugar 2 tablespoons at a time.

♣ Spoon into ungreased tube pan. Bake for 50 to 60 minutes or until cake tests done. Cool cake in pan on wire rack.

To assemble the cake:

♣ Remove cake from pan and cut into 4 layers. Return top layer to pan. Sprinkle with mixture of wine and rum. Spread with 1 portion of the filling. Repeat using remaining cake layers and fillings.

♣ Chill for 24 hours.

♣ Unmold cake onto serving plate. Spread whipped cream over top and side of cake.

Italian Christmas Cookies

A young cookie lover watched these special Christmas treats being prepared over the years by an elderly relative and came up with these measurements for the ingredients. The originals were made by dumping a partially filled bag of flour on the table, cracking a dozen eggs into it, adding handfuls of other ingredients and kneading until it was right.

Yield: 6 dozen

1/2 cup butter or margarine, softened
1 cup sugar
6 eggs
juice and grated rind of 1 orange
6 cups flour
2 tablespoons baking powder
1 cup confectioners' sugar
lemon juice
nonpareils

Note: Cookies may be frozen after cooling thoroughly and before glazing.

✤ Preheat oven to 350 degrees. Grease cookie sheet.
✤ Cream butter and sugar in mixer bowl until light and fluffy. Beat in eggs 1 at a time. Add orange juice and rind.
✤ Add flour and baking powder; mix well. Knead until no longer sticky, kneading in additional flour if needed; dough will be stiff.
✤ Shape into 1/2x3-inch ropes; tie into knots. Place on prepared cookie sheet. Bake for 12 to 15 minutes or until golden brown. Remove to wire rack to cool.
✤ Combine confectioners' sugar with enough lemon juice to make a thick glaze. Drizzle over cookies; sprinkle with candies.

Korabia (Greek Cookies)

Yield: 6 dozen

2 cups unsalted butter, softened
3/4 cup confectioners' sugar
1 egg yolk, beaten
1 teaspoon vanilla extract
1/4 teaspoon baking soda
1 teaspoon warm water
3 1/2 cups (or more) cake flour
confectioners' sugar

Variation: May add 1/2 cup ground roasted almonds if desired.

✤ Preheat oven to 350 degrees. Cover cookie sheet with waxed paper.
✤ Cream butter, 3/4 cup confectioners' sugar and egg yolk in mixer bowl until smooth. Add vanilla and baking soda dissolved in warm water; mix well. Add just enough flour to form a soft dough; mix until smooth.
✤ Shape into small crescents; place on prepared cookie sheet. Bake for 20 minutes.
✤ Coat hot cookies with confectioners' sugar. Cool on wire rack.

Lemon Sponge Pie

This is a recipe from the store and restaurant opened by Tom and Mary Castagna in Westerly, Rhode Island, in 1925. She baked 40 or more pies each day, as well as many cakes, and this pie was a family favorite.

Yield: 6 to 8 servings

¼ cup butter, softened
1 cup sugar
3 tablespoons cake flour
¼ teaspoon salt
juice and grated rind of 1 lemon
3 egg yolks, lightly beaten
2 cups milk
3 egg whites
1 unbaked 9-inch pie shell

✤ Preheat oven to 325 degrees.
✤ Cream butter and sugar in mixer bowl until light and fluffy. Add flour, salt, lemon juice and lemon rind; mix well. Add egg yolks, stirring until smooth. Add milk; mix well.
✤ Beat egg whites in mixer bowl until soft peaks form. Fold into lemon mixture.
✤ Spoon into pie shell. Bake for 1 hour.

The Castagnas started a small fruit and vegetable stand three days after their wedding in 1920. It was later combined with a luncheonette and soda fountain. When it outgrew its location they put up a building across the street from their original location, which is now owned by China Village. The Castagnas were the first to sell Birdseye Frozen Foods when the concept was new and made their own ice cream, candies and pies. They both lived into their 90s.

Ricotta Pie

Yield: 8 servings

For the pastry:

2½ cups flour
½ teaspoon salt
¼ cup sugar
½ cup shortening
3 extra large egg yolks, beaten
1 teaspoon vanilla extract

For the filling:

3 eggs
3 egg whites
1 cup sugar
1 tablespoon vanilla extract
2 pounds ricotta cheese
¼ cup flour
⅛ teaspoon salt

Garnish:

1 egg, beaten
confectioners' sugar

To make the pastry:

* Sift flour, salt and sugar into bowl. Cut in shortening until crumbly. Add mixture of egg yolks and vanilla; mix well to form dough, adding a small amount of water if needed.
* Chill, wrapped in plastic wrap, for 1 hour. Divide into 2 portions. Roll 1 portion into circle on floured surface; fit into deep 10-inch pie plate. Roll remaining portion into circle; cut into strips and reserve.

To make the filling:

* Beat 3 eggs and 3 egg whites in mixer bowl until foamy. Add sugar and vanilla; beat until thick and lemon-colored.
* Combine ricotta cheese, flour and salt in mixer bowl. Add egg mixture; mix well.

To make the pie:

* Preheat oven to 350 degrees. Spoon ricotta filling into pie shell.
* Arrange pastry strips in lattice design over top of pie; brush with 1 beaten egg.
* Bake for 50 to 60 minutes or until knife inserted in center comes out clean. Cool on wire rack. Garnish with confectioners' sugar.

Middle East

*N*ine thousand years ago in the hills of Kurdistan, men first herded sheep, and women first planted wheat. These two developments allowed nomadic tribes to form settlements for the first time. Over the years the settlements flourished and coped with the alien concepts of ownership, permanent housing, food surpluses, and bartering. Eventually the population outgrew the land, and some moved to a place called Mesopotamia at the plain of the Tigress and Euphrates rivers—The Fertile Crescent. Complex, government-organized irrigation systems created more food surpluses, and writing was invented to keep track of inventories, rents, and taxes! And thus civilization was born.

Sophisticated refinements to the basic wheat and lamb diet have occurred over the centuries to create a food tapestry woven with herbs and spices and wrapped in colorful presentation. In Iran, in fact, there is a saying that feasting the eyes is the first pleasure of a good meal. Flowers are used for flavor as well as for visual effect. The flower petals from the bitter orange tree and pink damask roses are distilled to create two potent "flower waters" used in many sweet dishes and beverages. (Look for them where you buy fine toiletries, as they are so fragrant they are often sold with the colognes!)

Lamb is still the favored meat today. Beef, goat, and camel are eaten far less often, and pork is forbidden by most religions in the region. Diets feature many grains, including bulgur and couscous, and other staples include eggplant, lentils, yogurt, olive oil, and chickpeas. There is quite a variety of breads, and desserts usually consist of dried fruits, nuts, and honey—perhaps wrapped in the paper-thin phyllo dough that only an advanced civilization could produce!

Now if we could just do something about those taxes . . . .

Middle East

Sohan Assaly (Slivered Almonds in Honey)

This distinctively flavored recipe makes a wonderful snack or dessert item. The cook, however, should be undisturbed during preparation.

Yield: 3 dozen

1/4 teaspoon saffron threads
1 tablespoon rose water
1/4 cup water
1/2 cup sugar
1/2 cup honey
8 ounces slivered almonds
1/2 cup butter
2 tablespoons finely chopped pistachios
parchment paper

Note: Place Sohan Assaly on layers of waxed paper when ready to store in container.

* Dissolve saffron in rose water.
* Bring 1/4 cup water and sugar to a rolling boil in heavy shallow saucepan. Boil for 7 minutes, stirring constantly. Add honey and almonds. Cook for 5 to 6 minutes or until golden brown and almonds begin to brown.
* Add butter. Cook for 5 minutes, stirring constantly. Stir in the rose water and saffron mixture. Cook for 2 to 3 minutes, stirring constantly. Drop by teaspoonfuls 1 inch apart onto parchment-lined trays. Sprinkle immediately with chopped pistachios.
* Cool for 20 minutes. Store in airtight container.

Hummus (Chickpea Dip)

Yield: 1 cup

1/4 cup olive oil
1   16-ounce can chickpeas
2 tablespoons tahini (sesame seed paste)
4 to 5 cloves of garlic, crushed
juice of 1 or 2 lemons
salt and pepper to taste

Garnish:
parsley

* Reserve 1 teaspoon olive oil. Combine peas, tahini, garlic and lemon juice in food processor container. Process until smooth, adding remaining olive oil. Add salt and pepper.
* Spoon into serving dish. Make an indentation in top. Drizzle reserved olive oil in indentation. Garnish with parsley.
* Serve with warm pita bread cut into triangles.

Shawrhba Ibd-Jash (Lebanese Chicken Soup)

This recipe is a specialty of the Diana Restaurant in Groton, Connecticut.

Yield: 8 servings

1 chicken, cut up, skinned
2 cloves of garlic, chopped
1 medium onion, chopped
cinnamon, salt and pepper to taste
1 cup sliced carrots
1 cup sliced celery
½ cup uncooked rice
¼ to ½ cup pignoli
1 cup uncooked noodles

Garnish:

parsley

♣ Rinse chicken well. Combine with water to cover in large saucepan. Bring to a boil, skimming off foam; reduce heat.

♣ Add garlic, onion, cinnamon, salt and pepper. Stir in carrots, celery and rice. Simmer for 15 minutes or until vegetables are tender-crisp.

♣ Add pignoli and noodles. Cook until rice and noodles are tender. Adjust seasonings and skim fat from surface. Ladle into soup bowls. Garnish servings with parsley.

Shurit Ads (Egyptian Lentil Soup)

Yield: 4 servings

2 tablespoons minced onion
1 tablespoon butter
1 cup dried lentils
4 cups chicken stock
1 medium onion, finely chopped
1 large tomato, chopped
2 large cloves of garlic, minced
1½ teaspoons cumin
½ teaspoon salt
1 tablespoon butter
4 lemon wedges

♣ Sauté 2 tablespoons minced onion in 1 tablespoon butter in sauté pan; set aside. Rinse and sort lentils.

♣ Bring chicken stock to a boil in large heavy saucepan over high heat. Add lentils, 1 chopped onion, tomato and garlic; reduce heat.

♣ Simmer, partially covered, for 45 minutes or until lentils are tender.

♣ Purée soup in food processor and return to saucepan. Stir in cumin and salt. Simmer for several minutes. Stir in 1 tablespoon butter.

♣ Ladle into serving bowls. Top with reserved sautéed onion. Serve with lemon wedges.

Salad-e Gojeh Khiar (Herbed Tomato and Cucumber Salad)

Yield: 4 servings

4 small tomatoes
3 tablespoons olive oil
juice of 1 lemon
1 large clove of garlic, crushed
1/2 teaspoon salt
1/2 teaspoon pepper
2 scallions with tops, chopped
3 radishes, sliced
1/2 cup minced fresh parsley
1/4 cup minced fresh mint
1/4 cup minced fresh dillweed
1 long English cucumber, peeled, chopped

✤ Drop tomatoes into boiling water in saucepan for 10 seconds. Skin tomatoes and cut into quarters.

✤ Combine olive oil, lemon juice, garlic, salt and pepper in medium bowl. Add scallions, radishes, parsley, mint and dillweed; mix well.

✤ Add tomatoes and cucumber; mix gently. Serve immediately or slightly chilled.

Z'Lata B'Lahaana (Orange and Cabbage Salad)

Yield: 6 servings

3 cups finely shredded cabbage
salt to taste
1 cup orange juice
2 tablespoons lemon juice
1/2 teaspoon sugar
salt and pepper to taste
Sections of 1 orange

✤ Rinse cabbage in colander; drain. Sprinkle with salt. Let stand for 1 hour. Rinse with cold water, pressing to remove excess liquid.

✤ Combine orange juice, lemon juice, sugar, salt and pepper in large bowl; mix well. Add cabbage; toss to mix well.

✤ Chill until serving time. Toss again just before serving. Top with orange sections.

When substituting dried herbs for fresh herbs, here is a general rule of thumb: dried herbs are 2 to 3 times as strong as fresh herbs and quantities should be adjusted accordingly.

Tabouli

Yield: 10 servings

2 bunches parsley, finely chopped
1 head romaine lettuce, finely chopped
2 tomatoes, finely chopped
2 cucumbers, finely chopped
½ bunch green onions, finely chopped
½ cup bulgur, rehydrated (see below)
juice and grated rind of 1 lemon
½ cup olive oil
salt and pepper to taste
chopped fresh mint to taste

+ Combine parsley, lettuce, tomatoes, cucumbers and onions in bowl.
+ Add bulgur, lemon juice and grated lemon rind, olive oil, salt and pepper. Add mint; mix well. Chill until serving time.

Bulgur, sometimes called parboiled wheat, represents the oldest recorded use of wheat and originated in the Near East. It is whole wheat that has been cooked, dried, partially debranned and cracked into coarse pieces. To rehydrate bulgur, soak it in twice its volume of hot water in a bowl and let it stand until the water has been absorbed or the bulgur is tender, approximately 30 minutes. Drain and use it in salads or as a substitute for rice or potatoes in cooked dishes.

Koofteh Berenji (Rice and Meatballs)

Yield: 8 servings

½ cup dried split peas
½ cup uncooked rice
½ teaspoon salt
4 cups water
3 eggs
½ teaspoon salt
½ teaspoon pepper
½ large onion, chopped
2 pounds ground beef
¼ cup chopped fresh parsley
¼ cup chopped fresh mint
¼ cup chopped fresh dillweed
1 tablespoon dried marjoram
1½ teaspoons dried tarragon
1 bunch scallions with tops, chopped
1½ large onions, chopped
2 teaspoons minced garlic
¼ cup oil
1 tablespoon tomato paste
2   14-ounce cans low-sodium beef broth
1 cup water
¼ cup lemon juice
1 teaspoon turmeric
1½ teaspoons salt
¼ teaspoon saffron
1 tablespoon hot water
plain yogurt

✤ Rinse and sort peas. Cook peas and rice with ½ teaspoon salt in 4 cups water in saucepan for 20 minutes; drain and set aside.

✤ Beat eggs with ½ teaspoon salt and pepper in bowl. Add ½ onion, ground beef, parsley, mint, dillweed, marjoram, tarragon, scallions and peas and rice mixture; mix well. Shape into large meatballs.

✤ Brown 1½ onions and garlic in oil in large heavy saucepan. Add tomato paste, beef broth, 1 cup water, lemon juice, turmeric and 1½ teaspoons salt. Stir in saffron dissolved in 1 tablespoon hot water.

✤ Bring to a boil; reduce heat. Add meatballs. Simmer, covered, for 45 minutes, basting tops of meatballs occasionally. Simmer, uncovered, for 15 minutes longer.

✤ Spoon meatballs into serving bowls; ladle broth over meatballs. Serve with yogurt and bread.

Kibbe

Yield: 6 servings

1 cup bulgur
2 cups warm water
2 large onions, chopped
2 tablespoons olive oil
5 tablespoons pine nuts
1 tablespoon butter or margarine
salt to taste
2 pounds ground lamb
1 small onion, chopped
1 clove of garlic, minced
1/4 teaspoon allspice
1/8 teaspoon ground cloves
1 tablespoon crushed dried mint leaves
1 teaspoon oregano
salt and pepper to taste
6 tablespoons plain yogurt (optional)

* Soak bulgur in 2 cups warm water in bowl for 30 minutes.
* Sauté 2 onions in olive oil in skillet until tender. Cool. Sauté pine nuts in butter in skillet. Reserve a few of the pine nuts. Combine remaining pine nuts with sautéed onions in bowl; mix well. Season with salt; set aside.
* Preheat oven to 400 degrees.
* Drain cracked wheat. Combine with ground lamb, 1 onion, garlic, allspice, cloves, mint, oregano, salt and pepper in bowl; mix well with hands.
* Press half the lamb mixture over bottom and side of baking pan. Spread onion and pine nut mixture in prepared pan. Pat remaining lamb mixture over top.
* Score top in diamond pattern; sprinkle with reserved pine nuts.
* Bake for 30 to 45 minutes or until done to taste. Top each serving with 1 tablespoon yogurt.

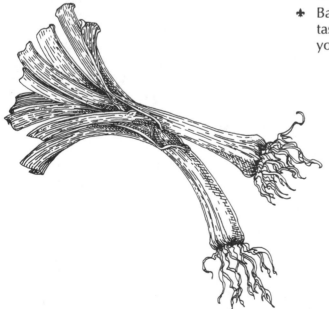

Maklubi (Chicken and Eggplant Casserole)

Yield: 5 to 6 servings

2 chickens, cut up, skinned
2 cups uncooked rice
2 cups chicken stock
2 medium eggplant, peeled, sliced
1/4 cup olive oil
1   46-ounce can tomato juice
1 cup water
pepper to taste

Garnish:

3/4 cup roasted walnuts
1 sliced tomato
chopped parsley

- Preheat oven to 350 degrees.
- Rinse chicken well. Bring to a boil in water to cover in large saucepan; skim off foam. Reduce heat and simmer for 10 minutes; drain.
- Cook rice partially in chicken stock in saucepan for 10 minutes; drain.
- Sauté eggplant in olive oil in large skillet until brown on both sides.
- Alternate layers of chicken and eggplant in large baking dish, spreading rice between layers.
- Combine tomato juice, water and pepper in bowl; mix well. Pour over layers.
- Bake, covered, until chicken and rice are tender and liquid has been absorbed.
- Garnish with walnuts, tomato and parsley.

Maklubi, and other tastes of the Middle East, comes to southeastern Connecticut through the doors of the Diana Restaurant in Groton. The Saad family, originally from Lebanon, and whose first restaurant was in Monrovia, Liberia, West Africa, opened the Diana Restaurant 11 years ago. Everything at the Diana Restaurant is zesty, fresh and prepared to order personally by a member of the Saad family.

Badinjan Bes Sinyah (Eggplant Casserole)

Yield: 4 to 6 servings

1½ to 2 pounds eggplant, peeled
salt
2 large onions, sliced
¼ teaspoon turmeric
½ teaspoon pepper
½ cup (or less) olive oil
3 large tomatoes, chopped
salt to taste
2 teaspoons sugar
¼ teaspoon cinnamon

Garnish:
1 tablespoon chopped fresh parsley

✦ Slice eggplant ½ inch thick. Sprinkle with salt; let stand for 30 minutes.

✦ Preheat oven to 350 degrees.

✦ Sauté onions with turmeric and pepper in 3 tablespoons of the olive oil in large sauté pan. Add tomatoes; reduce heat. Simmer for 15 minutes. Add salt to taste and mixture of sugar and cinnamon.

✦ Pat eggplant dry with paper towel. Brown in 2 or 3 batches in remaining olive oil in large sauté pan.

✦ Place eggplant in baking dish; top with tomato mixture. Bake for 30 minutes. Serve hot, garnished with parsley.

Shejar B'dehen (Zucchini and Rice)

Yield: 4 servings

3 tablespoons uncooked rice
1 small onion, finely chopped
3 tablespoons butter
½ teaspoon turmeric
½ teaspoon pepper
1 pound small zucchini, coarsely chopped
1½ cups tomato juice

✦ Soak rice in hot water in bowl for 2 to 3 hours; drain.

✦ Sauté onion in butter in saucepan over low heat until tender. Sprinkle with turmeric and pepper.

✦ Add zucchini. Cook for 2 minutes. Stir in rice and tomato juice. Cook, covered, over medium-low heat for 20 minutes or until rice is tender and liquid is nearly absorbed.

Chelo

Yield: 6 to 8 servings

3 cups uncooked basmati rice or Persian rice
2 quarts water
2 tablespoons salt
2 quarts water
1 tablespoon salt
3/4 cup melted butter
2 tablespoons hot water
2 tablespoons yogurt
1/2 teaspoon saffron
2 tablespoons hot water

Variation: May use American rice instead of basmati, cooking it for 10 minutes instead of 6 minutes during first cooking period.

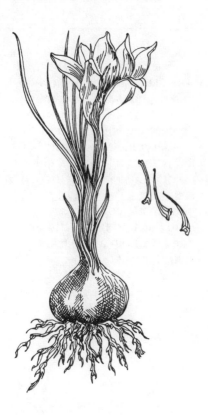

✤ Rinse rice from 3 to 5 times and drain. Combine with 2 quarts water and 2 tablespoons salt in bowl. Soak for 2 hours to overnight; drain.

✤ Bring 2 quarts fresh water and 1 tablespoon salt to a boil in large nonstick saucepan. Stir in rice. Cook for 6 minutes, stirring gently 2 times. Drain in colander and rinse with lukewarm water.

✤ Melt half the butter in saucepan. Stir in 2 tablespoons water and yogurt. Mound rice in saucepan. Pour mixture of remaining butter and 2 tablespoons hot water over rice. Cover with foil and lid.

✤ Cook over medium heat for 10 minutes; reduce heat. Cook for 50 minutes longer. Cool for 5 minutes without removing lid.

✤ Mix saffron with a serving spoon of rice; set aside.

✤ Spoon loose rice onto serving platter, leaving crusty portion in saucepan. Sprinkle saffron and rice mixture over top. Break crusty rice from bottom of saucepan into pieces and arrange around edge of platter.

Turkish Bulgur

Yield: 4 servings

1 cup chicken stock
1 cup tomato juice
1 cup uncooked bulgur
2 to 3 tablespoons butter
1/4 teaspoon cinnamon
1/8 teaspoon ground cloves
1/8 teaspoon ground allspice
1/4 cup raisins
1/4 cup slivered almonds
1 tablespoon sliced black olives

+ Heat chicken stock and tomato juice in saucepan. Set aside to cool.
+ Brown bulgur in butter in large saucepan. Add tomato juice mixture.
+ Simmer, covered, over low heat for 45 minutes or until liquid is absorbed. Stir in cinnamon, cloves, allspice, raisins, almonds and olives.
+ Cook just until heated through. Serve hot.

Homemade Yogurt

Yield: 1 quart

1 quart fresh whole milk
1/2 cup dry milk powder (optional)
3 tablespoons plain yogurt with acidophilus culture

+ Wash all utensils in hot soapy water; rinse in scalding water.
+ Scald milk in saucepan. Cool to lukewarm.
+ Stir a small amount of the warm milk into dry milk; stir dry milk into warm milk. Stir in yogurt.
+ Pour into clean glasses or jars; cover with plastic wrap. Place in pan of 100 to 110-degree water. Maintain temperature by placing pan in 100 to 110-degree oven or covering with towel and placing over pilot light on gas stovetop.
+ Let stand for 4 to 5 hours or until thickened. Store in refrigerator.

Like many Americans, Middle Easterners believe that yogurt is the supreme health food. It is believed to confer long life and good looks, prolong youth and fortify the soul. In Iran, girls use it as a facial. Like a good sourdough, the culture for homemade yogurt is saved from batch to batch and even dried on cloth and packed away for use on trips.

Pita Bread

When baking, these flat breads split into two distinct layers, which can be separated into a pocket to hold anything from sandwich fillings to shish kabob.

Yield: 10 servings

1 tablespoon sugar
2 cups 95 to 115-degree water
1 envelope dry yeast
1 cup all-purpose flour
½ cup whole wheat flour
1 tablespoon salt
4½ cups (about) all-purpose flour
cornmeal

✤ Stir sugar into warm water in bowl until dissolved. Stir in yeast. Let stand for 6 minutes.

✤ Stir in 1 cup all-purpose flour, whole wheat flour and salt. Add 4 cups all-purpose flour, mixing to form dough.

✤ Knead for 4 minutes on floured surface, kneading in additional flour if needed. Let rest for several minutes.

✤ Knead for 5 minutes longer or until smooth and elastic. Place in greased bowl, turning to grease surface. Let rise in warm place for 2 hours or until doubled in bulk.

✤ Divide dough into 10 portions. Roll each portion into ⅛ to ¼-inch thick circle on lightly floured surface. Let rest for 15 minutes.

✤ Preheat oven to 500 degrees. Sprinkle baking sheets with cornmeal.

✤ Place 1 or 2 circles on each baking sheet. Place on lowest oven rack. Bake for 1 minute. Move to higher oven rack. Bake for 3 to 7 minutes or until bread is puffed and light brown.

✤ Remove to wire rack to cool. Store in airtight container.

Note: Serve with soups, stews and hummus.

Leavened bread was developed by the Egyptians about 5,000 years ago! At first, bread was unleavened. Perhaps it was an Egyptian grandmother who noticed that when she waited too long to put her dough into the oven it began to rise. Loaves of bread have been found in the tombs of Egyptian Kings buried over 3,500 years ago, and on the walls inside the pyramids there are paintings of bread being kneaded and baked.

In the Middle East, wheat bread is more than the staff of life. It is considered so sacred that a dropped piece of bread must be picked up and kissed in atonement.

Baklava

Yield: 24 servings

For the honey-orange syrup:

2/3 cup orange juice
1 cup honey
3/4 cup sugar
1 cinnamon stick
1 tablespoon lemon juice

For the baklava:

1 pound walnuts, finely chopped
2 teaspoons cinnamon
1 teaspoon grated lemon rind
1 teaspoon grated orange rind
1/2 cup sugar
1   12-ounce package phyllo dough
1 1/4 cups melted butter
whole cloves

> **W**alnuts were originally from ancient Persia. The name *English* walnuts is a misnomer since England does not produce walnuts commercially; it derives from the fact that English trading ships transported the nuts around the world.

To make the honey-orange syrup:

✦ Combine orange juice, honey, sugar and cinnamon stick in saucepan. Bring to a boil. Boil for 5 minutes or to 220 degrees on candy thermometer. Remove cinnamon stick. Stir in lemon juice. Set aside.

To make the baklava:

✦ Preheat oven to 350 degrees.

✦ Mix walnuts, cinnamon, lemon rind, orange rind and sugar in large bowl; set aside.

✦ Cut phyllo dough to fit 9x13-inch baking pan; cover with damp cloth to prevent drying out.

✦ Layer 5 sheets dough in baking pan, brushing each sheet with butter. Sprinkle with 3/4 cup walnut mixture. Layer 3 sheets phyllo dough over filling, brushing each sheet with butter. Repeat process until there are 7 layers of filling. Top with 5 sheets buttered phyllo.

✦ Cut through top 4 sheets phyllo with sharp knife in diamond pattern. Place whole clove in center of every third diamond to secure top layers.

✦ Bake for 1 hour. Cut completely through diamond design. Cool in pan on wire rack for 10 minutes. Pour honey-orange syrup over top. Let stand overnight.

Shirini (Kurdish Pumpkin Dessert)

Yield: 6 servings

¹/₄ cup honey
1 cup sugar
¹/₂ cup water
3 cups 1¹/₂-inch slices peeled fresh pumpkin
³/₄ cup finely chopped walnuts
cinnamon

Variation: Serve with whipped cream if desired.

* Combine honey, sugar and water in large saucepan; mix well. Simmer for 10 minutes or longer or until thick and syrupy, stirring frequently.
* Add pumpkin to syrup. Simmer over low heat until pumpkin is tender and glazed. Cool slightly for several minutes. Arrange on platter; sprinkle with walnuts and cinnamon.

Date Dreams

Yield: 3 dozen

1 cup shredded coconut
1 cup chopped dates
³/₄ cup sweetened condensed milk
1 cup chopped walnuts
2 teaspoons vanilla extract

* Preheat oven to 350 degrees. Grease cookie sheet.
* Process coconut in food processor until finely ground. Combine with dates, condensed milk, walnuts and vanilla in bowl; mix well.
* Drop by spoonfuls onto prepared cookie sheet. Bake for 8 to 10 minutes or until golden brown. Remove to wire rack to cool.

Lebanese Cookies

These cookies are delicious served with coffee.

Yield: 8 dozen

2 cups finely ground walnuts
¼ cup sugar
1 teaspoon grated orange rind
1 pound unsalted butter
¾ cup sugar
2 eggs
1 tablespoon brandy
4¾ cups flour, sifted

♣ Preheat oven to 350 degrees.

♣ Mix walnuts, ¼ cup sugar and orange rind in bowl; set aside.

♣ Cream butter in mixer bowl until light. Add ¾ cup sugar gradually, beating until fluffy.

♣ Beat each egg slightly and beat into creamed mixture 1 at a time. Add brandy and flour gradually, mixing to form dough. Chill for 10 to 15 minutes if necessary for ease in handling.

♣ Shape dough into 1-inch balls. Make indentation in each ball with thumb. Fill indentations with walnut mixture; pinch dough to cover filling completely.

♣ Place seam side down on cookie sheet; place cookie sheet on lower oven rack. Bake for 20 minutes. Move cookie sheet to upper oven rack. Bake for 5 minutes longer or until brown. Remove to wire rack to cool.

Scandinavia

It is reverence for nature and the resulting simplicity of cuisine that the Scandinavians have in common with Native Americans. The severe climate and rugged terrain kept the Nordic peoples more isolated than those of other European cultures, and so their diet seems relatively static and conservative in comparison.

Frigid winters demand a higher level of fat in diets, which does as much to keep these people warm as hot, spicy foods do to keep tropical inhabitants cooler. Winter not only affected which foods would be eaten, but how they would be prepared. Knäckbröd, the thin, dried bread of Sweden and Finland, evolved because farmhouse ovens were traditionally outside and were snowed under all winter. The farmer's wife would have to bake the great, flat rings of bread for months in advance of winter and string them over poles to dry. In Norway, even spring milk was preserved in barrels with tette, a meadow flower, making it drinkable all through the winter.

A short growing season resulted in a limited variety of vegetables, most often pickled for year-round eating. That there are so many ways to preserve fish is also a testament to the storage mentality that defined survival. The surprise is that many of these traditions continue today when modern conveniences make them unnecessary, demonstrating the great pride they have in their self-reliant heritage.

Let's not ignore the lighter aspects of Scandinavian living, namely the wonderful desserts and the invention of the boilermaker, a frothy beer following a toss of aquavit. So lift a glass, look long and hard into your companion's eyes, and toast the Viking spirit that survives those long, dark winters year after year, emerging triumphant every spring with a vigor most of us will never know.

Scandinavia

Gravlax with Sennepsaus (Smoked Salmon with Mustard-Dill Sauce)

This marinated fish dish may be served with Norwegian crispbread or toast as a gourmet first course or as a main feature at a brunch. Norwegians love to serve it as kvelds, or a light supper, to family and friends, accompanied by a chilled white wine.

Yield: 8 to 16 servings

For the mustard-dill sauce:

¼ cup Dijon or other sharp prepared mustard
1 teaspoon dry mustard
3 tablespoons sugar
2 tablespoons vinegar
⅓ cup oil
3 tablespoons chopped fresh dill or 1 tablespoon
   dried dill

For the salmon:

1   4 to 8-pound fat whole salmon or trout
2 tablespoons oil
2 teaspoons coarsely ground white pepper
¼ cup kosher salt
2 tablespoons sugar
chopped fresh dillweed
2 tablespoons brandy

To make the mustard-dill sauce:

✿ Combine prepared mustard, dry mustard, sugar and vinegar in bowl or food processor container, whisking or processing until smooth.

✿ Add oil very gradually, whisking or processing constantly until smooth. Stir in dill. Chill, covered, until serving time.

To prepare the salmon:

✿ Remove the head and tail of fish and cut into 2 fillets, discarding all bones. Brush with oil.

✿ Crush white pepper, salt and sugar in small bowl. Rub the mixture onto both sides of salmon. Sprinkle dillweed generously on large piece of foil. Layer fillets on foil, sprinkling layers with additional dillweed and any remaining salt mixture. Sprinkle with brandy.

✿ Fold up foil to enclose salmon; seal tightly. Place on large platter; top with weight. Chill for 48 hours, turning packet every 12 hours to marinate evenly.

✿ Scrape away excess seasonings; place salmon on serving plate. Cut diagonally into very thin slices. Serve with mustard-dill sauce.

> When gravlax is presented as a main course, it is garnished with lemon wedges as well as the mustard sauce and served with toast and perhaps a cucumber salad.

Piirakat (Karelian Pasties)

Karelia is a region long-disputed over by Finland and the Soviet Union. Karelian émigrés to Finland brought with them a tasty cuisine influenced by Russian traditions. These boat-shaped pasties are still carried by fishermen and lumbermen for lunch.

Yield: 8 servings

For the egg butter:
4 hard-boiled eggs
½ cup butter, softened
¼ teaspoon salt
¼ teaspoon pepper

For the filling:
¾ cup uncooked medium grain rice
½ teaspoon salt
1½ cups water
¾ cup milk
¼ cup butter
1 egg, slightly beaten
¼ teaspoon pepper

For the pasties:
½ cup rye flour
½ cup wheat flour
¼ teaspoon salt
9 tablespoons water
¼ cup butter
½ cup water

To make the egg butter:
✤ Mash warm eggs with butter in bowl. Season with salt and pepper. Place in refrigerator just until chilled.

To make the filling:
✤ Cook rice with salt in water in saucepan for 20 minutes or until water is absorbed. Add milk. Simmer until milk is absorbed. Stir in butter, egg and pepper. Adjust seasonings; set aside.

To make the pasties:
✤ Preheat oven to 475 degrees.
✤ Mix rye flour, wheat flour and salt in bowl. Add 9 tablespoons water gradually, mixing to form stiff dough. Shape into 15-inch rope. Cut into 25 portions.
✤ Roll each portion into thin circle on floured surface. Sprinkle additional flour between circles; brush off excess.
✤ Spoon 1½ tablespoons filling down center of each circle. Crimp both edges of each circle at the same time with fingertips, starting at center; pasties will be oval in shape.
✤ Place on ungreased baking sheet. Bake for 12 to 15 minutes or until light golden brown. Heat butter and ½ cup water in saucepan until butter melts. Dip hot pasties into butter mixture. Place on platter lined with waxed paper and towel; cover and keep warm. Serve with egg butter on the side.

Fiskesuppe (Fish Soup)

Yield: 6 to 8 servings

1 pound whiting
1 pound scrod
1 pound salmon or flounder
1 medium onion
1 bay leaf
2 pounds potatoes, peeled, chopped
2½ cups milk
salt and pepper to taste
½ cup whipping cream
¼ cup butter
fresh dill to taste

✤ Skin and bone whiting, scrod and salmon; cut into large pieces. Combine with onion and bay leaf in saucepan. Add water to nearly cover. Simmer until fish flakes easily.

✤ Cook potatoes in milk in saucepan until tender. Add salt and pepper.

✤ Add fish to saucepan with potatoes. Strain fish stock into saucepan. Adjust seasonings. Stir in cream, butter and a generous amount of dill; do not reheat. Ladle into soup bowls.

Mumu's Fruit Soup

This is served for special holiday breakfasts with freshly baked sweet bread in Finland.

Yield: 8 to 10 servings

1 cup dried apricots
1 cup dried pears or ½ cup dried pears and
    ½ cup dried apples
1 cup dried pitted prunes
1 cup dried currants
3 cinnamon sticks
4 cups water
¼ cup sugar
2 tablespoons quick-cooking tapioca
½ teaspoon cardamom
¼ teaspoon salt

Note: May add water if needed for desired consistency.

✦ Combine apricots, pears, prunes, currants, cinnamon sticks and water in large stainless steel saucepan.

✦ Bring to a boil; reduce heat. Simmer for 30 minutes or until fruit is tender.

✦ Add sugar, tapioca, cardamom and salt. Bring to a boil; reduce heat. Simmer for 15 minutes.

✦ Discard cinnamon sticks. Chill until serving time. Ladle into soup bowls.

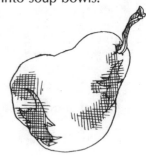

Sweet and Sour Cucumber Salad

This is a traditional Scandinavian favorite, with slight variations in each country. In Denmark, where sour salads are not as popular, the lemon juice or vinegar may be reduced by half; in Finland, sour cream may be added. In all cases, it is best made with fresh dill and the cucumbers must be sliced paper thin.

Yield: 12 servings

1/2 cup lemon juice or white wine vinegar
1/2 cup sugar
1 teaspoon salt
white pepper to taste
2 large European-style cucumbers, very thinly
  sliced
1/4 cup chopped fresh dill or 4 teaspoons dried
  dillweed

Garnish:

fresh dill sprigs

* Combine lemon juice, sugar, salt and pepper in bowl; mix well. Add cucumbers.
* Sprinkle with chopped dill. Chill for 3 hours or longer. Garnish with dill sprigs.

Sildesalat (Herring Salad)

Yield: 10 servings

1 salted herring
3 to 4 pickled beets, chopped
7 tart apples, chopped
3 to 4 pickled cucumbers, chopped
1/4 cup butter
3 tablespoons flour
3/4 cup bouillon
1/2 cup vinegar from pickled beets
1 teaspoon light French mustard

Garnish:

2 hard-boiled eggs and chopped watercress

* Soak herring in cold water in bowl for 6 to 8 hours; drain. Remove skin and bones; cut into small pieces.
* Combine herring with beets, apples and cucumbers in bowl; mix gently.
* Melt butter in saucepan. Stir in flour. Cook for several minutes. Stir in bouillon, vinegar and mustard. Cook until thickened, stirring constantly; remove from heat.
* Stir sauce until cool. Add herring mixture; mix gently. Garnish with chopped eggs and watercress.

Rosolli

Yield: 6 servings

For the salad:
1/2 cup chopped salted herring (optional)
1/2 pound potatoes
1 pound carrots
salt to taste
1/2 pound beets without tops, peeled, cubed
1/2 cup each chopped onion and dill pickle
1 clove of garlic, pressed
1/4 teaspoon salt
freshly ground white pepper to taste

For the dressing:
3/4 cup whipping cream
1 tablespoon sugar
2 tablespoons vinegar
1 to 3 teaspoons dry mustard or to taste
2 tablespoons reserved beet cooking liquid
1/2 teaspoon salt

To make the salad:

♣ Soak herring in cold water in bowl for 6 to 8 hours; drain. Remove skin and bones; cut into small pieces.

♣ Cook potatoes and carrots in salted boiling water in saucepan for 20 minutes or until tender; drain. Cool. Cut into small pieces.

♣ Cook beets in salted boiling water in saucepan for 30 minutes or until tender; drain, reserving 2 tablespoons cooking liquid. Cool.

♣ Combine potatoes, carrots, beets, onion, pickle and herring in bowl. Add garlic, 1/4 teaspoon salt and pepper; mix well. Chill.

To make the dressing:

♣ Whip cream in mixer bowl until slightly thickened. Add sugar, vinegar, dry mustard, reserved beet liquid and salt; mix well. Serve with salad.

Får-i-Kål (Lamb with Cabbage)

Yield: 6 servings

2 to 3 pounds lamb shoulder roast
1 large head cabbage
2 to 3 tablespoons peppercorns
flour
salt

Note: May make ahead and reheat to improve flavor.

♣ Cut lamb into 3-inch pieces. Shred half the cabbage coarsely; shred remaining cabbage finely. Tie peppercorns in cheesecloth bags.

♣ Alternate layers of lamb, coarsely chopped cabbage and pepper in saucepan until all ingredients are used, sprinkling layers with flour and salt. Fill saucepan halfway with water.

♣ Simmer until meat is partially cooked, stirring occasionally and adding water if needed.

♣ Add finely chopped cabbage. Simmer until lamb is tender and mixture is of desired consistency. Discard pepper bags. Serve with boiled potatoes.

Pytt i panna (Put-in-the-Pan)

In Sweden, this is served piping hot with raw egg yolks or fried eggs, fresh cucumber salad or pickled beets.

Yield: 4 servings

8 to 10 medium potatoes, chopped
3 tablespoons butter
2 or 3 red or yellow onions, chopped
2 cups finely chopped cooked lamb
1 teaspoon salt
1/2 teaspoon pepper

✤ Cook potatoes in butter in skillet until tender and brown; remove with slotted spoon.
✤ Sauté onions in butter remaining in skillet until tender and brown. Add lamb. Cook until light brown.
✤ Return potatoes to skillet. Season with salt and pepper. Cook over low heat for 5 minutes. Serve piping hot.

Norwegian Meatballs

There are many versions of Scandinavian meatballs. The basic differences lie in the liquid used (water, milk, cream, or even club soda) and the spice (nutmeg, ginger, allspice). Regardless of the details, they make a wonderful buffet item.

Yield: 6 servings

3/4 pound ground beef
1/2 pound ground veal
1/4 pound ground pork
1 1/2 cups soft bread crumbs
1 cup half and half or light cream
1/2 cup chopped onion
1 tablespoon butter
1 egg
1/4 teaspoon ginger
nutmeg and pepper to taste
1 1/2 teaspoons salt
1   10-ounce can cream of mushroom soup
1/2 soup can water
1/4 teaspoon beef bouillon granules

✤ Grind beef, veal and pork together 2 times. Soak bread crumbs in half and half in bowl for 5 minutes.
✤ Sauté onion in butter in skillet until tender but not brown.
✤ Combine ground meats, soaked bread crumbs, onion, egg, ginger, nutmeg, pepper and salt in bowl; mix well.
✤ Shape into meatballs. Brown in skillet. Remove to heavy saucepan or slow cooker.
✤ Combine soup, water and bouillon. Pour over meatballs. Simmer until cooked through. Serve over noodles.

Salmon and Whitefish Mousse

Fish mousse or fish pudding is traditionally made from Norwegian codfish. Now the food processor does the work that was originally done with a wooden spoon.

Yield: 18 servings

For the mousse:

1½ pounds salmon fillet, skinned, cubed
¾ pound whitefish fillet, skinned, cubed
¼ cup dry white wine
2 tablespoons fresh lemon juice
3 eggs
2 egg whites
1½ tablespoons potato flour or cornstarch
2 cups whipping cream
2 teaspoons salt
¼ teaspoon freshly ground white pepper

For the caviar sauce:

1 cup sour cream
2 tablespoons lemon juice
¼ cup fresh whitefish caviar or red salmon caviar

Garnish:

fresh dill sprigs

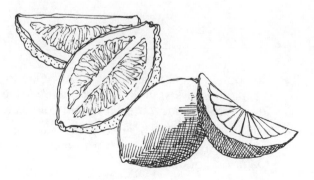

To make the mousse:

* Combine fish with wine and lemon juice in stainless steel bowl. Marinate in refrigerator for 2 to 24 hours.
* Put fish through meat grinder fitted with fine disk 3 times or purée in food processor. Return to steel bowl. Chill for 1 hour longer.
* Preheat oven to 400 degrees. Butter 2-quart loaf pan or terrine.
* Beat fish in large mixer bowl at high speed until smooth. Add eggs, egg whites, potato flour, cream, salt and white pepper; beat until light and fluffy.
* Spoon into prepared loaf pan. Cover with waxed paper and foil; place in large baking pan. Fill baking pan with water halfway up side of loaf pan.
* Bake for 1½ hours or until mousse is set and fish is cooked through.

To make the caviar sauce:

* Combine sour cream and lemon juice in bowl; mix well. Fold in caviar.

To serve the mousse:

* Unmold mousse onto serving plate. Garnish with dill sprigs. Serve hot or chilled with caviar sauce.

Swedish Brown Beans

This is an updated version of a dish traditionally served with ham, Swedish meatballs, roast beef or turkey at Christmas or for any special smörgåsbord or dinner.

Yield: 4 to 5 servings

2   19-ounce cans kidney beans
1 cup packed brown sugar
1 tablespoon wine vinegar
1 small onion, chopped
salt to taste
1 tablespoon cornstarch
2 tablespoons water
2 tablespoons butter

✦ Combine undrained beans, brown sugar, vinegar, onion and salt in medium saucepan; mix well. Simmer for 1 to 3 hours, stirring occasionally.

✦ Stir in mixture of cornstarch and water if needed for desired consistency. Cook until thickened, stirring constantly. Stir in butter.

Stuet Kaal (Norwegian Cabbage)

Yield: 4 servings

1½ pounds cabbage, coarsely shredded
salt to taste
1 cup sour cream
1 teaspoon caraway seeds
1 teaspoon salt
pepper to taste

✦ Cook cabbage in boiling salted water to cover in saucepan for 8 to 10 minutes or until tender-crisp; drain.

✦ Stir in sour cream, caraway seeds, 1 teaspoon salt and pepper. Cook just until heated through, stirring constantly.

Brunede Kartofler (Browned Potatoes)

Yield: 4 servings

1 pound small firm potatoes
salt to taste
2½ tablespoons sugar
2 tablespoons butter

✦ Boil potatoes in salted water in saucepan for 12 minutes or just until tender; drain and peel. Press through sieve and rinse with cold water.

✦ Melt sugar in skillet over very low heat. Stir in butter. Cook until mixture forms a light brown foam. Add potatoes.

✦ Cook for several minutes or until glazed and golden brown, shaking skillet gently to coat evenly. Serve immediately.

Jansson's Frestelse (Mr. Jansson's Temptation)

This is a must on any Swedish smörgåsbord.

Yield: 4 to 5 servings

2 large yellow onions, finely chopped
14 to 16 Swedish anchovy fillets
6 medium potatoes, peeled, cut into thin strips
1 to 1½ cups whipping cream
1 tablespoon dry bread crumbs
1 to 2 tablespoons butter

+ Preheat oven to 425 degrees. Butter shallow baking dish.
+ Spread onions and anchovy fillets in prepared baking dish. Top with potatoes.
+ Add enough cream to cover potatoes. Sprinkle with bread crumbs; dot with butter.
+ Bake for 45 to 50 minutes or until potatoes are tender.

Variation: May add 1 to 2 tablespoons anchovy brine for stronger flavor.

The *smörgåsbord*, translated literally from the Swedish, means bread and butter table. It can consist of a simple tray of appetizers or enough elaborately prepared dishes to consist of a meal. It originated in the days of the Vikings, when guests helped themselves to food from a huge center table. A *smörgåsbord* usually includes a number of fish dishes, particularly herring, plus marinated vegetables, various types of pickles, salads and cold meats. It can also include hot dishes and, of course, dessert.

Spinach and Tomato Casserole

Yield: 6 servings

4 slices bacon, cut into 2-inch pieces
1 pound spinach, stems removed
salt and pepper to taste
3 medium tomatoes, peeled, sliced
4 ounces Swiss cheese, sliced

Variation: May substitute one 10-ounce package frozen spinach leaves for fresh spinach. Pour boiling water over spinach to thaw slightly; drain.

+ Preheat oven to 350 degrees.
+ Fry bacon in skillet until crisp; drain.
+ Arrange spinach in greased 1½-quart baking dish. Sprinkle with salt and pepper. Place tomato slices in single layer over spinach. Top with cheese; sprinkle with bacon.
+ Bake for 20 minutes or until cheese melts.

Kroppkakor (Swedish Potato Dumplings)

Serve leftovers for breakfast. Brown sliced dumpling in margarine and serve with gravy.

Yield: 6 servings

6 medium potatoes, chopped
2 tablespoons finely chopped onion
1 tablespoon butter or margarine
1 egg
1 cup flour
½ teaspoon salt
chopped salt pork to taste
1 cup chopped steak
1 10-ounce can cream of mushroom soup

* Cook potatoes in water in saucepan until tender; drain. Mash potatoes by hand; measure 3 cups. Add onion and butter; mix well. Cool to room temperature. Add egg, flour and salt; mix well.
* Cook salt pork and steak in skillet until brown, stirring constantly.
* Pat some of the potato mixture between floured hands. Add some of the meat mixture. Shape potato into a ball around filling, covering completely; ball should be slightly smaller than a tennis ball. Repeat with remaining ingredients, reserving any leftover meat for gravy.
* Drop dumplings into boiling water in large saucepan. Cook, covered, for 10 minutes or just until dumplings float to the top; do not overcook. Remove with slotted spoon.
* Stir soup into drippings and leftover meat filling in skillet. Cook until heated through. May add water to make gravy consistency. Serve over dumplings.

Æbleflæsk (Bacon and Apples)

Yield: 8 servings

2 pounds apples
8 slices bacon
sugar to taste

* Core apples. Cut each apple into 8 wedges.
* Cook bacon in skillet until crisp; remove to warm plate.
* Add apples to drippings in skillet. Cook until tender, but not soft, turning gently. Sprinkle with sugar.
* Place apples in serving dish; arrange bacon over top.

Lucia Crown

Yield: 1 crown

1½ cups flour
1 envelope dry yeast
¾ cup chopped blanched almonds
½ cup sugar
½ teaspoon cardamom
pinch of saffron (optional)
¾ cup evaporated milk
¼ cup water
5 tablespoons butter or margarine
2 eggs
2½ to 3 cups flour
2 cups sifted confectioners' sugar
1 teaspoon vanilla extract
2 tablespoons milk
¼ cup slivered dried apricots

In pre-Christian times, people celebrated the return of the sun in December, when they knew the days would start growing longer and sunshine would gradually replace darkness. This ancient winter festival is the source of the Swedish celebration of St. Lucia's Day on December 13 before the Christmas season. Wearing a long white dress and a crown of candles, the oldest daughter of a Swedish family carries saffron-colored yeast bread or buns, to her parents on the morning of St. Lucia Day. May add candles to the bread to use as a centerpiece.

* Combine 1½ cups flour and yeast with ½ cup almonds, sugar, cardamom and saffron in bowl. Heat evaporated milk, water and butter in saucepan to 120 degrees. Add to yeast mixture; mix well. Add 1 egg; mix well.

* Add enough remaining flour to make soft dough.

* Knead on floured surface for 5 minutes. Divide into 4 equal portions. Roll and pull 3 portions into 20-inch ropes.

* Braid ropes on greased baking sheet, shaping into 8- or 9-inch ring; press ends to seal.

* Divide remaining portion into halves. Roll and pull into 2 narrow 18-inch ropes. Twist ropes together; place on top of braid, pressing ends to seal.

* Brush with 1 beaten egg. Let rise in warm place for 3 hours or until almost doubled in bulk.

* Preheat oven to 350 degrees. Bake crown for 30 to 35 minutes or until bread tests done and is golden brown, covering loosely with foil if necessary to prevent overbrowning. Remove to wire rack to cool.

* Blend confectioners' sugar with vanilla and enough milk to make spreading consistency. Spread over crown. Decorate with apricots and remaining ¼ cup almonds.

Lefse

Years ago, women baked lefse on the kitchen range and used a flat wooden stick for turning.

Yield: 36 servings

8 cups hot mashed or riced cooked potatoes
1/2 cup whipping cream
1/2 cup butter or margarine
1 tablespoon (scant) salt
3 to 4 cups flour

Note: A large heavy rolling pin such as is used in Norway is good to use for rolling out the batter. To prevent sticking, a white stocking is sometimes put on the pin.

* Combine potatoes with cream, butter and salt. Chill for several hours to overnight.
* Combine potato mixture with enough flour to make stiff dough; mix well. Shape into 1 1/2-inch balls. Roll balls thin on floured surface; keep cool.
* Preheat lefse griddle or pancake griddle to 400 degrees.
* Bake lefse on griddle until bubbles and brown spots appear, turning once.
* Serve warm or cool between paper towels and chill or freeze until needed. Serve with butter and sugar.

Pandekager (Pancakes)

These thin pancakes are served with stewed apples, ligonberries or other fruit, jam, chopped almonds mixed with sugar or custard cream.

Yield: 8 servings

4 eggs
6 tablespoons sugar
6 tablespoons melted butter
salt to taste
2 cups flour
grated rind of 1 lemon
1 1/2 cups milk
1/2 cup beer
melted butter

* Combine eggs, sugar, 6 tablespoons butter and salt in bowl; mix well. Mix flour with lemon rind in small bowl. Add to egg mixture alternately with milk and beer, mixing until moistened after each addition.
* Chill for 1 hour or longer.
* Pour in very thin layer into butter in heated skillet; shake pan to spread batter over bottom. Bake over high heat until edge begins to brown, shaking occasionally to prevent sticking. Turn pancake. Cook until brown.
* Repeat with remaining batter.

Joulutortut (Christmas Prune Tarts)

These are traditionally served in Finland after Christmas dinner with gingerbread cookies and coffee.

Yield: 3 dozen

1 pound dried pitted prunes
1 cup water
1/2 cup sugar
4 cups flour
1 pound butter
3/4 cup cold water
1 egg yolk, beaten

Variation: May use frozen puff pastry for these tarts.

* Cook prunes in water in saucepan until tender. Stir in sugar.
* Mix flour with 1 cup butter in bowl until crumbly. Add water; mix to form dough. Chill for 30 minutes.
* Roll dough on floured surface; dot with some of the remaining butter. Fold in 4 sides of dough to cover butter. Chill in refrigerator. Repeat process 3 more times.
* Preheat oven to 400 degrees.
* Roll dough on floured surface. Cut into 3-inch squares. Cut the corners of each square diagonally toward center.
* Place 1 spoonful filling in center of each square. Turn down alternate corners to form pinwheels; press centers to seal. Place on baking sheet. Brush with egg yolk. Bake for 15 minutes.

Kærnemælkskoldskål (Cold Buttermilk Soup)

This soup may be served as part of a light meal or as an unusual dessert.

Yield: 6 servings

6 tablespoons sugar
2 egg yolks
lemon juice to taste
4 cups buttermilk

Garnish:

2 cups whipped cream
1 1/2 ounces blanched slivered almonds
strawberry jam

* Combine sugar and egg yolks in mixer bowl; beat until thick and lemon-colored. Stir in lemon juice.
* Add buttermilk gradually, mixing constantly. Ladle into soup bowls. Garnish with whipped cream, almonds and strawberry jam. Serve very cold.

Rødgrød med Fløde (Fruit Jelly with Cream)

This Danish dish is popular on a hot summer day.

Yield: 10 servings

1²/₃ pounds red currants
1²/₃ pounds raspberries
8 cups water
sugar to taste
vanilla extract to taste
¹/₂ cup potato flour or cornstarch

Garnish:
sugar
slivered almonds
whipped cream

✤ Cook currants and raspberries in water in saucepan. Press through fine sieve or cloth; return liquid to saucepan.

✤ Stir in sugar and vanilla. Blend ¹/₄ cup of the liquid with potato flour.

✤ Bring remaining juice to a boil. Stir in potato flour mixture. Cook until thickened, stirring constantly. Spoon into serving dish. Garnish with sugar and slivered almonds. Serve with whipped cream.

Torta

Yield: 12 servings

¹/₂ cup butter, softened
¹/₂ cup sugar
4 egg yolks
1 cup flour
1 teaspoon baking powder
5 tablespoons milk
¹/₂ teaspoon almond extract
4 egg whites
1 cup sugar
³/₄ cup chopped almonds
whipped cream

✤ Preheat oven to 350 degrees.

✤ Cream butter and ¹/₂ cup sugar in mixer bowl until light and fluffy. Add egg yolks; beat until lemon-colored.

✤ Sift flour and baking powder together. Add to creamed mixture alternately with milk, mixing well after each addition. Mix in almond extract. Spread in 2 round 9-inch baking pans.

✤ Beat egg whites in mixer bowl until soft peaks form. Add 1 cup sugar gradually, beating constantly until stiff peaks form.

✤ Spread meringue over batter in pans; sprinkle with almonds.

✤ Bake for 20 minutes. Remove carefully to wire rack to cool.

✤ Place 1 layer meringue side down on serving plate. Spread generously with whipped cream. Top with remaining layer meringue side up.

Swedish Nuts

Yield: 4 cups

¹/₂ cup butter
3¹/₂ cups salted mixed nuts without peanuts
2 egg whites
1 cup sugar
¹/₂ teaspoon salt

* Preheat oven to 325 degrees. Melt butter in 10x15-inch baking pan.
* Spread nuts on baking sheet. Roast for 20 minutes or until light brown.
* Beat egg whites in mixer bowl until stiff peaks form. Fold in sugar, salt and nuts.
* Spread in prepared baking pan. Bake for 30 minutes, stirring every 10 minutes.

Swedish Apple Pie

This elegant pie is somewhat different from a regular apple pie but is easy to make.

Yield: 6 to 8 servings

For the topping:

¹/₃ cup sugar
¹/₃ cup flour
1 teaspoon cinnamon
¹/₄ cup butter, softened

For the pie:

2 cups sliced apples
2 tablespoons water
2 tablespoons flour
³/₄ cup sugar
salt to taste
1 egg
1 teaspoon vanilla extract
1 cup sour cream
1 unbaked 8 or 9-inch pie shell

To make the topping:

* Combine sugar, flour, cinnamon and butter in bowl; mix until crumbly.

To make the pie:

* Preheat oven to 350 degrees.
* Cook apples in water in saucepan until tender. Mash apples slightly.
* Add flour, sugar and salt; mix well. Add mixture of egg and vanilla. Beat sour cream until fluffy. Fold into apple mixture. Spoon into pie shell.
* Bake for 40 minutes. Sprinkle with topping mixture. Bake for 15 minutes longer.

Grandmother's Spritz

These are crisp, buttery cookies. The recipe from a Swedish mor-mor, or grandmother, has been made for generations who feel that the cookies are best when shaped into S's and O's.

Yield: 6 dozen

1 cup butter, softened
3/4 cup sugar
1 egg yolk
1 teaspoon almond extract
2 cups sifted flour
1 teaspoon baking powder
1/8 teaspoon salt

Variation: May pipe into strips and shape into S's and O's with fingers. May substitute vanilla extract for almond extract and increase sugar slightly.

✦ Preheat oven to 350 to 375 degrees.
✦ Cream butter and sugar at medium speed in mixer bowl or with wooden spoon until light and fluffy. Add egg yolk and almond extract.
✦ Sift flour, baking powder and salt together. Add to creamed mixture, beating at low speed to form dough.
✦ Spoon into pastry bag fitted with star tip. Pipe into 2-inch S's and O's on ungreased cookie sheet.
✦ Bake for 8 to 10 minutes or until edges begin to brown. Remove to wire rack to cool.

Swedish grandmothers frequently used an ingredient called salt of hartshorn, which was made from the antlers of a deer and predated baking powder as a rising agent by several centuries. It makes cookies crisper and lighter than baking powder, and although it emits an odor of ammonia during baking, the cookies will bear no trace of the smell. It is produced chemically now and can be purchased as *aqua ammoniae* (ammonium carbonate).

Swedish cookies should be crisp enough to snap without crumbling, yet so delicate that they almost dissolve in the mouth.

The cookie recipe at left was that of Thelma Andersson Swody's grandmother, Sofia Andersson, who immigrated here from Kristinehamn, Sweden, on June 15, 1922. She lived with Thelma's parents on their dairy farm, Sunnybrook, in Narragansett, Rhode Island. Thelma has many loving memories of this special lady, who helped raise the four young children after Thelma's father drowned in 1930, and her mother ran the dairy farm. These cookies represent only one of her talents.

The lady in the apron is mor-mor—Sofia Andersson!

Old Swedish Cookies

Yield: 1½ dozen

½ cup butter, softened
2 tablespoons confectioners' sugar
1 cup flour
1¼ cups packed brown sugar
2 tablespoons flour
1 teaspoon baking powder
2 eggs, beaten
½ cup coconut
1 cup chopped nuts
1 teaspoon vanilla extract

✤ Preheat oven to 350 degrees.
✤ Combine butter, confectioners' sugar and 1 cup flour in bowl; mix well by hand. Press into 9x9-inch baking pan.
✤ Bake for 25 minutes or until light brown.
✤ Combine brown sugar, 2 tablespoons flour, baking powder, eggs, coconut, nuts and vanilla in bowl; mix well. Spoon over baked layer.
✤ Bake for 25 minutes longer. Cool on wire rack. Cut into bars.

Sandbakkels (Shell-Shaped Cookies)

Yield: 4 dozen

1 cup butter, softened
1 cup (heaping) confectioners' sugar
1 large egg
1 teaspoon almond extract
1 teaspoon vanilla extract
3 to 4 cups flour

Variation: May add finely ground walnuts and reduce flour slightly.

✤ Preheat oven to 350 degrees.
✤ Cream butter in mixer bowl until light. Add confectioners' sugar gradually, mixing constantly until fluffy. Beat in egg and flavorings. Add enough flour to form dough; mix well.
✤ Press evenly into sandbakkel tins. Bake for 10 to 12 minutes or until light brown. Tap tins gently to remove cookies. Cool on wire rack.

Scandinavian Rosettes

These delicate rosettes, often made at Christmas, look a lot like snowflakes.

Yield: 6 dozen

2 eggs
2 teaspoons sugar
1 cup milk
1 cup flour
1/2 teaspoon salt
oil for frying
confectioners' sugar

* Beat eggs lightly in bowl. Add sugar; mix well. Stir in milk.
* Sift in flour and salt together; mix until smooth.
* Heat 2 1/2 inches oil in pan slightly larger than rosette iron. Dip rosette iron into heated oil; drain excess oil on paper towel.
* Dip heated iron 3/4 of the way into batter. Place coated iron in heated oil.
* Fry for 20 to 35 seconds or until puffed and light golden brown. Remove rosette with fork. Sprinkle with confectioners' sugar. Repeat process with remaining batter.

Gingerbread

Yield: 9 servings

2 tablespoons orange marmalade
1 cup molasses
1/2 cup buttermilk
1 egg, slightly beaten
2 cups flour
1/2 cup sugar
1/2 teaspoon salt
1 teaspoon baking soda
1 teaspoon ground ginger
1 teaspoon ground cinnamon
1 teaspoon ground allspice
1/2 cup melted butter or slightly less canola oil
8 ounces cream cheese, softened
2 tablespoons Grand Marnier
confectioners' sugar

* Preheat oven to 350 degrees.
* Combine marmalade, molasses, buttermilk and egg in bowl; mix well.
* Sift flour, sugar, salt, baking soda, ginger, cinnamon and allspice into large bowl. Add molasses mixture; mix well. Add butter or oil; stir just until blended.
* Pour into greased 9x9-inch baking pan. Bake for 25 to 35 minutes or until tester comes out clean. Cool on wire rack.
* Whip cream cheese, Grand Marnier and enough confectioners' sugar in bowl to form a spreadable frosting. Frost gingerbread when slightly warm. Serve immediately.

Glögg

This is a traditional December holiday drink.

Yield: 4 to 6 servings

1   26-ounce bottle of dry red wine
1 cup sugar
peel of 1 orange, cut into strips
1 cinnamon stick
5 cloves
6 cardamom seeds, crushed
½ cup Port wine or sweet vermouth
½ cup aquavit
½ cup slivered almonds
½ cup raisins

* Combine dry red wine, sugar, orange peel, cinnamon, cloves and cardamom in saucepan; mix well. Let stand for 4 to 6 hours.
* Cook just until heated through; do not boil. Remove from heat. Stir in wine and aquavit.
* Sprinkle almonds and raisins into cups. Strain warm glögg into prepared cups.

Mumma

Yield: 6 servings

3 bottles of Porter beer, chilled
2 bottles of dark beer
1 deciliter (approximately 3½ ounces) Madeira
1 bottle of sockerdricka or sweetened carbonated water such as Sprite

* Combine beers and wine in tall glass pitcher. Stir in sockerdricka. Serve at once.

Note: Do not use soda water or mineral water in this drink.

Aquavit, the popular Scandinavian drink, comes in many flavors. It can be made with such ingredients as caraway, anise, fennel and coriander. It is very powerful and is meant to be consumed with food.

One of the most unusual aquavits comes from Norway. It is Linie Aquavit, linie meaning equator. This popular drink actually makes two crossings of the equator in the holds of ships in well-seasoned oak casks. When it is finally bottled, the label bears the name of the ship on which the aquavit traveled and the dates of the voyage.

United Kingdom & Ireland

Centuries ago in pagan Celtic Ireland, royalty held precise beliefs regarding hospitality. The royal cook was instructed to treat the Court Poet especially well with the finest cuts of meat. The fear was that culinary offense might result in public satirization by the author, whose freedom of movement among the kingdoms was unusual in a society largely based on slavery. Literary reverence is a tradition that continued throughout the ages. In more recent recollections, George Bernard Shaw, a vegetarian for the last 70 of his 94 years, would not have been impressed by the royal cook's carnivorous offerings. When he was caught up in the bicycling craze in Victorian England, he described the ideal diet for becoming a champion cyclist as brown bread and black currant jam. He did, however, develop quite a sweet tooth in his later years, and probably supported the old Irish country superstition of "nipping the cake". This was the custom of breaking off a small piece of cake, when freshly baked, to avert bad luck.

Today, ancient plants such as nettle and sorrel are still consumed as well as shellfish, which we know was eaten by the early inhabitants in 8,000 B.C. The revered potato was only introduced in the seventeenth century from the New World, but was quickly adopted by the peasants as a mainstay of their diet. The rich land supports great numbers of sheep, and cereal crops of wheat, barley, corn, oats, and rye have been plentiful, even during the famines of the 1840s and 1850s, when unfortunately they were reserved by absentee land owners for export purposes only.

A long and rich history is tied to the contemporary diet in the United Kingdom and Ireland, well worth further reading.

United Kingdom & Ireland

Sausage Rolls

Yield: 12 servings

1/4 cup finely chopped onion
1 tablespoon oil
3/4 pound sausage
1/4 teaspoon ground fresh nutmeg
pepper to taste
1 sheet puff pastry, thawed
1 egg, beaten
salt to taste
1 teaspoon water

* Preheat oven to 450 degrees.
* Sauté onion in oil in skillet until tender; drain. Combine onion, sausage, nutmeg and pepper in bowl; mix well. Shape into 3/4x3-inch rolls.
* Cook sausage rolls in skillet for 5 minutes or until brown on all sides, turning frequently; drain.
* Roll puff pastry 1/4 inch thick on lightly floured surface. Cut into 3x4-inch rectangles. Roll 1 sausage roll in each pastry rectangle; seal edge with water. Place seam side down on baking sheet; slash top of pastry diagonally several times. Brush with mixture of egg, salt and water.
* Bake for 10 minutes or until brown. Serve warm.

Watercress Dip

Yield: 12 servings

1 medium bunch watercress
2/3 cup mayonnaise
6 ounces cream cheese, softened
1/4 cup finely chopped onion
1 clove of garlic, finely chopped
1 teaspoon vinegar
1 teaspoon lemon juice
1/4 teaspoon tarragon
pepper to taste

* Chop watercress in food processor. Add mayonnaise, cream cheese, onion, garlic, vinegar, lemon juice, tarragon and pepper. Process until blended.
* Serve with raw vegetables and assorted crackers.

Leek Soup with Noodles

The leek is the national symbol of Wales.

Yield: 6 servings

6 or 7 medium leeks, trimmed,
2 tablespoons butter
4 cups beef stock
1 cup medium noodles
milk
salt and pepper to taste
grated cheese

✤ Slice leeks lengthwise; cut into thin slices. Cook leeks, covered, in butter in saucepan over low heat for 10 minutes, stirring occasionally. Stir in stock. Bring to a boil; reduce heat. Simmer for 20 minutes, stirring occasionally.

✤ Add noodles; mix well. Cook until noodles are tender, stirring occasionally. Stir in enough milk to make desired consistency. Cook until heated through. Season with salt and pepper.

✤ Ladle into soup bowls; sprinkle with grated cheese.

Scallop Soup

Yield: 4 servings

3/4 pound scallops, whole or coarsely chopped
3 slices bacon, chopped
2 large potatoes, peeled, chopped
1 tablespoon butter
2 1/2 cups milk
1 1/4 cups fish stock
2/3 cup chopped seeded tomatoes
1/4 teaspoon mace
salt and pepper to taste
2 tablespoons heavy cream
chopped fresh parsley

✤ Rinse scallops in cold water; drain. Sauté bacon and potatoes in butter in saucepan until bacon is partially cooked. Add milk and fish stock; mix well. Cook just to the boiling point, stirring occasionally; reduce heat.

✤ Simmer, covered, for 20 minutes. Stir in scallops and tomatoes. Cook just until scallops become firm. Season with mace, salt and pepper. Stir in cream.

✤ Ladle into soup bowls; sprinkle with parsley.

Orange and Watercress Salad

Yield: 6 servings

3 oranges, peeled
several sprigs of watercress
2 tablespoons oil
1 teaspoon vinegar
2 teaspoons lemon juice

Garnish:
coarsely chopped watercress

* Remove the white pith from oranges; slice crosswise. Place in bowl.
* Chop several sprigs of watercress finely. Combine with oil, vinegar and lemon juice in bowl; mix well.
* Pour oil mixture over orange slices. Let stand for 30 minutes. Garnish with coarsely chopped watercress.

Spinach Salad

Yield: 4 to 6 servings

1/2 cup walnut pieces, coarsely chopped
10 ounces spinach, rinsed, trimmed, torn into pieces
2 red apples, unpeeled, cut into wedges
1 teaspoon lemon juice
5 tablespoons walnut oil
3 tablespoons canola oil
2 1/2 tablespoons raspberry vinegar or any fruit-flavored vinegar
salt and pepper to taste
1/2 teaspoon sesame seeds

* Preheat oven to 350 degrees.
* Roast walnut pieces on baking sheet for 5 to 8 minutes or until fragrant.
* Place spinach in salad bowl. Toss with mixture of apple wedges and lemon juice. Add walnuts; mix well.
* Whisk walnut oil and canola oil in bowl. Stir in raspberry vinegar. Season with salt and pepper. Pour over spinach mixture; sprinkle with sesame seeds.

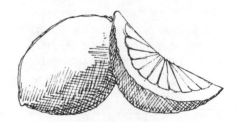

Cornish Pasty

The Cornish Pasty was for centuries the working man's midday meal. The classic pasty contained chopped vegetables, and meat when times were favorable. It is sometimes known as a "loggan," which is a pasty containing no potatoes, or as a "tiddy oggy," the local name for potato.

Yield: 4 servings

6 ounces stew beef, trimmed
2 potatoes, peeled, coarsely grated
1 small rutabaga, peeled, coarsely grated
1 onion, finely chopped
2¼ cups flour
salt to taste
½ cup shortening
2½ tablespoons butter
3 tablespoons ice water
salt and freshly ground pepper to taste
3 tablespoons butter, cut into 4 pieces
1 egg, beaten

* Preheat oven to 425 degrees.
* Chop beef in blender or food processor. Combine beef with potatoes, rutabaga and onion in bowl.
* Combine flour and salt in bowl. Cut in shortening and butter until crumbly. Add ice water; mix well.
* Roll pastry on lightly floured surface. Cut out 4 circles using large saucer as guide.
* Spoon beef mixture in center of each pastry circle; season with salt and pepper. Top with butter.
* Dampen edges of pastry with water. Draw up 2 edges to meet to enclose filling. Pinch and twist the pastry together to form fluted and curved pattern. Cut air vent in 1 side of each pasty.
* Brush with egg.
* Place on buttered baking sheet. Bake for 10 minutes. Reduce oven temperature to 350 degrees. Bake for 30 minutes.

Nearly one third of the work force in Ireland is employed in agriculture. The land is fertile and yields a heavy bounty. Meals tend to be high in calories and are meant to satisfy the hearty appetite of the working man. Most dishes are simple and uncomplicated, allowing the true flavor of the dish to come through without masking it with a sauce.

Whiskey Steaks

Yield: 4 servings

4 filet mignon steaks
freshly ground pepper
2 tablespoons olive oil
½ cup Irish whiskey
½ cup whipping cream
2 tablespoons finely chopped parsley

* Rub both sides of steaks with freshly ground pepper. Brown steaks on both sides in olive oil in heavy skillet for 5 minutes or until desired degree of doneness; drain.
* Stir in whiskey, flaming steaks for 1 minute. Transfer steaks to warm serving platter.
* Stir cream and parsley into pan drippings. Cook until slightly reduced in volume, stirring constantly. Pour over steaks. Serve immediately.

Dublin Pork and Apples

Yield: 6 servings

4 medium onions, thickly sliced
1 tablespoon oil
6 thick pork chops, trimmed
flour
salt and pepper to taste
1 tablespoon brown sugar
½ cup stock
nutmeg to taste
4 large apples, peeled, cored, sliced
¼ cup sultanas or golden raisins
½ cup cream
1 teaspoon currant jelly

Garnish:
parsley

* Sauté onions in oil in heavy saucepan for 2 minutes. Remove onions to plate.
* Dredge pork chops in mixture of flour, salt and pepper. Cook pork chops in saucepan over medium heat until brown on both sides; reduce heat. Top with brown sugar, stock and onions. Simmer, covered, for 1¼ hours or bake in 300-degree oven.
* Stir in nutmeg, apples and sultanas. Cook just until apples are tender, stirring frequently. Stir in cream and currant jelly; adjust seasonings. Cook just until heated through, stirring frequently. Garnish with parsley.

Medley Picnic Pie

A wartime economy dish, this versatile pie converts easily to a vegetarian dish by replacing the meats with seasonal fresh-cooked vegetables.

Yield: 6 servings

2¼ cups flour
salt to taste
½ cup shortening
2½ tablespoons margarine
3 tablespoons ice water
½ cup shredded Cheddar cheese
5 eggs
1 egg yolk
1 teaspoon (heaping) *fines herbes*
1 medium potato, cooked, peeled, sliced
2 medium onions, finely chopped
2 cloves of garlic, finely chopped
1 tablespoon olive oil
½ teaspoon sage
4 precooked pork sausages, sliced into halves
1 potato, cooked, peeled, sliced
½ teaspoon thyme
½ cup shredded Cheddar cheese
6 rashers of smoked bacon, cut into pieces
½ cup shredded Cheddar cheese
1 egg, beaten
1 tablespoon water

Note: Serve hot or cold in lunch boxes, for snacks or, with a salad, as an evening meal.

* Preheat oven to 350 degrees.
* Combine flour and salt in bowl. Cut in shortening and margarine until crumbly. Add ice water; mix well. Roll into rectangle on lightly floured surface. Line baking dish with pastry, leaving 1 inch for overlap; sprinkle with ½ cup cheese. Cut small circle from remaining pastry; set aside.
* Break eggs in dish 1 at a time, keeping yolks in tact. Pour each egg over cheese. Add remaining whole egg yolk. Season with salt and ⅓ of the mixed herbs.
* Arrange 1 sliced potato over eggs. Sauté onions and garlic in olive oil in skillet until onions are tender. Sprinkle ½ of the onion mixture over the potato slices. Sprinkle with sage. Layer sausage in circle. Top with 1 sliced potato, thyme, half the remaining mixed herbs and ½ cup cheese.
* Arrange cut bacon in circle. Top with remaining onion mixture; sprinkle with ½ cup shredded cheese. Sprinkle with remaining mixed herbs.
* Bring in edges of pastry. Place reserved pastry circle in center. Brush pastry with mixture of egg and water; do not seal edges.
* Bake for 45 to 60 minutes or until brown and bubbly.

Chicken Pie with Wild Mushrooms

Yield: 6 servings

1 pound boneless chicken breasts
1/2 pound wild mushrooms, trimmed
2 to 4 tablespoons butter
2 tablespoons oil
2 leeks, thinly sliced
3 carrots, sliced
salt and pepper to taste
3 tablespoons flour
1 1/2 cups chicken stock
1/2 cup whipping cream
1 cup frozen peas, thawed
2 scallions with tops, chopped
3 tablespoons chopped parsley
1/4 teaspoon nutmeg
1/2 to 1 teaspoon tarragon
1 unbaked pie shell

Variation: Decorate top of pie with additional pastry shaped into leaves or other interesting shapes.

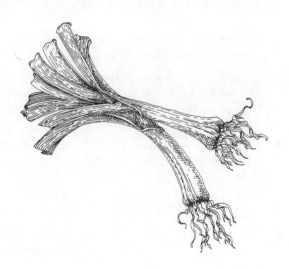

* Preheat oven to 450 degrees.
* Rinse chicken and pat dry. Cut into bite-sized pieces.
* Sauté wild mushrooms in 2 tablespoons butter in skillet for 5 minutes or until brown. Transfer to bowl with slotted spoon.
* Heat oil in buttered skillet. Sauté leeks and carrots in skillet. Cook, covered, for 10 minutes, stirring occasionally. Transfer to bowl with mushrooms.
* Sauté chicken in skillet until brown on all sides and tender; season with salt and pepper. Transfer to bowl with vegetables.
* Add enough butter to pan drippings to measure 3 tablespoons. Add flour; mix well. Cook over medium-high heat for 3 minutes or until thickened, stirring constantly. Stir in stock and cream slowly. Simmer until thickened, stirring constantly.
* Combine with chicken mixture in bowl. Stir in peas, scallions, parsley, nutmeg and tarragon. Spoon into 10-inch deep-dish pie pan. Cover with pie shell, crimping edges to seal; cut slits with sharp knife.
* Place in oven. Reduce temperature to 375 degrees. Bake for 45 minutes or until brown and bubbly.

Rabbit Stew

Yield: 6 servings

1 rabbit, cut into pieces
3 tablespoons butter
1 large onion, coarsely chopped
3 tablespoons flour
2 cups stock
juice of 1 lemon
4 carrots, sliced
2 large potatoes, cut into 1-inch pieces
5 ounces mushrooms, cut into quarters
salt and pepper to taste

* Preheat oven to 375 degrees.
* Rinse rabbit and pat dry. Melt butter in ovenproof pan. Brown rabbit on both sides in butter. Transfer to platter.
* Sauté onion in same pan until tender. Stir in flour. Cook for 2 minutes or until thickened. Add stock and lemon juice slowly; mix well. Bring to a boil, stirring constantly.
* Add rabbit, carrots and potatoes; mix well.
* Bake for 1 hour. Stir in mushrooms. Bake for 30 minutes. Add salt and pepper. Serve immediately.

Pease Porridge

As the rhyme reminds us, some like it hot, some like it cold, some like it in the pot nine days old.

Yield: 6 servings

1 pound dried green split peas
2¹/₂ cups water
¹/₂ teaspoon salt
pepper to taste
2 tablespoons butter

Variation: May vary recipe by adding 1 egg and 1 egg yolk to puréed mixture.

* Sort peas; rinse. Bring peas, water, salt and pepper to a boil in saucepan; reduce heat. Simmer for 1 hour or until mixture is texture of mush, stirring occasionally.
* Spoon mixture into blender or food processor container. Process until puréed.
* Combine purée and butter in saucepan. Cook just until heated through, stirring occasionally. May add additional liquid if mixture is too thick.
* Spoon into 6 greased custard cups. Place in baking pan filled halfway with boiling water. Bake, covered, at 350 degrees for 1 hour. Invert onto serving plate. Serve with ham, pork or as a side dish.

Apple-Potato Mash

Yield: 4 to 6 servings

5 large potatoes, peeled, cut into quarters
salt to taste
2 large apples, peeled, cored, sliced
1 tablespoon water
1 tablespoon sugar
¼ cup cream
3 tablespoons butter

✤ Combine potatoes, salt and enough water to cover in saucepan. Cook, covered, until potatoes are tender; drain.

✤ Combine apples, water and sugar in saucepan. Cook until soft, stirring occasionally.

✤ Mash potatoes with cream in bowl. Stir in apples and butter. Serve with bacon or fried fish.

Beacán Bruithe (Baked Mushrooms)

Yield: 4 servings

16 large mushrooms
2 tablespoons melted butter or oil
½ cup finely chopped onions
¼ pound sweet sausage
seasoned bread crumbs to taste
½ teaspoon sage
salt and pepper to taste

✤ Preheat oven to 350 degrees.

✤ Remove stems from mushrooms; finely chop stems. Brush mushroom caps with melted butter. Arrange in shallow baking pan.

✤ Sauté onions and mushroom stems in remaining butter in skillet for several minutes. Add sausage; mix well. Cook until sausage is crumbly and onions are tender, stirring constantly; drain. Stir in bread crumbs, sage, salt and pepper. May add water if mixture is too dry.

✤ Stuff each mushroom cap with sausage mixture. Pour approximately ¼ cup water into baking pan. Bake for 15 to 20 minutes or until heated through.

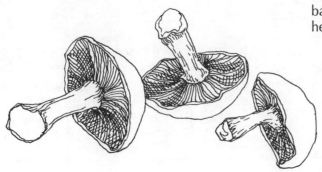

Bubble and Squeak

This Irish dish is named for the noise it makes in the pan as it cooks.

Yield: 6 to 8 servings

¼ cup butter or bacon drippings
1 small onion, chopped
2 cups cooked sliced cabbage
2 cups mashed potatoes

* Melt butter or drippings in large skillet. Add onion. Sauté until onion is translucent.
* Add cabbage and mashed potatoes. Press with spatula to form a cake. Cook over medium heat until well browned on bottom.
* Slide potato cake carefully onto plate. Flip back into skillet, browned side up.
* Cook until brown. Cut into wedges. Serve hot.

Colcannon

Yield: 8 to 10 servings

2 cups shredded cabbage
4 cups warm mashed potatoes
6 green onions, chopped
1 tablespoon chopped parsley
salt and pepper to taste
¼ cup margarine or butter
paprika to taste

* Preheat oven to 250 degrees.
* Steam cabbage in saucepan for 5 minutes. Stir cabbage into mashed potatoes in bowl. Add green onions and parsley; mix well. Season with salt and pepper.
* Spoon into baking dish; dot with margarine. Cut into serving pieces; sprinkle with paprika. Place in oven until serving time.

Scots Fried Potatoes

Yield: 2 to 3 servings

4 large potatoes, peeled
salt to taste
3 tablespoons fine bread crumbs
3 tablespoons finely ground ham
2 teaspoons water
4 eggs, beaten
oil for frying

* Boil potatoes in salted water in saucepan until tender-crisp. Cool. Cut into ⅛-inch thick slices.
* Combine bread crumbs, ham, water and eggs in bowl; mix well. Coat potato slices with mixture. Cook in hot oil in skillet until brown on both sides, turning once; drain.

Mrs. Burpee's Apple Chutney

Yield: 20 pints

40 tart cooking apples, peeled, cored
1½ pounds seeded muscat raisins
1½ pounds currants
¾ pound chopped citron
½ cup dried hot chili peppers, crushed
½ cup chopped gingerroot
¼ cup finely chopped garlic
4 large onions, cut into quarters
½ cup crystallized ginger
6 pounds sugar
3 quarts cider vinegar
1 tablespoon nutmeg
1 tablespoon ground ginger
1 tablespoon cumin seeds

✤ Grind apples, raisins, currants, citron, chili peppers, gingerroot, garlic, onions and preserved ginger in meat chopper, using fine blade.

✤ Bring sugar and vinegar to a boil in stockpot. Stir in nutmeg, ground ginger, cumin seeds and ground apple mixture. Return to a boil; reduce heat. Cook for 6 to 8 hours or until thickened, stirring frequently.

✤ Ladle into sterilized jars, leaving ½ inch headspace; seal with 2-piece lids.

Mustard Pickles

Yield: 12 pints

10 pounds small pickling onions
3 cucumbers, chopped
flowerets of 1 head cauliflower
3 pounds green bell peppers, chopped
4 large green tomatoes, chopped
1¾ cups salt
1 tablespoon turmeric
3 cups flour
4 cups sugar
½ teaspoon celery salt
¼ cup dry mustard
2 quarts white vinegar

✤ Combine onions, cucumbers, cauliflowerets, green peppers, tomatoes and salt with enough water to cover in bowl. Soak overnight.

✤ Bring vegetable mixture to a boil in stockpot; drain. Add turmeric, flour, sugar, celery salt, dry mustard and 6 cups vinegar. Bring to a boil. Cook until thickened, stirring constantly. Add remaining vinegar. Bring to a boil.

✤ Ladle into sterilized jars, leaving ½ inch headspace. Cool. Seal with 2-piece lids.

Date and Nut Bread

Yield: l loaf

2¼ cups sifted flour
½ teaspoon baking soda
2 tablespoons baking powder
½ teaspoon salt
½ teaspoon cinnamon
¼ teaspoon nutmeg
1 cup packed light brown sugar
1 egg, beaten
1 cup buttermilk
2 tablespoons melted butter
1   8-ounce package dates
1 cup coarsely chopped walnuts

Note: May soak dates in a small amount of boiling water to soften.

* Preheat oven to 350 degrees.
* Sift flour, baking soda, baking powder, salt, cinnamon and nutmeg in bowl; mix well. Stir in brown sugar.
* Beat egg, buttermilk and butter in bowl until blended. Stir into flour mixture. Add dates and walnuts; mix well.
* Spoon into buttered and floured loaf pan. Bake for 1¼ hours. Cool slightly in pan. Invert onto wire rack to cool completely.

Irish Soda Bread

A slice of Irish Soda Bread and a comforting cup of tea combine for a perfect break on a busy day.

Yield: 12 servings

3 cups flour
½ cup sugar
1 tablespoon caraway seeds
1 tablespoon baking powder
1 teaspoon salt
1 teaspoon baking soda
¾ pound raisins
1¾ cups buttermilk
2 eggs
1 tablespoon melted margarine

* Preheat oven to 350 degrees
* Combine flour, sugar, caraway seeds, baking powder, salt, baking soda and raisins in bowl; mix well.
* Beat buttermilk and eggs in bowl for 30 seconds. Add margarine, beating for 10 seconds. Stir into flour mixture.
* Spoon into greased and floured 9-inch round cast-iron skillet or loaf pan. Bake for 50 minutes or until brown.

Tea-Time Scones

Yield: 18 to 24 servings

3 cups self-rising flour
1¼ teaspoons salt
2½ teaspoons baking powder
2½ tablespoons sugar
6 tablespoons butter
¾ cup milk
butter
strawberry jam
½ cup plus 2 tablespoons fresh cream, stiffly
  beaten

Variation: May substitute whipping cream for fresh cream.

* Preheat oven to 450 degrees. Preheat baking sheet.
* Sift flour, salt, baking powder and sugar in bowl; mix well. Cut in 6 tablespoons butter until crumbly. Stir in milk gradually.
* Knead on lightly floured surface until smooth. Roll ½ inch thick; cut 2-inch circles with plain or fluted cutter. Place on warm baking sheet; brush with additional milk. Bake for 10 to 12 minutes or until brown.
* Split warm scones into halves; fill with butter, strawberry jam and whipped cream.

Eckeles Cakes

Yield: 12 servings

1 cup melted margarine
2 cups flour
½ cup sour cream
¼ teaspoon salt
1   11-ounce package currants
2 to 3 tablespoons sugar

* Preheat oven to 400 degrees.
* Combine margarine, flour, sour cream and salt in bowl; mix well. Chill for 2 to 3 hours.
* Combine currants and enough water to cover in saucepan. Boil until soft; drain. Stir in sugar.
* Roll chilled dough on lightly floured surface. Cut into 3-inch circles.
* Spoon currant mixture in center of half the circles; top with remaining circles. Seal edges with fork dipped in milk and sugar. Place on ungreased baking sheet.
* Bake for 20 minutes.

Christmas Pudding

The recipe for this traditional holiday dessert was given to Charles Chapin's maternal grandmother in 1890 by a neightbor, Mrs. Gardner, who brought it from England. It has become a Chapin holiday tradition since then.

Yield: 8 to 12 servings

For the hard sauce:

¼ cup butter
1 teaspoon boiling water
1 cup confectioners' sugar
1 teaspoon lemon extract or sherry
fresh orange juice to taste
grated orange rind to taste
whipped cream

For the pudding:

¾ loaf white bread
1¾ cups milk
4 eggs, beaten
¾ cup packed brown sugar
2 tablespoons (rounded) ground suet
5 ounces citron, ground
1½ teaspoons nutmeg
1½ teaspoons cinnamon
½ teaspoon ground cloves
½ teaspoon mace
¾ 15-ounce package raisins
¾ 11-ounce package currants
grated rind of 1 lemon

Note: Flavor improves with aging.

To make the hard sauce:

✤ Combine butter, boiling water, confectioners' sugar, lemon extract, orange juice and orange rind in double boiler; mix well.

✤ Cook over boiling water until blended, stirring constantly. Stir in whipped cream just before serving.

To make the pudding:

✤ Soak bread in milk in bowl until soft. Add eggs, brown sugar, suet, citron, nutmeg, cinnamon, cloves, mace, raisins, currants and lemon rind; mix well.

✤ Spoon into pudding mold. Steam in 2-quart steamer for 3½ hours.

✤ Store, tightly covered, in cool place.

✤ Serve with hard sauce.

To steam puddings, use molds with tightly fitting lids. Grease the mold, sprinkle it with sugar and fill two-thirds full. Place it on a trivet over one inch of boiling water in a pan large enough to allow for circulation of the steam. Begin over high heat and reduce the heat to low as steam builds up.

Plum Puddings

Yield: 24 servings

For the hard sauce:

1 cup unsalted butter
1 cup confectioners' sugar
¼ cup rum, cognac or sherry
⅛ teaspoon salt

For the foamy sauce:

½ cup butter
1 cup confectioners' sugar
1 egg, beaten
2 tablespoons hot water
1 teaspoon vanilla extract or 2 tablespoons cognac
⅛ teaspoon salt

For the puddings:

¾ pound ground beef suet
1¼ cups flour
1 teaspoon nutmeg
2 slices firm white bread, crusts removed, crumbled
½ teaspoon salt
1   15-ounce package seeded muscat raisins,
     stems removed
1   15-ounce package black raisins
2   11-ounce packages currants
1½ pounds mixed candied fruit, finely chopped
½ pound pitted dates, chopped
⅓ pound whole candied cherries, cut into halves
¼ pound candied pineapple, chopped
grated rind of 1 lemon
1 cup plus 2 tablespoons packed brown sugar
5 eggs, beaten
1 cup cool strong black coffee
cognac or rum (optional)

Note: Use a large covered roaster for steaming 2 layers of puddings. Separate layers with a cake rack.

To make the hard sauce:

* Cream butter and confectioners' sugar in mixer bowl until light and fluffy. Beat in rum and salt until blended.
* Chill in refrigerator.

To make the foamy sauce:

* Cream butter in mixer bowl until light and fluffy. Add confectioners' sugar, egg and hot water; mix well.
* Place bowl over hot water. Beat until thickened. Stir in vanilla and salt.

To make the puddings:

* Combine suet, flour, nutmeg, bread crumbs and salt in large bowl; mix well. Add muscat raisins, tossing to coat.
* Stir in raisins, currants, candied fruit, dates, cherries, pineapple and lemon rind. Add brown sugar, eggs and coffee; mix well.
* Pack firmly into 3 pudding molds or basins. Place in pan filled halfway with hot water.
* Bring water to a boil; reduce heat. Steam, covered, for 4 hours, adding additional water as needed. Cool. Pour cognac or rum over puddings.
* Serve with hard sauce or foamy sauce.
* Store, covered with foil or plastic wrap, in refrigerator. Reheat by steaming for 1 hour.

Irish Rice Pudding

Yield: 4 to 6 servings

4 cups milk
1 to 1¼ cups half and half or cream
½ cup rice
½ to ¾ cup sugar
1 tablespoon vanilla extract
cinnamon and nutmeg to taste

♣ Preheat oven to 350 degrees.
♣ Combine milk, half and half, rice, sugar, vanilla, cinnamon and nutmeg in bowl; mix well. Pour into baking dish.
♣ Bake for 45 minutes, stirring occasionally. Reduce oven temperature to 300 degrees. Bake for 1 hour, stirring occasionally. Do not stir during last 15 minutes of baking.

Raspberry Trifle

This is the perfect dessert after a heavy holiday meal.

Yield: 8 to 12 servings

1   3-ounce package raspberry gelatin
½ cup boiling water
4 cups frozen raspberries with juice, partially
    thawed
3 cups milk
¼ cup sugar
1½ tablespoons flour
5 egg yolks, beaten
1 teaspoon vanilla extract
1 homemade pound cake, thinly sliced
½ cup sherry
½ cup slivered almonds
½ cup chopped pecans
slivered almonds
1 cup whipping cream
sugar to taste

♣ Dissolve gelatin in boiling water in bowl. Stir in raspberries and juice. Cool.
♣ Heat milk in double boiler over boiling water. Combine ¼ cup sugar and flour in bowl; mix well. Stir in egg yolks. Whisk in warm milk.
♣ Pour mixture into double boiler. Cook over boiling water until thickened, stirring constantly. Stir in vanilla. Cool to room temperature.
♣ Line 3-quart glass bowl with ⅓ of the pound cake. Sprinkle with ⅓ of the sherry, ⅓ of the almonds, ⅓ of the pecans and ⅓ of the raspberry mixture. Layer remaining pound cake, sherry, almonds, pecans, raspberry mixture and custard in order listed ½ at a time. Sprinkle with slivered almonds.
♣ Beat whipping cream and sugar to taste in mixer bowl until stiff peaks form. Spread over top.

Eggnog

Yield: 20 servings

12 egg whites
1/2 cup sugar
12 egg yolks
1 cup sugar
1/4 teaspoon salt
4 cups whipping cream
4 cups milk
4 cups bourbon
1 cup rum
freshly grated nutmeg

Note: To avoid danger of salmonella, use 1 1/2 cups egg substitute for fresh egg yolks.

✤ Beat egg whites in mixer bowl until soft peaks form. Add 1/2 cup sugar, beating constantly until stiff peaks form.

✤ Beat egg yolks in mixer bowl until creamy. Beat in 1 cup sugar and salt. Fold beaten egg whites into beaten egg yolks.

✤ Beat whipping cream in mixer bowl until soft peaks form. Fold into egg mixture. Stir in milk and bourbon. Add rum; mix well. Store in refrigerator.

✤ Sprinkle with nutmeg just before serving.

Irish Coffee

Yield: 1 serving

1 cup hot strong coffee
2 teaspoons brown sugar
1 1/2 ounces Irish whiskey
whipped cream
sugar and vanilla extract to taste

✤ Pour hot water into stemmed glass or glass mug. Let stand until glass is warm; discard water. Add a small amount of hot coffee to glass. Let stand for several seconds.

✤ Add coffee until glass is filled halfway. Stir in brown sugar until dissolved. Add whiskey; mix well. Pour in remaining coffee. Serve with whipped cream flavored with sugar and vanilla.

In both the north of England and in Scotland, *high tea* is eaten later in the day than afternoon tea, about 5:00 or 6:00 p.m., and is a much more substantial meal, even replacing dinner. You are expected to do justice to this uniquely British meal, which is comprised of some or all of the following: tea; a cooked savoury; a cold savoury; ham with chutneys, mustards and pickles, etc.; fruit tarts; scones with homemade jams, butter or cream; crusty breads and cheeses; and sandwiches, pies and cakes! Use this recipe to ensure the success of your high teas.

A Perfect Cup of Tea

* Pour hot water into teapot. Let stand while water comes to a boil in teakettle.

* Discard water in teapot. Add 1 teaspoon of tea per person plus 1 for the teapot. Pour in required amount of boiling water. Let steep, covered, for 3 to 5 minutes.

* Strain into teacups. Serve with milk or lemon slices. Decant remaining tea into another teapot.

Western Europe

*T*here are two distinct styles of eating in Western Europe: the sophisticated, haute cuisine of the great urban centers and the simpler, heartier fare of the countrysides. Together they offer world-renowned breads, pastries, truffles, sausages, cheeses, wines, beers, and champagnes. What glorious contributions to the food world!

The grand cuisine of France was first defined by La Varenne in 1651, made more grandiose after the French Revolution by Carême, and was finally re-simplified for the twentieth century by Auguste Escoffier, the "father" of classical French cooking taught today. Similar documentation had taken place in other European countries by the end of the sixteenth century.

Today's European city dwellers, for the most part, eat well, often, and leisurely. Respites for coffee and pastry are taken as much for the gossiping as for the food and may happen late in the evening as frequently as late in the afternoon. Dinners may take hours, as every facet of a meal is savored. Perhaps it is this leisurely pace, and not the recently touted consumption of red wine, that keeps cholesterol levels down. In any event, great chefs are as prized as the composers, writers, and painters with whom they are grouped when the term "artist" is used.

The abundant countrysides offer simpler, more wholesome foods likely to be grown where they are eaten. Bread, cheese, and wine for lunch is typical, finished off with fresh fruit. Sausages, stews, roast chicken, or rabbit for dinner complement the down-to-earth nature of the people. The eagerly-awaited arrivals of new wines, spring vegetables, and fall harvest festivals are all occasions that promote a feeling of harmony with the cycles of nature.

We would do well to emulate the excellence found in either style.

Western Europe

Bleu Cheese Dip

Yield: 1¹/3 cups

³/4 cup sour cream
¹/4 cup milk
¹/3 cup crumbled bleu cheese

✤ Combine sour cream, milk and bleu cheese in bowl; mix well.
✤ Serve with assorted crackers or vegetables.

Fried Mussel Pancakes

Mussels are very popular along the French and Belgian coastline.

Yield: 2 servings

2¹/2 pounds fresh whole mussels
5 tablespoons flour
1¹/2 tablespoons cornstarch
1 teaspoon salt
¹/2 cup water
2 eggs, beaten
2 green onions, finely sliced
1 tablespoon chopped cilantro
¹/4 teaspoon ground pepper
1 teaspoon oil

Garnish:
2 limes, cut into quarters
sprigs of cilantro
Kikoman sauce

✤ Preheat oven to 350 degrees.
✤ Rinse mussels in cold water; scrub to remove beards. Arrange on baking sheet. Bake for 5 minutes or until shells pop open. Cool. Discard any shells which do not open.
✤ Pry open shells; remove mussel meat. Rinse mussels; drain.
✤ Cut mussels lengthwise into halves.
✤ Sift flour, cornstarch and salt in bowl; mix well. Add water and eggs, beating until smooth. Stir in mussels, green onions, cilantro and pepper.
✤ Heat lightly greased 10-inch skillet over medium-high heat. Pour ¹/2 of the batter into the skillet. Bake for 2 minutes or until top is set, rotating pan to insure even baking. Remove from heat. Place plate over skillet; invert pancake onto plate. Return skillet to heat. Slide pancake into skillet. Bake for 1 minute or until set. Flip onto serving plate. Repeat process with remaining batter. Garnish with lime wedges and sprigs of cilantro. Serve with Kikoman sauce.

Tomato Yogurt Dip

Yield: 10 servings

1 cup plain yogurt
½ cup chopped tomato
1 teaspoon tomato paste
1 teaspoon ground coriander
salt and pepper to taste

✤ Combine yogurt, tomato, tomato paste and coriander in bowl; mix well. Season with salt and pepper.
✤ Serve with assorted crackers or vegetables.

Zucchini Strata

Yield: 12 servings

1½ cups sliced mushrooms
3 tablespoons oil
¾ cup chopped green bell pepper
1½ cups chopped or sliced zucchini
¾ cup chopped white onion
1 large clove of garlic, crushed
6 eggs
¼ cup light cream
2 cups cubed bread
16 ounces cream cheese, chopped
1½ cups shredded medium Cheddar cheese
¼ teaspoon salt
freshly ground pepper

✤ Preheat oven to 350 degrees.
✤ Sauté mushrooms in oil in skillet until tender. Remove to platter.
✤ Sauté green pepper, zucchini, onion and garlic in same skillet until zucchini is tender; drain. Stir in mushrooms.
✤ Beat eggs and cream in mixer bowl until blended. Stir in vegetable mixture. Add bread, cream cheese, Cheddar cheese, salt and pepper; mix well.
✤ Pour into greased 16-inch round baking dish or 2 greased 8-inch round baking dishes. Bake for 1 hour. Let stand for 10 to 15 minutes before slicing.

Melksnysels (Milk Noodles)

When Pauline Rix's Dutch grandmother took an Englishman as her groom in 1890, his diet changed drastically because she did not savor "English" cooking. At 71, she can still clearly recall how the grandchildren looked forward to these noodles when the family gathered for feasting and fellowship.

Yield: 6 servings

2 eggs, beaten
5 cups milk
2 cups flour
salt to taste
2 tablespoons butter
cinnamon and sugar mixture to taste

* Combine eggs and 1 cup milk in bowl; mix well. Add sifted mixture of flour and salt; mix well. Stir in just enough milk until stiff dough forms. Knead well.
* Roll into thin rectangle on lightly floured surface. Dust with additional flour; cut into thin strips.
* Heat remaining milk just to the boiling point in saucepan. Add butter and dough strips. Simmer until noodles are tender.
* Ladle noodle mixture into soup bowls; sprinkle with mixture of cinnamon and sugar.

Soupe de Bruxelles (Cream of Belgian Endive Soup)

Yield: 4 servings

2 heads Belgian endive, stems removed
1 medium onion, chopped
1 medium potato, chopped
1 small clove of garlic, finely chopped
3 tablespoons butter or margarine
2 cups chicken broth
1/2 cup whipping cream
1 egg yolk, beaten
salt and pepper to taste
1/8 teaspoon nutmeg

* Reserve several center leaves of endive for garnish. Chop remaining endive; set aside.
* Sauté onion, potato and garlic in butter in skillet until potato is tender. Stir in endive. Cook until tender, stirring frequently.
* Spoon endive mixture into blender container. Add chicken broth. Process until smooth. Return to skillet. Cook until heated through, stirring occasionally.
* Stir in mixture of cream and egg yolk gradually. Cook just until heated through. Season with salt and pepper.
* Serve hot or cold. Ladle into soup bowls. Garnish with reserved endive leaves; sprinkle with nutmeg.

Rettichsalat (Radish Salad)

Yield: 4 servings

2 bunches radishes, thinly sliced
salt to taste
1 tablespoon olive oil
2 tablespoons vinegar
1 teaspoon chopped chives
pepper to taste
½ cup sour cream (optional)

✤ Place radishes in bowl; sprinkle with salt. Let stand for 10 minutes; drain.

✤ Combine olive oil, vinegar, chives and pepper in bowl; mix well. Pour over radishes, tossing to coat.

✤ Marinate in refrigerator until serving time. Stir in sour cream just before serving.

Sauerkraut Salad

Yield: 10 to 12 servings

5   16-ounce cans sauerkraut
6 slices bacon
6 tablespoons olive oil
1 large onion, finely chopped
3 cloves of garlic, finely chopped
3 tablespoons finely chopped parsley
3 tablespoons finely chopped celery
2   8-ounce cans tomato sauce
salt and pepper to taste

✤ Rinse sauerkraut; drain.

✤ Fry bacon in skillet until crisp; drain. Add olive oil, onion, garlic, parlsey and celery; mix well. Cook until vegetables are brown, stirring constantly.

✤ Add sauerkraut; mix well. Cook for 20 minutes. Stir in tomato sauce and enough water to cover; season with salt and pepper. Bring to a boil; reduce heat. Simmer, covered, for 2 hours, stirring occasionally.

Sauerkraut is practically the German national dish. German cooks use it not only as an accompaniment to meat, but combine it with fruits or other vegetables to create a variety of side dishes. Sauerkraut is simply shredded cabbage and salt that is left to ferment, and its preparation has remained the same since it was recorded by the ancient Romans, who acquired it from the Orient. The method was forgotten by Europeans until the 13th century, when the conquering Tartars reintroduced it to Austria and it subsequently traveled to an appreciative Germany.

Slow-Cooker Boeuf Bourguignon

Yield: 6 to 8 servings

6 slices bacon, cut into 1/2-inch pieces
3 pounds beef rump, cut into 1 1/2-inch pieces
1 large onion, chopped
4 large carrots, sliced
2 cups beef broth
1/2 cup Burgundy
1 1/2 teaspoons salt
1/2 teaspoon pepper
1/4 cup tomato sauce
4 large cloves of garlic, finely chopped
1 bay leaf
1 teaspoon thyme
2 teaspoons parsley
2 tablespoons cornstarch
3 tablespoons water
16 ounces mushrooms, cut into halves
1/2 cup Burgundy

♣ Fry bacon in skillet until crisp. Transfer to plate.
♣ Add beef to skillet. Cook until brown on all sides, stirring constantly. Transfer to slow cooker.
♣ Add onion and carrots to skillet. Cook until onion is brown, stirring constantly. Remove from heat. Deglaze skillet with beef broth and 1/2 cup Burgundy. Pour mixture over beef. Add salt, pepper, bacon, tomato sauce, garlic, bay leaf, thyme and parsley; mix well.
♣ Cook, covered, on Low for 8 hours, stirring occasionally. Discard bay leaf. Stir in mixture of cornstarch and water. Add mushrooms and 1/2 cup Burgundy; mix well. Cook for 2 hours or until beef is tender, stirring occasionally. Serve over brown rice.

Rouladen

When Barbara Curphey was a child and her German mother made this dish, the smell of it cooking nearly drove her mad. She could hardly wait for dinner!

Yield: 4 servings

1 1/4 to 1 3/4 pounds beef round steak
salt and pepper to taste
6 tablespoons prepared mustard
6 tablespoons chopped onion
4 slices bacon
4 dill pickles

♣ Season steak with salt and pepper. Pound 1/4 to 1/2 inch thick with meat mallet. Cut into four 3x6-inch strips.
♣ Spread 1 1/2 tablespoons mustard on each strip. Layer each strip with 1 1/2 tablespoons onion, 1 slice bacon and 1 dill pickle. Roll to enclose filling; secure with wooden pick.
♣ Place in heavy saucepan. Cook, covered, over low heat for 2 1/2 to 3 hours or until beef is tender, turning occasionally. May add water if rouladen becomes too dry.
♣ Serve with buttered spaetzle or noodles.

Sauerbraten

This recipe, served with potato pancakes and red cabbage, has been in William Campbell's family for three generations.

Yield: 6 to 8 servings

1   4 to 5-pound beef bottom round roast
2 medium onions, sliced
1 carrot, sliced
1 stalk celery, sliced
2 cups red wine vinegar
1 tablespoon salt
1 tablespoon mixed pickling spice
1 sprig of parsley
1 teaspoon thyme
butter
olive oil
salt and pepper to taste
5 tablespoons cornstarch
¼ cup water

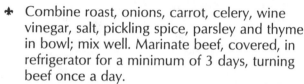

* Combine roast, onions, carrot, celery, wine vinegar, salt, pickling spice, parsley and thyme in bowl; mix well. Marinate beef, covered, in refrigerator for a minimum of 3 days, turning beef once a day.

* Brown roast on all sides in mixture of butter and olive oil in heavy saucepan. Strain marinade; pour over roast. Simmer for 3 to 4 hours or until tender. Transfer roast to warm platter. Bring pan drippings to a boil; season with salt and pepper. Stir in mixture of cornstarch and water gradually. Cook until thickened or until desired consistency, stirring constantly. Serve with roast.

German Skillet Supper

Yield: 4 servings

6 slices bacon
1 medium cabbage, cut into 6 wedges
1 medium onion, chopped
¼ cup water
2 tablespoons sugar
1 pound Polish kielbasa sausage, cut into 6 pieces

* Fry bacon in skillet until crisp. Drain, reserving 2 tablespoons drippings; crumble bacon.

* Bring reserved drippings, cabbage, onion, water and sugar to a boil in saucepan; reduce heat. Cook, covered, over medium heat for 10 minutes, stirring occasionally. Add kielbasa; mix well. Cook, covered, for 10 minutes, stirring occasionally. Sprinkle with bacon.

Asparagus and Ham Saucy Crêpes

Yield: 12 servings

For the crêpes:

12   3x4-inch thin slices boiled ham
12   ½ x½x5-inch pieces of Gruyère cheese
12 stalks asparagus
12 non-dessert crêpes

For the onion sauce:

2 medium onions, chopped
3 tablespoons butter
1½ cups whipping cream
¼ teaspoon cayenne pepper
¼ teaspoon salt

Garnish:

¼ cup chopped fresh parsley
¼ cup chopped fresh chives

To make the crêpes:

✦ Preheat oven to 350 degrees.
✦ Layer ham, cheese and asparagus on crêpes; roll to enclose filling. Arrange in 9x13-inch baking dish sprayed with nonstick cooking spray. Bake for 20 minutes.

To make the onion sauce:

✦ Sauté onions in butter in skillet for 5 minutes. Stir in cream, cayenne pepper and salt. Bring to a boil; reduce heat. Simmer for 15 minutes, stirring frequently.

To assemble the crêpes:

✦ Spoon onion sauce over crêpes; sprinkle with parsley and chives.

Noodles Marmaduke

Yield: 4 servings

¼ cup chopped onion
1 pound ground beef
½ pound mushrooms, sliced
1 clove of garlic, finely chopped (optional)
¼ cup butter
3 to 5 tablespoons red wine
3 tablespoons lemon juice
1   11-ounce can beef consommé
1 teaspoon salt
pepper to taste
3 cups uncooked noodles
1 cup sour cream
chopped parsley

✦ Sauté onion, ground beef, mushrooms and garlic in butter in large skillet, stirring until beef is crumbly; drain. Stir in wine, lemon juice, consommé, salt and pepper. Simmer for 15 minutes, stirring occasionally.
✦ Add noodles to mixture; mix well. Cook, covered, for 5 minutes or until noodles are tender.
✦ Stir in sour cream just before serving. Cook just until heated through, stirring constantly. Sprinkle with parsley.
✦ Serve with green salad and French bread.

Brockel Bohnen (Broken Beans)

During wine grape harvest and apple and pear harvest in Germany, this hearty dish was often served. Families working in the brisk air in the orchards and vineyards needed such sustaining foods.

Yield: 4 to 6 servings

1 pound green beans, trimmed, broken into pieces
1 tablespoon butter
1 tablespoon flour
salt and pepper to taste
marjoram to taste
3 large potatoes, peeled, thinly sliced

✤ Sauté green beans in butter in saucepan over low heat. Stir in flour. Cook until blended, stirring constantly. Add enough water to cover; mix well. Bring to a boil, stirring constantly; reduce heat. Stir in salt, pepper and marjoram. Simmer for 5 minutes, stirring occasionally.

✤ Add potatoes; mix well. Add additional water if desired. Bring to a boil; reduce heat. Cook, covered, for 30 minutes.

✤ Mash potatoes and green beans until creamy mixture forms. Serve with sausage, pork chops or any type of meat.

Belgian Endive au Gratin

Yield: 4 servings

8 heads Belgian endive, stems removed
juice of 1 lemon
1 teaspoon salt
8 thin slices ham
2 tablespoons butter or margarine
2 tablespoons flour
1/2 cup half and half
1/2 cup shredded Jarlsberg cheese
1/4 cup dry white wine
nutmeg to taste
2 tablespoons grated Parmesan cheese

Garnish:
chopped parsley
chopped tomato

✤ Preheat oven to 400 degrees.

✤ Combine endive and enough water to cover in saucepan. Stir in lemon juice and salt. Simmer, covered, for 10 minutes; drain.

✤ Wrap 1 ham slice around each endive. Arrange in buttered baking dish.

✤ Melt butter in saucepan. Stir in flour. Cook until bubbly, stirring constantly. Add half and half, Jarlsberg cheese, wine and nutmeg gradually; mix well. Cook until thickened, stirring constantly.

✤ Spoon over endive; sprinkle with Parmesan cheese. Bake for 10 minutes. Brown under broiler.

✤ Garnish with chopped parsley and chopped tomato.

Hot German Potato Salad

Yield: 6 to 8 servings

6 slices bacon, finely chopped
1 medium onion, finely chopped
1/3 cup vinegar
1/2 cup chopped parsley
1/2 cup water
2 teaspoons flour
1 tablespoon sugar
1 1/2 teaspoons salt
1/4 teaspoon pepper
1 1/2 pounds potatoes, cooked, sliced

* Fry bacon in skillet until crisp; drain on paper towel, reserving 1 teaspoon drippings in skillet.
* Sauté onion in reserved drippings for 2 minutes. Stir in bacon, vinegar, parsley, water, flour, sugar, salt and pepper. Cook until thickened, stirring constantly.
* Add potatoes; mix well. Serve warm.

Lyonnaise Potatoes

Yield: 4 servings

1 large onion, sliced
2 tablespoons butter
6 medium potatoes, chopped
1/2 teaspoon browning sauce
salt and pepper to taste

* Sauté onion in butter in large skillet until tender. Add potatoes and enough water to cover; mix well. Cook, covered, until potatoes are tender.
* Stir in browning sauce, salt and pepper. Serve with pork chops.

Pickled Beets

Yield: variable

2 cups strained beet water
1 cup white vinegar
1 cup sugar
1 teaspoon pickling spice
chopped, peeled, cooked beets

* Bring beet water to a boil in saucepan. Stir in vinegar and sugar. Add pickling spice which has been tied in cheesecloth or placed in small strainer. Stir in beets until covered by mixture.
* Bring mixture to a boil, stirring occasionally. Remove pickling spice. Spoon into sterilized jars leaving 2 1/2 inch headspace; seal with 2-piece lids. Process in boiling water bath.

Dumpfnudla (Dumplings)

Yield: 4 to 6 servings

For the sauce:

1 large onion, finely chopped
2 tablespoons shortening
2 tablespoons flour
1¹/₂ cups water
1 teaspoon salt
2 teaspoons sugar
1¹/₂ tablespoons white vinegar

For the dumplings:

2 eggs, beaten
³/₄ cup milk
2 cups flour
¹/₂ teaspoon salt
2 teaspoons baking powder

For the potatoes:

1 cup water
¹/₂ teaspoon salt
1 tablespoon shortening
1 large potato, sliced

To make the sauce:

♣ Brown onion in 2 tablespoons shortening in skillet. Stir in 2 tablespoons flour. Cook until flour is light brown, stirring constantly.

♣ Add 1¹/₂ cups water, 1 teaspoon salt, sugar and vinegar; mix well. Cook until onion is tender, stirring occasionally.

To make the dumplings:

♣ Combine eggs, milk, 2 cups flour, ¹/₂ teaspoon salt and baking powder in bowl; mix well.

To prepare the potatoes:

♣ Place 1 cup water, ¹/₂ teaspoon salt and 1 tablespoon shortening into two 12-inch skillets. Arrange potato slices in single layer over bottoms of skillets. Cook, covered, until tender; drain.

To assemble and cook the dish:

♣ Drop dumplings by tablespoons into skillets with potato mixture. Cook, covered, over medium heat for 15 minutes or until frying sounds can be heard. Do not peek. Serve with onion sauce.

This was a fast recipe for Josephine Eckman's mother to make when she was working in the field. She would go in 30 minutes before the menfolk and whip up a dish of *Dumpfnudla*, which was always served with watermelon. The best part was the crusty potatoes with dumplings attached. Josephine's children savor this recipe now, and even enjoy it in the winter, without watermelon.

Grandmother Rohlff's Stollen

Yield: 2 loaves

1 cup mixed raisins (black, golden and/or muscat)
1/2 cup currants
1 cup chopped candied mixed fruit
1/4 cup brandy
1 cup warm milk
3/4 cup butter
2 envelopes dry yeast
1/2 cup sugar
1 cup unbleached flour
2 eggs, beaten
2 teaspoons ground cardamom
1/2 teaspoon ground nutmeg
grated rind of 1 lemon
grated rind of 1 orange
1/2 cup chopped pecans
4 to 5 cups unbleached flour
melted butter
confectioners' sugar

Note: May bake in 2 loaf pans.

* Combine raisins, currants, candied fruit and brandy in bowl; mix well.

* Heat milk and butter in saucepan until butter melts, stirring constantly. Cool to 105 to 115 degrees. Combine milk mixture with yeast, sugar and 1 cup flour in bowl; mix well. Let stand for 15 minutes. Stir in eggs, cardamom, nutmeg, lemon rind and orange rind. Let rise, covered, for 30 minutes or until light and bubbly.

* Add raisin mixture and pecans; mix well. Add enough remaining flour to make stiff dough.

* Knead on lightly floured surface until smooth and elastic. Place in greased bowl, turning to coat surface. Let rise, covered, in warm place for 50 minutes or until doubled in bulk.

* Divide dough into 2 portions. Roll 1 portion into 9x12-inch oval on lightly floured surface. Fold long side over to within 1 inch of opposite side. Place on greased baking sheet. Repeat process for remaining dough. Let rise, covered, in warm place for 40 to 45 minutes or until doubled in bulk.

* Preheat oven to 350 degrees.

* Bake for 45 minutes. Cool. Brush with melted butter; sprinkle with confectioners' sugar.

Champagne Rolls

Yield: 24 rolls

1 package dry yeast
1 tablespoon sugar
1/4 cup warm water
1/4 cup all-purpose flour
1 cup warm water
1 cup Champagne, at room temperature
2 tablespoons oil
1 tablespoon salt
6 to 7 cups unbleached flour
cornmeal

> Champagne, that wonder-ful bubbly drink first captured by Dom Perignon in the 17th century, must legally be called simply Mousseux—*Sparkling*—if it comes from any province in France but the one for which it is named.

✤ Combine yeast, sugar, 1/4 cup water and 1/4 cup all-purpose flour in small bowl. Mixture will be heavy and lumpy. Cover and set aside. Let stand for 10 minutes or until very active and bubbly.

✤ Combine remaining 1 cup water, Champagne, oil and salt in large bowl. Stir until salt is dissolved. Add yeast mixture. Add unbleached flour 1 cup at a time, stirring until dough pulls cleanly away from side of bowl.

✤ Transfer dough to a floured board. Knead for 5 to 10 minutes, adding just enough unbleached flour to keep dough from sticking to board or hands.

✤ Place dough in greased bowl. Cover with plastic wrap and clean towel. Let rise in warm place for 1 hour or until doubled in bulk.

✤ Divide dough into 4 portions. Cut each portion into 6 pieces. Shape each piece into a ball. Place about 2 inches apart on cornmeal-dusted baking sheet. Dust with unbleached flour; slash center of each roll. Let rise for 15 or 20 minutes longer.

✤ Preheat oven to 400 degrees. Bake for 15 to 18 minutes or until golden brown. Serve warm.

Blitz Torte (Lightening Cake)

This recipe, which originated in Germany, makes an elegant birthday cake when the candles are added. It is named Lightening Cake because it disappears as quickly as lightening flashes.

Yield: 6 to 8 servings

1/2 cup butter
1/2 cup sugar
4 egg yolks
1 cup flour
4 teaspoons milk
1 teaspoon vanilla extract
1/2 teaspoon baking soda
4 egg whites
1 cup sugar
2 drops of vanilla extract
2   10-ounce packages frozen sliced strawberries, thawed
2 cups whipped cream, whipped

Variation: May substitute fresh strawberries, raspberries, pineapple, blueberries or peaches for frozen strawberries. None of the other ingredients should be substituted.

✤ Preheat oven to 375 degrees. Grease and flour two 9-inch round baking pans.

✤ Cream butter, 1/2 cup sugar and egg yolks in blender until light and fluffy. Add flour, milk, 1 teaspoon vanilla and baking soda. Process until blended.

✤ Spread mixture in prepared baking pans.

✤ Beat egg whites in mixer bowl until soft peaks form. Add sugar and 2 drops of vanilla gradually, beating constantly until stiff peaks form. Spread over prepared layers. Bake for 20 minutes. Remove to wire rack to cool.

✤ Place 1 baked layer on large platter. Arrange 1 package strawberries with juice over baked layer. Top with 1/2 of the whipped cream. Place remaining baked layer over whipped cream. Top with remaining package of strawberries with juice and remaining whipped cream.

✤ Arrange candles in top of torte if desired; slice. Serve immediately.

French Breakfast Puffs

Yield: 12 servings

1 1/2 cups flour
1 1/2 teaspoons baking powder
1/2 teaspoon salt
1/4 teaspoon nutmeg
2/3 cup butter
1 cup sugar
1 egg
1/2 cup milk
1 teaspoon cinnamon

✤ Preheat oven to 350 degrees. Mix flour, baking powder, salt and nutmeg together.

✤ Cream 1/3 cup butter, 1/2 cup sugar and egg in mixer bowl until light and fluffy. Stir in dry ingredients alternately with milk.

✤ Fill greased muffin cups 2/3 full. Bake for 20 to 25 minutes or until light golden brown.

✤ Dip puffs in 1/3 cup melted butter; roll in mixture of 1/2 cup sugar and cinnamon. Serve hot.

German Apple Cake

Yield: 16 servings

3 cups flour
1 tablespoon baking powder
1 teaspoon salt
4 eggs
2 cups sugar
1 cup oil
1/2 cup orange juice
2 1/2 teaspoons vanilla extract
4 cups thinly sliced peeled apples
2 teaspoons cinnamon
3 tablespoons sugar
confectioners' sugar (optional)

Variation: Use unpeeled apples for a little added color.

✤ Preheat oven to 350 degrees.
✤ Mix flour, baking powder and salt together.
✤ Beat eggs and 2 cups sugar in mixer bowl until creamy. Add dry ingredients alternately with mixture of oil and orange juice; mix well. Beat in vanilla.
✤ Spoon 1/2 of the batter into greased and floured 10-inch tube pan. Arrange half the apples over batter. Combine cinnamon and 3 tablespoons sugar in bowl; mix well. Sprinkle 1/2 of the mixture over apples. Top with remaining batter and apples; sprinkle with remaining cinnamon mixture.
✤ Bake for 1 hour and 10 minutes or until cake tests done. Cool in pan for 1 hour. Invert onto wire rack. Sprinkle with confectioners' sugar.

Individual Shaum Tortes

Yield: 10 to 12 servings

9 egg whites
salt to taste
1 1/4 teaspoons baking powder
3 cups sugar
1 tablespoon white vinegar
1 teaspoon vanilla extract

✤ Preheat oven to 250 degrees. Line baking sheet with waxed paper.
✤ Beat egg whites, salt and baking powder in mixer bowl at high speed until soft peaks form. Add sugar gradually, beating constantly at medium speed until stiff peaks form. Beat in vinegar and vanilla.
✤ Mound 2 to 3 tablespoons onto prepared baking sheet. Repeat process until all of mixture is used.
✤ Bake for 45 minutes; turn off oven. Let stand in oven with door closed for 15 minutes. Open door. Let stand for 15 minutes.
✤ Serve tortes with fruit and ice cream or yogurt.

German Twists

Growing up in the midwest, Joan Lillquist has fond memories of the intriguing German woman next door who made these fabulous cookies and shared the recipe with her mother.

Yield: 8 dozen

For the cookies:

4 cups flour
2 cups large curd cottage cheese
1 cup butter, softened
1 cup margarine, softened
1½ pounds pecans, finely chopped
1½ cups packed brown sugar

For the glaze:

1   1-pound package confectioners' sugar
½ to 1 cup milk

To make the cookies:

✤ Combine flour, cottage cheese, butter and margarine in bowl; mix well. Chill, covered, overnight.

✤ Preheat oven to 375 degrees.

✤ Combine pecans and brown sugar in bowl; mix well.

✤ Divide dough into 6 portions. Roll each portion into 12-inch circle on surface sprinkled with confectioners' sugar. Cut each circle into 16 wedges, like a pizza. Sprinkle each circle with ⅙ of pecan mixture.

✤ Roll each wedge up from wide end. Shape into crescents on baking sheet. Repeat process with remaining dough.

✤ Bake for 15 to 18 minutes or until brown.

To glaze the cookies:

✤ Drizzle warm twists with mixture of confectioners' sugar and milk.

Nuss Plaetzchen

Sehr gut! And low in fat too!

Yield: 2 to 3 dozen

2 cups sugar
3 eggs
1 cup flour
1 teaspoon baking powder
2 cups chopped pecans
1 teaspoon vanilla extract

✤ Preheat oven to 350 degrees.

✤ Beat sugar and eggs in mixer bowl until thickened. Stir in flour, baking powder, pecans and vanilla.

✤ Drop by teaspoonfuls onto greased cookie sheet. Bake for 10 minutes. Remove to wire rack to cool completely.

Icebox Cookies

Yield: 4 dozen

2 cups packed brown sugar
1 cup butter or margarine, softened
2 eggs, beaten
1 teaspoon baking soda
4 cups flour
1 teaspoon vanilla extract
1 cup chopped pecans

❖ Cream brown sugar and butter in mixer bowl until light and fluffy. Beat in eggs. Add sifted mixture of baking soda and flour; mix well. Stir in vanilla and pecans.

❖ Shape dough into rolls as thick as the size cookies you desire. Chill for 3 to 4 hours or until firm.

❖ Preheat oven to 400 degrees.

❖ Slice rolls into slices approximately 1/4 inch thick. Place slices on cookie sheets.

❖ Bake for 10 minutes or until brown. Remove to wire rack to cool completely.

Weihnachts Plaetzchen

Yield: 3 to 4 dozen

1 teaspoon baking powder
1 1/2 tablespoons milk
2/3 cup packed brown sugar
1/2 cup butter, softened
1 egg, beaten
1/4 cup grape wine
1 pound candied pineapple
1/2 pound candied red cherries
1/2 pound candied green cherries
4 cups chopped pecans
1 teaspoon cinnamon
1 teaspoon allspice
1/2 teaspoon salt
1 1/2 cups flour

❖ Preheat oven to 250 degrees.

❖ Dissolve baking powder in milk in cup; mix well.

❖ Cream brown sugar and butter in mixer bowl until light and fluffy. Add egg; mix well.

❖ Stir in baking powder mixture and wine. Add pineapple, cherries, pecans and mixture of cinnamon, allspice, salt and flour; mix well.

❖ Drop by spoonfuls onto greased and floured baking sheet. Bake for 25 minutes or until brown.

Appendix

Mail Order Sources

For many of us, unique and exotic ingredients are now quite commonplace in our large supermarkets, gourmet shops, and urban ethnic markets. Look to your closest city for sources, and ask ethnic organizations and social clubs where to buy ingredients. Usually they are more than happy to promote their culture. If you are still at a loss, many of the sources listed below offer a catalog of their offerings.

Asian

Kam Man Foods
200 Canal Street
New York, NY 10013
(212) 571-0330
(Chinese)

Katagiri
224 E. 59th Street
New York, NY 10022
(212) 755-3566
(Japanese)

Brazilian

Coisa Nossa
46 W. 46 Street
New York, NY 10036
(212) 719-4779

Eastern European

For a free copy of **The Kielbasa Trail**, a Guide to Eastern European Foods in Central Connecticut, contact:
Connecticut River Valley and
   Shoreline Visitors Council
393 Main Street
Middletown, CT 06457-3309
(203) 347-0028
(800) 486-3346

Flours and Spices

Pete's Spice
174 First Avenue
New York, NY 10009
(212) 254-8773

General Gourmet Shops

Balducci's
Mail Order Division
11-02 Queens Plaza South
Long Island City, NY 11101
(800) 822-1444
(800) 247-2450 (NY only)

Dean & Deluca
Mail Order Department
560 Broadway
New York, NY 10012
(212) 431-1691
(800) 221-7714

Zabar's
2245 Broadway
New York, NY 10024
(212) 496-1234

Mail Order Sources

Eastern Indian

Bazaar of India
1331 University Avenue
Berkeley, CA 94702
(415) 586-4110

Foods of India
121 Lexington Avenue
New York, NY 10016
(212) 683-4419

Seema Enterprises
10616 Page Avenue
St. Louis, MO 63132
(314) 423-9990

Italian

Manganaro Foods
488 Ninth Avenue
New York, NY 10018
(212) 563-5331
(800) 4-SALAMI

Mexican

Kitchen Food Shop
218 Eighth Avenue
New York, NY 10011
(212) 243-4433

Middle Eastern

K. Kalustyan
123 Lexington Avenue
New York, NY 10016
(212) 683-8458

Middle East Market
2054 San Pablo
Berkeley, CA 94702
(415) 548-2213

Portuguese Sausage

Sardinha's
206 Brownell Street
Fall River, MA 02720
(508) 674-2511

Scandinavian

Fredricksen and Johannesen
7719 Fifth Avenue
Brooklyn, NY 11220
(718) 745-5980

Old Denmark
133 E. 65 Street
New York, NY 10021
(212) 744-2533

Spices and Dried Herbs

Paprika Weiss
1546 Second Avenue
New York, NY 10028
(212) 288-6117
(for European and Hungarian spices)

Penzey's Spice House, Ltd.
1921 S. West Avenue
Waukesha, WI 53186
(414) 574-0277

Spice and Sweet Mahal
135 Lexington Avenue
New York, NY 10016
(212) 683-0900
(for Asian and Indian spices)

The Spice House
1048 North Third Street
Milwaukee, WI 53203
(414) 272-0977

This list does not constitute an endorsement of any firm listed.

Index of Foreign Titles

Index of Recipes

index of recipes

SEAFOOD SECRETS

Martini Bait, Put On The Pot, Luxurious Lobster, Light the Fire, and *Top It Off* are only a beginning to the tempting chapters in our collection of over 400 seafood recipes. From simple to elegant, these imaginative recipes can enhance cooking and dining experiences both ashore and afloat! This delectable repertoire of family favorites is amusingly illustrated by Sally Caldwell Fisher. Spiral bound, 9¼ inches by 8 inches, 256 pages, $14.95.

THE MYSTIC SEAPORT ALL SEASONS

Compiled from recipes in the private files of Mystic Seaport Museum members, this exciting cookbook offers traditional as well as new and unusual ideas for entertaining throughout the year. Illustrated by Sally Caldwell Fisher, the cookbook is filled with tips, culinary lore, and a treasure of recipes pertaining to each season. Spiral bound, 9¼ inches by 8 inches, 248 pages, $14.95.

Christmas Memories Cookbook

Block Island Turkey and *Captain Cooke's Plum Pudding* are only a sampling of the recipes in this collection. Recreate imaginative variations on classic New England cooking. Great for year-round entertaining and original gift ideas. Ample pages for "recording your" favorite holiday menus and recipes. Spiral bound, 9¼ inches by 8 inches, 272 pages, $14.95.

HOLIDAY COOKBOOK for Kids

Here is an illustrated, full-color, step by step guide for a wide range of holiday dishes kids can cook themselves (or with a little help). Stories of holiday origins will delight as well. Wire bound, 6 inches by 9 inches, 56 pages, $12.95.

Global Feast Cookbook

This book will transport you around the world with its unique collection of 350 very special family heirloom recipes. Hundreds of anecdotes, histories, family photographs, and illustrations combine to create Mystic Seaport's most readable cookbook ever. Spiral bound, 9¼ inches by 8 inches, 256 pages, $15.95.

MOVEABLE FEASTS COOKBOOK

The book for everyone who has ever planned a concert in the park, a trek through the woods, a day on a boat, or any meal to go. Our newest cookbook not only has hundreds of tantalizing recipes for all kinds of excursions but it also plans out a whole exciting menu from *Pepper Soup* to *Pecan Tarts*. These creative recipes will make all *Moveable Feasts* occasions to remember. Delightfully illustrated by Sally Caldwell Fisher. Spiral bound, 9¼ inches by 8 inches, 256 pages, $14.95.

ORDER BLANK

Mail to: Mystic Seaport Museum Stores, 47 Greenmanville Avenue, Mystic, CT 06355 or call 1-800-331-BOOK (2665)

Please send me:

____ copies of *Global Feast Cookbook*
      @15.95 ea._____
____ copies of *Moveable Feasts Cookbook*
      @14.95 ea._____
____ copies of *Seafood Secrets Cookbook*
      @14.95 ea._____
____ copies of *All Seasons Cookbook*
      @14.95 ea._____
____ copies of *Christmas Memories Cookbook*
      @14.95 ea._____
____ copies of *Holiday Cookbook for Kids*
      @12.95 ea._____

CT residents add 6% Sales Tax: _____

Packing and shipping: ___$4.50___

Total: _____

Name _____

Address _____

City _____ State ____ Zip _____

☐ Check ☐ VISA ☐ AMEX ☐ MC   Exp. Date _____

Credit
Card No. | | | | | | | | | | | | | | | | |

Signature _____

All prices subject to change without notice.